再来看《剑10》Test 1 里的例题:

Do you think your weekends are long enough? [Why / Why not?]

典型的 5 分答案:

They're too short. I get up late on Saturday and Sunday. I need more time to have fun.

典型的 6 分答案:

No. My weekends are not long enough for me to do all the things I like, such as shopping and playing sports. And I still feel tired on Monday when I go back to school.

典型的 7 分答案:

Like most people, *I have two-day weekends. But I have too much stuff to do at weekends —* cleaning my room, working out *at the gym*, hanging out *with friends ... I just don't have enough time for them. Three-day weekends* would be better.

继续看《剑10》Test 2 里的例题:

Do you think all children should learn to play a musical instrument? [Why ? / Why not?]

典型的 5 分答案:

All children should learn to play a musical instrument because they can enjoy music when they play it.

典型的 6 分答案:

I think they should. Studying is very stressful. Playing a musical instrument helps children relax. It's an important skill all children should have.

典型的 7 分答案:

Yes, *they should because playing a musical instrument can* reduce stress. *It can also help children* improve their concentration. *Playing a musical instrument, like the piano or a guitar, is also a good way for them to* express themselves.

再来比较一下《剑9》Test 2 里面不同分数段的答案：

Do you enjoy looking for gifts for people? [Why / Why not?]

典型的 5 分答案：

Sure, because when I look for gifts, I want to show people I love them very much.

典型的 6 分答案：

Yes. I have many friends and I need to celebrate their birthday or other happy events. Finding the perfect gifts for them is exciting.

典型的 7 分答案：

Yes, I do because selecting the right gifts can be *fun and enjoyable*. I always try to consider my friends' *interests and personality* when I select gifts for them. I can't afford expensive gifts, but I believe it's the *thought* that counts.

还有《剑9》Test 3 里的实例：

Do you sometimes prefer to send a text message instead of telephoning? [Why? / Why not?]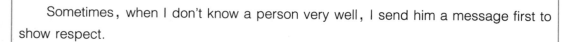

典型的 5 分答案：

Sometimes, when I don't know a person very well, I send him a message first to show respect.

典型的 6 分答案：

I send more messages than I call people. They don't make people annoyed, and I spend little money sending text messages.

典型的 7 分答案：

Yes. I prefer to text when the message isn't *an urgent one*, because that allows the receiver more time to think about how to reply. Texting is also *much cheaper* than calling.

IELTS SPEAKING

All of you wish to use English freely during the IELTS Speaking Test, but making this wish a reality remains a puzzle for most of you out there.

十天突破

雅思口语 剑11版

慎小嶷 / 编著

Pat's Ten-Day Step-by-Step Guide
to the Speaking Test

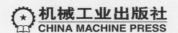

机械工业出版社
CHINA MACHINE PRESS

本书正文按照天数划分内容，在十天里紧密结合《剑11》对最新雅思口语考试的应试策略进行了详尽的剖析，并结合《剑11》的考题特点提供了富有针对性的语言点讲解。

本书作者 Pat 老师有多年的英语国家生活经历，在使用地道英语表达对 IELTS 口语题库进行透析的同时，还对中国考生容易陷入的误区进行了非常中肯的提醒。词汇学习手册汇集了地道口语常用表达法的精华，考生可以随身携带、随时学习。

本书的音频部分均由英籍专业人士朗读，便于考生模仿和练习。

本书作者对于真实的英语国家生活和中国学生的口语瓶颈均有极为深刻的了解，并著有畅销书《十天突破雅思写作》和《十天突破 IELTS 写作完整真题库与 6-9 分范文全解》。

图书在版编目（CIP）数据

慎小嶷十天突破雅思口语：剑 11 版／慎小嶷编著. —6 版.
—北京：机械工业出版社，2016.4（2016.7重印）
ISBN 978－7－111－53456－3

Ⅰ.①慎…　Ⅱ.①慎…　Ⅲ.①IELTS－口语－自学参考资料
Ⅳ.①H319.9

中国版本图书馆 CIP 数据核字（2016）第 063699 号

机械工业出版社（北京市百万庄大街 22 号　邮政编码 100037）
策划编辑：孟玉琴　　　责任编辑：孟玉琴　于　雷
版式设计：张文贵
责任印制：乔　宇
保定市中画美凯印刷有限公司印刷
2016 年 7 月第 6 版·第 7 次印刷
184mm×260mm·28.1875 印张·4 插页·735 千字
标准书号：ISBN 978－7－111－53456－3
定价：72.00 元（赠学习手册）

凡购本书，如有缺页，倒页，脱页，由本社发行部调换
电话服务　　　　　　　　　　　网络服务
服务咨询热线：（010）88361066　机 工 官 网：www.cmpbook.com
读者购书热线：（010）68326294　机 工 官 博：weibo.com/cmp1952
　　　　　　　（010）88379203　教育服务网：www.cmpedu.com
封面无防伪标均为盗版　　　　金 书 网：www.golden-book.com

IELTS 口语的"脉"

你是谁

对 the IELTS Speaking Test 的持续跟踪让 Pat 深感在考场里真实出现的雅思口试话题极为广泛。事实上，它们几乎已经涵盖到了英美日常生活里的所有领域。

以 2016 年 7 月 9 日下午为例，就轮换出现了从 a creative person 到 a sport that helps you keep fit 等跨度很大的 28 道卡片话题。如果再加上当天出现的第一、三部分考题经过排列组合后的可能性则更会远多于此。

与 Cambridge ESOL 出题者们明显"有备而来"相比，多数国内口语考生（希望您是一个例外）则仍处在采取顽固拖延战术或者根本就没有战术、慌不择路的"非正规军"状态。下面的官方统计数据残酷展现了这支"非正规军"在 IELTS Speaking Test 中是怎样被剑桥击溃的：

Mean Band Score for the Most Frequent Countries or Regions of Origin
(Source: www.ielts.org)

Place of Origin	Speaking	Place of Origin	Speaking
Germany	7.3	Greece	6.5
Philippines	6.9	Colombia	6.4
Nigeria	6.8	Egypt	6.4
Sri Lanka	6.7	Iran, Islamic Republic of	6.4
France	6.6	Italy	6.4
Malaysia	6.6	Mexico	6.4
Russian Federation	6.6	Brazil	6.3
Spain	6.6	Sudan	6.2

Place of Origin	Speaking	Place of Origin	Speaking
Hong Kong	6. 1	Vietnam	5. 8
Indonesia	6. 1	Korea, Republic of	5. 7
Jordan	6. 1	Iraq	5. 6
Nepal	6. 1	Kuwait	5. 6
Pakistan	6. 1	Libya	5. 6
Bangladesh	6	Saudi Arabia	5. 6
Taiwan	6	Uzbekistan	5. 6
India	5. 9	Japan	5. 5
Thailand	5. 9	Qatar	5. 5
Kazakhstan	5. 8	Turkey	5. 5
Oman	5. 8	China(People's Republic of)	5. 4
Syrian Arab Republic	5. 8	United Arab Emirates	5. 3

结论　　在 IELTS 考生最多的 40 个国家或地区中，中国大陆考生的口语成绩平均值（mean band score）仅高于 United Arab Emirates（阿联酋），而低于其他全部亚、非、欧国家和地区，也包括不少文化被普遍认为比中国文化更加"内向"的国家。很显然，导致这种分数差距的根本原因并不是缺少肢体语言，也不是缺乏目光交流，而只能是实打实的语言能力问题。咱们也许真的应该反思一下：我们是不是一直都把错了 IELTS 口语的脉？

考官是谁

我们生活在"阿尔法狗"（AlphaGo）已经击败了人类棋圣、无人驾驶汽车（self-driving cars）的综合表现正全面赶超人类驾驶汽车的时代。但 IELTS 口试仍然坚持了"人—人对话"的形式，而没有像其他很多口语考试那样为了节省成本和方便考试安排改用"人—机对话"。主办方 British Council 这样坚持的利和弊都很明显：考生在今后的海外留学生活里要进行的也是"人—人对话"。所以，IELTS 口试可以更准确地反映出考生与当地人面对面的**实际交流能力**（face-to-face communication skills）。但另一方面，examiner 的个人素质就有可能会对考生的表现产生影响。

在中国的互联网上，雅思考官往往会被描述成黑洞般的暗物质。"印度大妈"、"光头杀手"、"灭绝师太"、"5 分中年男"、"扔身份证的不耐烦 MM"，"像 Nikita 里面一个 killer 的冷面 SG"，"热情、然并卵的笑面虎老爷爷"、"拒绝 eye contact 的杀马特"，"酷似 Breaking Bad 里 Mr. White 的眼镜蜀黍" ……国内同学们关于口语考官的种种轶闻已经足以写成一本精彩的武侠小说（a swordplay and chivalry novel）了。但这些故事的盛传，恰恰证明了多数考官其实都是普通人。

事实上，不仅是雅思口试，到目前为止世界上的任何一种口试（包括求职时要做的 interview）都难以实现绝对的标准化，IELTS 确实难以排除 examiners 评分不负责任的可能性，但口语考官们总体来说还是敬业的。Pat 自己在中国从事雅思培训期间接触到了十几位现任和前任的 IELTS 口语 examiners，我可以非常肯定地说他们/她们无一例外都是"正常"人。而且相对于英美社会的整体情况而言，客观地说这些考官的平均文化素质是不错的，如果连这些人您看了都觉着"不顺眼"，真等到您到国外长期学习、生活时恐怕就得"大跌眼镜"了。

而且，在评分能力方面，他们/她们全都体现出了下面的 5 个共同点：

❶ They are native English speakers.

这确保了考官们能够使用并且充分理解在英美被 native speakers 普遍接受的英文，但同时这也意味着他们/她们也许无法理解在英语国家里"罕见"的英文。

❷ They at least have an undergraduate degree.

您肯定知道 degree 和 diploma 的区别，其实口语考官们的整体教育背景在英美社会中是不算低的，但长成什么样儿那是人家的自由……

❸ They have Teaching English as a Foreign Language（TEFL）qualifications.

这说明口语考官们是把从事语言相关工作当成自己 career path（职业发展方向）的重要部分，所以多数考官的心态其实并不像传说中的"口语杀手"打分那么"潇洒"。

❹ They need to get re-certified every two years.

考官资质每两年都是需要再次重新认证的，除非彻底不想干了，否则一般没必要让自己的打分多次被 remark 推翻。

❺ They have at least three years of English teaching experience.

三年英语教学经验也不算是很短了。这一条其实确保了多数考官对孩子们的"症结"还是能适当有所体谅的，但这同时也往往意味着考官对常见的"技巧"其实玩儿得比你还熟。

结论 IELTS speaking 的本质就是和你的考官用英语进行一次尽可能充分的交流。对口语考官的过度恐惧或者过度谄媚（butter up the examiner）都是没有必要的，你只需要像尊重其他人一样去尊重考官就够了，考官注意力的真正焦点其实是你的语言。

怎样使用本书收效最大

正是基于以上这些原因，在创作本书的全过程里，Pat 始终希望能够把在我身边的英语母语者们每天正使用着的真实口语和他们/她们的实际生活状态介绍给中国的同学们。坦白地说，写这样一本书并不轻松，因为在分析每个 IELTS 话题时我其实都是在不自量力地扮演着一个"文化传播者"的角色。

但是令 Pat 感到欣慰的，除了中国考生朋友们越洋寄来的 thank-you notes 之外，还有下面这个令人振奋的事实：

《剑11》出版之前已经开始在中国大陆发行的《十天口语》上一版里 Pat 着力推荐的 a variety of，tend to，is supposed to，regularly，normally，attract，aimed at，atmosphere，approach，open-minded，exchange information，sustainable，preserve，explore，insight，spot，layout…等等实用表达均在《剑11》文本里密集地现身，这强有力地证明了《十天口语》对剑桥官方所偏爱的口语风格的把握是准确的并带有一定前瞻性的。That's the best compliment a test-prep book author can possibly get，right?

对于备考时间比较充裕的同学，Pat 希望您能够经常翻阅您手中的这本书。我可以肯定地说本书里的每句话都是自己用心写的，值得您花时间细读，看这样的书不会浪费您宝贵的时间。即使只是每次浏览三、五分钟，您也能获取一些此时此刻正在英语国家被 native speakers 真实使用着的词句。出国之后您就会明白：真实的英文口语其实是简洁有效的，反而比用来"唬人"的英语好学。跟 native speakers 卖弄"大词"只能像跟一个思想传统的人炫耀你多么熟悉 Fifty Shades of Grey 一样不靠谱。

对于考试已经迫在眉睫但还没开始准备的同学来说（Pat 深知这样心理素质"过好"的同学虽然正在减少，但却永远不会彻底消失），请您立刻停止拖延战术，登录 blog. sina. com. cn/ieltsguru 打印出本月口语预测题，然后按照下面的顺序选读本书：Day1（esp. Question 2）→ Day 3（通读）→Day 4（第一节）→ Day 6（至少结合音频把单词发音的那部分练一练）→Day 8（不要背答案，但是应该熟悉高分答案的语言风格）→ Day 9（熟悉高分答案的语言风格）→ 本书附赠的《IELTS 口语高频词汇和短语速查手册》里标星号的词汇和短语。

结论 充分了解每个月的出题动向是必要的，同时我们必须注意积累地道的英文表达和对当代英美文化的适当了解。只有这样，您才能踏踏实实地提高自己的英语交流能力。也只有这样，您才算是真正把住了 IELTS 口语的"脉"。

☆ 致谢

　　本书参与协助编写工作的人员有：李丹、朱燕林、杨津英、张俊兰、樊顺玲、张淑琴、苏惠英、于辉、张洪霞、朱卡亚、孟建章、冉继华、宋琪、李玉亚、宋笑颜、孔庆桐、李广荣、王福利、苗春瑞、刘礼、兰印玲、孟玉敏、苏琴英、王玉丰、王军、朱瑾瑾、苏锡武、张会分、李佩香、袁毅、朱达斌、朱露西、孟平珍、崔文勤、卢朝臣、杨荣莲、陈杰学、孙国庆、智月仙、王丽沙、杨振国、孙晓荣、张智萍、王洪玲、徐建英、余团林、刘国强、董维川、孙三伶、史凤华、林淑芬、冷江豫、赵焱、李玉凤、刘昭文、宋文顺、白淑平、孙国栋、杨兴普、田桂祥、李正其、苏汉寿、朱文辉、李坤煌、李雄伟、林君凤、毛干斌、刘宝钗、李杰、刘建龙、李云香、苏惠心、尚纯义。

My deepest appreciation goes to my parents and my sister Meg, without whom I wouldn't possibly have embarked upon this " cottage industry". Your loving and unwavering support means everything to me.

Special kudos goes to Ms Meng Yu-qin, the editor of this book, whose intelligence and resourcefulness make a real difference in the creation of this book.

Most of all, I wish to dedicate this book to the students who made up my classes in the Global IELTS Institute (Beijing) . Their example has continually spurred me to keep working on this book. I hope it will be a nice reminder of our delightful time together.

小巍

2016 年 7 月写于新泽西

Pat 英文自序

Preface

The speaking section is often the most daunting part of the IELTS Test. Ironically, many IELTS candidates perform poorly in the speaking section because they over-prepare for it. The "error-free" templates and picture-perfect "model answers" committed to memory make the entire preparation process a strategic failure — few people would try to learn the piano if they were only interested in playing the Liszt Sonata in B minor, right?

To achieve a high score in the speaking section of the IELTS Test, you must understand what the examiner realistically wants. Personal preferences vary when it comes to words, structures and concepts, but all examiners value spontaneity. It is fairly easy for them to spot thoughtless spouting of prepared answers, because there are few or no natural pauses in answers given by rote. In addition, candidates tend to hesitate noticeably when the examiner asks for further elaboration on a prepared response. This dramatic hesitation seriously erodes the candidate's credibility in proving English proficiency, which often results in score penalties.

Unlike many other preparation materials available for the speaking section of the IELTS Test, this book is not designed to be memorized by rote; rather, it is intended to develop the readers' spontaneous English conversation skills. Accordingly, all chapters are structured around subjects that are not only IELTS-oriented, but also current and thought-provoking. The perspective offered on each subject challenges you to think beyond its common treatment. Each subject is also presented with a one-step-beyond component, serving as a springboard for addressing related topics at a more sophisticated level.

It is true that speaking a second language is partly a talent, but it is mostly a skill. It will, like any other skill, improve with practical guidance and continued practice. I encourage you to actively use the English and test-taking techniques you will learn from this book. That will not only help you retain what you learn but also make you a more confident and competent IELTS candidate.

Pat,

July, *2016*

Contents

目　录

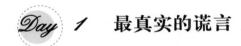

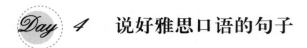

Day 4　说好雅思口语的句子

Day 5　雅思口语的段

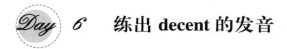

Day 6　练出 decent 的发音

Day 7　Part 1：短兵相接

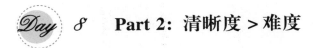

Day 8　Part 2: 清晰度 > 难度

Day 9　Part 3: 深入讨论的勇气

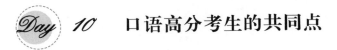

Day 10　口语高分考生的共同点

Pat回北京最爱做的事就是下馆子，除了因为自己是真正的吃货（I'm a foodie.）之外，也因为在美国和加拿大的餐馆里实在没什么好吃的菜，生活久了特别深刻的体会就是享受肺、折磨胃。而英国菜嘛……更是出了名儿的不"给力"，除了 fish 'n' chips。

有一次在北京的一家餐馆里，Pat突然发现英文菜单上很彪悍地写着"stir fly"（炒苍蝇）。我完全被老板的勇气震撼了，心想正常人胆子再大也不至于连苍蝇都敢吃，而且居然还是炒着吃。《舌尖上的中国》里绝对没介绍过这种怪异的做法（This bizarre "recipe" was absolutely not featured in A Bite of China.）。仔细研究之后，才发现原来应该是 stir–fried（炒的）。

还有一次，Pat看到一家北京餐馆的菜单上面对"干煸四季豆"这道菜的英文描述竟然是："This website is temporarily closed. Please check back later." 这显然是因为餐馆老板在网上搜索这个菜的英文名称，但是网站却没有正常运行而得到的不是答案的答案，属于真正的 lost in translation。

Pat还见到过"四喜丸子"被叫做 four happy meatballs（四个快乐的肉球儿），"鸡肉"被翻译成 muscle，《一代宗师》里的"念念不忘"被译成 read, read and don't forget，而中国的经典古语"知之为知之，不知为不知，是知也"竟被翻译成："Know is know. No know is no know. That's know."

No sweat.

The Ten-Day Series on IELTS

Day 1

最真实的谎言
True Lies

Using lies as alibis
Is the same game
Played in different ways
It's just a waste of time
Made for gullible minds

长期困扰中国口语考生的 10 个问题

○ 口语考试是不是必须回答"积极"的答案？口试是不是一定要回答"新颖"的答案？

○ 口语考官打分的依据到底是什么？

○ 口语需要 templates 吗？

○ 发音在口语评分里到底有多重要？

○ 如何选择口语考点？

○ 看口语机经有用吗？

○ 口语考试要不要"套磁"？

○ 考官问的问题压根儿就没有听懂怎么办？

○ IELTS 口语考时事么？

○ 怎样客观看待口试的 Predictions？

Pat's Answers

1 口语考试是不是只能回答"积极"的答案？口试是不是一定要回答"新颖"的答案？ (***Do I have to sound positive or optimistic? Do I have to give the examiner completely original or creative answers?***)

国内考生甚至一些培训教师普遍相信下面的错误观点：

A 你不能给考官 "I don't like..." "Actually, I don't know much about..." "Well, I disagree..." 这类否定语气的答案。

B 你必须要给出非常有创意 (original)、与众不同 (unique)、引人入胜 (engaging) 的答案才能拿高分。

我们来看看一位真实的口语考官是怎样理解这个问题的 (Clark: 29)：

One important point to emphasize (强调) here is that the marking system does **NOT** include references to the following points:

* Interesting content

* Amusing or funny answers

* Body language

* The truth

* Appearance or dress

更加发人深思 (thought-provoking) 的是，这位考官同时还给出了自己评分的实例 (Ibid, 29)： "I interviewed a young lady who was arrogant (傲慢的), impolite, impatient and quite rude — but I awarded this lady a score of 8 because her spoken English matched the descriptions in the marking system (评分体系) for band score 8."

像这样一个已经是集所有讨厌于一身 (obnoxious, intolerable)，而且也并没有为了讨好考官而展示"事业线" (cleavage) 的女士，因为英语说得并没有明显问题，还是从考官那里拿走了口语 8 分的高分。在真实考官的眼里，IELTS 口试并不是"主要看气质" (It's not about whether the examiner finds the candidate attractive or not.)。

而我在北京时的同事，口语考官 Martin Renner 就更加直白地说："It's not what you say. It's how you say it."

这两位货真价实的考官的肺腑之言完全符合 Pat 自己对学生口语成绩的长期跟踪调查：口语的分数，只看你的英语水平和答案是否具体、充实，和所谓的"别出心裁"或者是否"积极"完全没有关系。说得更直接一点：考官坐到口试的小房间里的任务不是考查智商，也不是进行"心理分析"，雅思主办方交给他/她的唯一任务是要确定考生的英语口语水平到底怎样。我们需要做的，只是努力去说正确的、流利的英文，但是实在没必要再给自己强加更多的条条框框了（hard and fast rules）。

British Council 官方给出的这段话是对这个问题的解答最合适的结束语："Examiners are only interested in your language and your ability to communicate. That is all they are assessing and judging."

2 口语考官的评分到底依据什么？(*How should I interpret the rating system?*)

同学们都知道口语有四项评分标准，但是那个标准很学术，一般考生难以望其项背。通过下面的这个表格，我们可以总结出一个更好理解的"草根版"口语评分标准。

Pat 总结的"草根版"雅思口试评分标准

	5分	6分	7分
Fluency & Coherence 流利度和连贯度	句子中经常出现不必要的停顿，而且缺乏口语的衔接，还有些同学过度使用"er…""ah…"这些 fillers，甚至中间出现长时间没话说"干在那儿"（get put on the spot）的尴尬情况。而5分得主的另一个极端是超级流畅，说话完全没有轻重缓急，甚至已经听不出来喘气，看不到眨眼，同时答案里却充斥着像 moreover 这样在真实	能说出完整的句子，但是每隔几句一定会有不连贯的地方。有可能出现较长时间的令人尴尬的停顿，但是次数不多	语速比较自然，有合理的衔接，只在很少的地方由于思考答案出现了不必要的停顿或者内容跳跃

	5分	6分	7分
	的英美生活里绝没有人说的"奥特曼"连接词，这种考生在说中文时都没有的灵异现象（supernatural phenomenon）只能被考官解读为你是在背书		
Grammar 语法	不能准确区分单词是否要加ed或者s，甚至会出现he/she不分的情况	每隔几句都有少量的时态或者单复数错误	基础语法错误已经基本消除，但仍存在一些高端的语法错误（比如少数介词或者连词使用不准确）
Pronunciation 发音	考官可以听懂你的内容，但某些地方他/她需要仔细分辨才能听懂，考官不会享受和你的对话，只希望考试时间快点过去	考官能比较容易地听懂你的内容，但仍然有些单词发音明显是错误的，语调上不是很自然	发音自然，但还是偶尔出现发音错误，考官已经开始享受和你的交谈过程
Vocabulary 词汇量	使用小学或初一单词过多，这是其中一种可能。 但对国内考生而言还有另一种更常见的可能，就是字典英语痕迹明显，使用大量在国外生活里从来不用的超级大词，Pat管这叫"词汇恐怖主义"（verbal terrorism）	用词已经比较准确，在适当的时候可以用出来一些有难度的词汇，但遗憾的是，这些难词大约有1/3是被错误使用的	可以分辨在哪些地方应该用小词，哪些地方可以用大一点的词汇，偶尔有用词不当，但是不影响整体意思的表达

下面我们用《剑11》Test 1 里面的一道考题来说明低分与高分口语答案的区别：

Do you prefer eating out or eating at home? [Why?]

典型的 5 分答案：

Eating out is easier than eating at home and the food is very delicious.

典型的 6 分答案：

I prefer eating out because it helps me save time. And restaurant food tastes better than the food I cook at home.

典型的 7 分答案：

I prefer eating out because restaurants provide a variety of food to choose from. Eating out is also a good way to relax and socialise with friends.

我们还可以通过《剑11》的下面这道考题来体会低档、中档与高档分数之间的差异：

Do you watch cookery programmes on TV? [Why? Why not?]

典型的 5 分答案：

Yes, I watch cookery programmes on TV. They are interesting. They show how to make food.

典型的 6 分答案：

Yes, I do. They teach me how to cook well. The food cooked on those shows looks beautiful, and the hosts are very funny.

典型的 7 分答案：

Yes, I do because TV chefs have great cooking skills. I can really learn from them and improve my own cooking. Many of them also have a good sense of humour. I particularly like cookery programmes that teach people how to cook healthy food.

我们还可以通过《剑 8》Test 4 里面的考题来看看口语 7 分到底是怎样炼成的:

Do you enjoy the advertisements on television?

典型的 5 分答案:

No，I don't. I think they are very boring.

典型的 6 分答案:

I don't like them. Advertisements on television just waste my time. They suddenly stop interesting TV shows and the things they try to sell are useless.

典型的 7 分答案:

I enjoy some of them because they are creative and entertaining，and they can provide useful information about new products. But it's true sometimes advertisements really spoil the fun of watching TV.

下面再用一个每场考试 Part 1 都有人被问到的常考问题实例来说明一下 5 → 6 → 7 的飞跃 (leap)：

What's your favourite subject at school?

典型的 5 分答案:

It's English because English is very useful and interesting.

典型的 6 分答案:

It's maths because maths makes us smart and maths is very useful for learning some other subjects such as chemistry.

典型的 7 分答案:

Hmm, I guess it's PE, which stands for physical education. Sometimes we call it the gym class. PE not just helps us keep fit, it also helps us reduce stress and improve our memory.

再来看一个 5 → 6 → 7 的三级跳 (hop，skip，jump)：

What's your favourite season?

典型的 5 分答案：

    I like winter best. I enjoy the snow in winter. It's so beautiful.

典型的 6 分答案：

    It's spring because everything is fresh in spring. Sometimes we have light rain. Spring is gentle and comfortable.

典型的 7 分答案：

    Well, I would say… summer. Actually, the summer in my city is really hot… scorching! But in summer, my friends and I have lots of free time, so we can hang out together in places like shopping malls or Starbucks. And in summer we can just wear very casual clothes like T-shirts and shorts…

我们的结论

    ☆ 5 分是挣扎着说出来的（或者另一个极端是无比流利地"喷"出来的），和考官的交流要不然就是基本无效，要不然就是特别机械生硬，更像"人机对话"

    ☆ 6 分是思考着说出来的，和考官的交流开始有效，但是并不充分而且也不是很流利

    ☆ 7 分是快速思考之后比较连贯地说出来的，但中间仍然会有正常呼吸和短暂思考所需要的自然停顿（natural pauses）。和考官的交流比较充分，而且已经具有一定的层次感，但偶尔会出现不导致严重误解的语法、用词或者发音错误

3 口语要准备模板吗？（*Will templates work?*）

近期刚听过一个口语模板，实在太经典了，必须记录在这儿：

    ……如果考官问你的问题你答不出来，可以深情地跟考官委婉地说，"Hmm, that is a very good question. Let me think about it…"然后眼珠转两圈儿（而且还明确规定必须是"两圈"），假装沉思之后猛然惊醒，对考官大声说，"Ah, Sir! I finally found a good answer to your question. But I'm not sure if I understood your question correctly…

So，could you please say your question again？"

I was dumbfounded by it. 这已经都不是卖萌了，这是真萌。如果学生敢在考场里用出这样的模板，后果肯定要比韩梅梅回答 "I'm fine. Thank you. And you？" 更严重。请鼓起勇气自己说吧，其实你没那么差。不论是中文还是英文，进行口头交流时如果频频使用模板会让 native speakers 觉得呆板甚至怪诞。

4 发音在口语评分中到底有多重要？（*How important will my pronunciation be during the actual test?*）

早在 2008 年 8 月，剑桥对口语考试的发音部分就推出了评分细则。这个标准听起来很美，但在实际评分过程中实施起来却很难（The examiners will have a hard time putting it to good use.）。想把发音这样不可能量化的内容去量化，最后只能变成画蛇添足（like gilding the lily）。所以：不必因为考试对发音有评分细则而过度焦虑甚至影响你和考官的正常交流。另一方面，努力提高自己的发音水平还是有必要的，而且这对您出国后的日常生活也会有实质帮助。本书的 Day 6 为您提供了实用的发音训练，可以帮助你在很短的时间内练出至少不让考官讨厌的发音（但是要达到让考官主动喜欢您的纯正发音确实需要一个比较长的学习和实践过程）。

5 如何选择口语考点？（*Where am I supposed to take the IELTS speaking test?*）

关于考点，我们可以明确三件事：

A 考题难度在全国的各考点没有任何差异。这听起来很绝对，但这么说的依据是 Pat 自己近十年来持续跟踪不同考点考题的实践。想特别提醒大家：全国所有考点在同一天的考题都是同步的。很多同学不理解这一点。其实如果好好看看网络上的当天考生回忆，您就会发现全国当天考题确实是同步的。

B 考官给你的打分会受其他考生水平的影响。口语考试是主观性考试，这就决定了它的评分必然带有主观性。完全标准化的口语评分不仅雅思没有，世界上也根本就不存在。Pat 也确实听到不少水平一般的北京孩子去外地考试考到 6.5 或者 7 分的实例，所以如果从总体来看，我们应该承认北京、上海、广州等大城市竞争更激烈一些。

C 具体到某一个考生，还是存在着不确定性（uncertainty）的。比如，有可能给你考试的那个考官天性（by nature）就是"刺儿头"（very cranky），或者也许你的考官说英语时带有较重的"外地"口音，再比如你为了去外地而长途旅行，导致考前没能休息好等等，这些细节的不确定因素无法完全排除（can't be ruled out）。

结论：总体上二三线城市口语打分的大环境确实要好一些，但还要看自己的行程安排是否方便，而且考官自己的个性特征（individuality）其实要比区域大环境更重要。

6 看口语机经有用吗？（*How can I use the collections of past test questions wisely?*）

口语机经是对过去考题的总结，挺好，但美中不足的（a fly in the ointment）就是题目数量惊人，对于非专业人士而言最好还是结合近期动态来准备效率更高。各位可以随时查看 Pat 的博客 blog. sina. com. cn/ieltsguru 上面公布的最新口语预测，帮助您节约宝贵的备考时间。

7 口语考试要不要 "套磁"？（*Am I supposed to butter up the examiner?*）

To tao or not to tao, that is the question.

像这类 "第二十二条军规"（*Catch 22*）似的问题其实永远会吵个没完。我们这样来看这个问题就能看得更清楚：套磁并不会明显加分，但是如果套不好却可能导致扣分，因为考官被套一点也不影响他/她用英语提出问题，可集中精力套磁却会让你没有精力去好好回答问题。再说，如果考官真的对你的套磁感兴趣了，他/她撇开考试真跟你聊起来了你吃得消吗？（Are you really up to it?）

比如，近期有个考生听考官是美国口音，为了实现跟考官 "零距离" 她就说自己的 "偶像" ——罗玉凤——也住在美国。没想到该考官正好看过 *People* 对凤姐的深度报道，追问了一大堆相关问题，直到考试结束还问该考生凤姐是不是已经在美国找到她的 dream guy 了。我们当然应该尊重考官，但像这种情况就纯属全力套磁而被 "逆袭"（lost the upper hand）的闹剧了。

8 考官问的问题我这个土人压根儿就没听懂怎么办？（*What can I possibly do if I don't fully understand a question?*）

IELTS 口语里的 Part 1 和 Part 3 都是问答题。在这两个部分里，如果遇到有的问题没听懂，国内同学们的通常做法是说，"I beg your pardon?"（在英美日常口语里人们更多时候其实会直接说 "Pardon?" 或者 "Pardon me?" 或者 "Sorry, could you please repeat that?"）

上面这几种说法对于话题轻松的 Part 1 都是可行、而且考官们也愿意接受的（British

Council 官方明确指出：You can ask the examiner to repeat a question if you did not hear it clearly.）。但 Pat 同时发现：对于话题比较正式的 Part 3，中国同学们听不懂问题有些时候是因为题目里存在着自己不熟悉的生词，那么仅仅要求考官重复一遍就未必能解决题目里有生词的问题了。

下面这两种方法可以确保您在 Part 3 即使遇到有生词的问题也至少不会被严重扣分：

◆ 如果您的考官态度比较客气，那么请跟他/她说，"Could you please rephrase（转述）the question?" 或者 "Sorry, could you please explain what you mean by…（你听不懂的部分）?" 如果他/她愿意换一种说法解释一下，你就应该可以顺利地躲开原题里的生词了。

◆ 如果对方的态度不温不火，或者你根本就看不清他/她的态度，你没有信心他/她会愿意替你转述，那么请直接告诉他/她，"Well, my best guess would be…" 这样说的好处是诚实，坦白承认你确实就是在猜，那么即使后面你所猜测的内容略有一点跑题，至少这道题他/她还可以原谅你，你集中精力认真听他/她的下一个问题就好了。

9 IELTS 口语考时事么？（*Am I supposed to constantly update my knowledge about current events for the speaking test?*）

最近有不少考生发来邮件问 Pat 如果近期考试的话是否要准备一些关于中美关系紧张（the rising tensions between China and the US）、"踢屁屁" 协定（TPP, The Trans-Pacific Partnership Agreement）、"小扎" 的清华座谈（Mark Zuckerberg's Q & A session at Tsinghua University）、明星涉毒（celebrities got arrested for using drugs）、甚至范爷和王思聪等名人的 "网络骂战"（celebrity spats on micro-blogging websites）、英国退欧公投（the British Brexit referendum）的相关信息，而且，每次到逢年过节的时候大家在来信问候之余也少不了要问问关于该节日的英语会不会在口试里被"盘查"。

这种担心是正常的，毕竟 IELTS 口试属于面对面的交流，很容易让人联想到考官是否会 "实时" 出题。但令人遗憾（也许是令人庆幸）的是：每一次 IELTS 口试的考题均是由剑桥统一提供的，整体来说考官个人并没有 "出题权"，而且 IELTS 口语不考查最新的时事知识。

《剑11》里给出的官方真题最真实地体现了雅思口试 "只考社会趋势，但不考具体时事"的准确定位：

   ❈ What kinds of home are most popular in your country?

   ❈ How easy is it to find a place to live in your country?

   ❈ What types of weather do people in your country dislike most?

   ❈ What are the most popular kinds of TV programmes in your country?

这种"只管趋势，但不管时事"的严格定位在一定程度上导致了口试话题的空洞与乏味，但想想考官一天下来要把有限的那几十个问题轮番问这么多不同的人，其实比你更郁闷，你的心理也就平衡了。更重要的是：考查范围明确也就保证了 IELTS 口语考题的难度对参加考试的全体考生来说是公平的。

所以，IELTS 口试的首要任务是考查你的英文口语表达能力。关注时事新闻（follow current events in the news）本身是一种很好的习惯，但你就不必为了准备口试而特意去突击时事新闻"涨姿势"了。

10 怎样正确看待口试的 **Predictions?**

对于备考时间很紧的考生们来说，不论英语水平高低，提前看看口语预测里的题目都是高效率的备战方法。而且，由于雅思口试是分阶段更换题库而不是每次考试都更换题库，因此口语预测的命中率还是挺高的。客观地说：准备口语预测不算是浪费生命。但有 3 点，Pat 要特别请您注意：（a）对于那些过于简单、你肯定能回答出来的预测题，可以跳过去不必准备，有重点地备考是明智而不是偷懒；（b）话题接近的考题完全可以合并。虽然你不是考官，但考官也不是你，考官就是一般人而不是 mind reader。当然，合并话题时必须自然，过于牵强那就不是合并了，而是无怨无悔地跑题；（c）Pat 坚决鼓励您把自己原创的想法加到预测题的答案里去，即使有点幼稚也比彻底放弃抵抗就地卧倒要可贵。至于如何扩展思路，学完 Day 8 便知。

❈   ❈   ❈

Okay, *let's get the show on the road.*

Day 2

IELTS 口语的本质是什么?
The Untold Story

Pat's Guide
To The IELTS Speaking Test

When I look into your big blue eyes,
I start to quiver and shake
Talk to me, talk to me,
All I want is just a nice little conversation

* *www.teachertube.com* *

对于从来没有近距离接触过外国人的那部分中国孩子,第一次进考场和考官面对面很可能会有"坐电椅"的感觉,有些女同学走出考场时说的第一句话甚至就是"吓死本宝宝了"。经常点击上面这个网址的 interviews(在页面上方的 search 栏里填入 interview 即可),能让你更了解地道英语的交谈风格和"LW"们说话时独特的面部表情,帮助您从战略上藐视敌人。

► *We take the test seriously, but we want to make it fun and interesting as well.*

Part 1 的实质是什么？

关键词：chat

IELTS 口语第一部分用剑桥的官方定义来说，是"关于你的背景、爱好、兴趣和习惯的基础问题"。但这听起来也太虚伪了吧？用普通人的话来讲，Part 1（俗称"趴 1"或者"趴忘"）的本质就是一个 chat，跟考官聊聊你自己的基本情况。从答案长度上来讲，每道题平均能回答 3 句话左右就相当不错了。当然，如果确实遇到了特别有感觉的题目，您也不必"嘴下留情"，尽管发挥好了，只要能确保流利、自然就成。

一般来说在国外聊天儿的时候人们是心态比较随意的（laid-back）。既然已经铁了心要去考官们的国家，那你就得按照他们的习惯来了。如果 Part 1 说得就跟背书（regurgitation）似的，人家就立刻会怀疑你跟他/她聊的诚意。因此，在 Part 1 里请您放松心态，跟 examiner 好好地练一次口语吧！

Part 1 的考题也是口试的三个部分里最"欢乐"的一个部分，因为它最贴近考生自己的生活。下面都是《剑 11》给出的 Part 1 真题：

◆ What kinds of food do you like eating most? [Why?]

◆ Who normally does the cooking in your home? [Why / Why not?]

◆ Do you watch cookery programmes on TV? [Why? / Why not?]

◆ Do you prefer eating out or eating at home? [Why?]

◆ How often do you go out with friends? [Why / Why not?]

◆ How friendly are you with your neighbours? [Why / Why not?]

◆ Which is more important to you, friends or family? [Why?]

◆ What type of photos do you like taking? [Why?]

◆ Do you like people taking photos of you? [Why / Why not?]

Part 2 的实质是什么？

关键词: description

口语的 Part 2（俗称"趴 2"或"趴吐"），剑桥的官方定义是"In Part 2, the examiner gives you a topic card. Then you have one minute to prepare and make notes. Then you'll be required to talk about the topic for one to two minutes."

Pat 注: 其实在全球很多考点，考官都已经不再是发一个卡片了，而是发一张大纸，上面在一个很小的角落里印着一个 topic 和几点提示。

Part 2 的本质是要求你做一个 description（描述）。为了更好地理解什么是"description"，您可以回想一下自己小时候上语文课的时候，老师向你描述一个事物和老师平时说话有什么不同。

"描述"和"闲聊"至少有下面两点不同:

☆ 描述时一定会有适当的思考和停顿（pause）。

我们说过，Part 1 基本可以看成是 chat，但是有些考生在 Part 2 因为正好遇到可以调动自己准备过的答案（a prepared answer），就直接把答案无比流畅地背出来。这明显不符合正常人描述的习惯。

☆ 描述需要有一定的规划，需要有秩序。

"描述"需要更加精确的语言。而且和 Part 1 与 Part 3 不同，Part 2 需要在同一个话题的不同方面之间做数次转换，所以对答案的秩序感要求更高一些。不过既然是口语，毕竟与写作的严谨度要求不同，所以也不用太呆板（rigid），口语最好的效果永远是轻松自然的。

比如下面这道题是《剑 11》Test 1 的 Part 2:

> Describe a house / apartment that someone you know lives in.
>
> You should say:

rekindle love for life.

> whose house / apartment this is
>
> where the house / apartment is
>
> what it looks like inside
>
> and explain what you like or dislike about this person's house / apartment.

下面这道题则是《剑 11》Test 3 的 Part 2：

> Describe a day when you thought the weather was perfect.
>
> You should say：
>
> > where you were on this day
> >
> > what the weather was like on this day
> >
> > what you did during the day
>
> and explain why you thought the weather was perfect on this day.

如果这些 topics 让您感到"无从下嘴"，没关系，我们将在 Day 8 里对完整的卡片真题库进行深入的探寻。

Help me through the hard times

↘ **Part 3** 的实质是什么?

关键词: discussion

"趴 3/趴睡"的本质是一个 discussion（讨论）。多数时候 Part 3 的问题都与 Part 2 的卡片话题相关，而且问题涉及的人群比较广泛：Part 1 的多数题是关于"you / your life"的，而 Part 3 的多数题则是关于"people"，"society"或者"your country"，甚至"the world / global issues"的。

> **既然 Part 3 是 discussion，那么在语言上就必然有下面三个特点：**
>
> ☆ 需要很强的层次感。不过您尽可以放心的是：本书已经为您总结出了 Part 3 讨论所需的全部常用逻辑结构，详见 Day 5，Day 9。
>
> ☆ 语言风格会比 Part 1 和 Part 2 更正式一些，无论从用词还是内容都会更 formal。
>
> ☆ 但好消息是：毕竟 Part 3 还是考口语而不是考写作，所以 Part 3 的答案也不必过于严肃，而且 Part 3 的考题难度与雅思作文题的难度相比还是有一定差距的，详情请见 Day 9。

比如《剑 11》Test 1 的 Part 2 卡片话题是 a house／apartment someone you know lives in，相应的 Part 3 就出现了下列问题：

◆ What kinds of home are most popular in your country?

◆ What do you think are the advantages of living in a house rather than an apartment?

◆ Do you think everyone would like to live in a larger home?

◆ Do you agree that there is a right age for young adults to stop living with their parents?

像这样的问题显然已经与 IELTS 写作里常考的 "more and more people are choosing to live alone" 话题有相似之处，但难度比写作考题还是要低。

◣ **Part 1** 的话题有范围吗？

Pat 认真总结了近九年里的全部口语 Part 1 话题。分析结果表明：不管是新题、旧题、半新半旧或者是半新不旧的题，都一定超不出下面的 20 个方面。其中颜色越亮的话题越放松（laid-back），颜色越暗的越"板"（stuffy）。您还将在后面的 Day 7 看到更深入的 Part 1 话题分析。

The Part-1 Topic Areas				
Studies	Language	Food	Nature	Sports & Outdoor Activities
Work	Weather & Season	Media	Collection	Pets
Building	Hometown	Arts	Clothing	Festivals, Holidays & Parties
People	Reading & Writing	Colours	Travel & Transport	Shopping

Part 1 考什么?

每个月在亚太考区最新出现的新题, Pat 都会及时在自己的博客 blog. sina. com. cn/ ieltsguru 的口语预测中为您及时公布。

下面这些真题是亚太区的一些 Part 1 考题实例 (Part 1 的完整 topic pool 请看 Day 7)。

Recent Part 1 Questions

The Start of the Test

Please switch off / turn off your mobile phone.

What's your full name? / Can you tell me your full name please?

Can I see your ID card please?

☞ ☆ What's your full name? / Can you tell me your full name please?

这是固定的问题,简单地回答 **My (full) name is…** 就很好了。如果您还不放心,一定想要解释名和姓,因为中文的姓名顺序和英文正好相反,所以最好别太具体地说你的 first name / last name 是什么,除非你的策略是想在一开始就弄晕考官 (Pat 的很多在中国有任教经历的英美朋友们都谈到过他们在中国时 "had to be careful about saying 'first name' and 'last name' to avoid confusion")。所以,如果您非要说清楚自己 "姓字名谁",那就还是脚踏实地地说 **My family name is… and my given name is…** 吧。

☞ ☆ Can I see your ID card please?

这个也是固定问题，回答 Here you are. 或者 Here you go. 都很好。

Hometown / Your House / Your flat / Housework

What do you like about your hometown?

Do you think your hometown is good for young people?

What would you change about your city?

What types of public transport can be found in your hometown?

Do you do housework?

☞ ☆ What would you change about your city?

这里的 would 表示只是你的希望，并不是必须能实现的。

☞ ☆ What types of public transport can be found in your hometown?

注意，很多中国同学爱说的 transportation 其实是美国的说法，英国考官会用 transport。

☞ ☆ Do you do housework?

最常见家务事儿的英文表达是: wash the dishes / do the dishes (洗碗)，do the laundry (洗衣服，在英美极少有人 wash clothes by hand)，take out the rubbish (倒垃圾，这是英式英语，而在美国则叫 take out the trash)，vacuum the floor (用吸尘器吸地板，Pat 注意到在中国吸尘器已经快成古董了，而英美的大多数家庭却还在"坚守"吸尘器)，mop the floor (擦地板)，clear the table after dinner (晚饭后收拾餐桌)，water the plants (浇花)，而且在地道英文里 spring cleaning (春季大扫除) 也是很常用的说法。

Your Studies / Your Work

Are you working or studying?

(对学生) What do you like about your studies?

What's your major? Do you like it?

What did you do on your first day in this school / university?

（对已经工作的考生）What do you like / dislike about your job?

☞ ☆ **What did you do on your first day in this school / university?**

国外学校入学的第一天经常被称为 Orientation Day，常见活动有 an orientation tour of the campus（其实也就是带着大家看看校园），a Welcome Meeting，a free lunch（但最近几年因为经济不行，很多学校已经赖掉了），在有些学校里还可以 meet the faculty and staff（和教职工见面）。

Hobbies & Habits

What do you usually do at weekends?

Do you often do things in a hurry?

Do you think sleep is important?

☞ ☆ **What do you usually do at weekends?**

注意，英国考官说"在周末"时会说 at weekends，而不说 on weekends。

☞ ☆ **Do you often do things in a hurry?**

Pat's answer: Yes, I do. I'm not very good at making plans or managing my time, so I'm often in a hurry to get things done, which can be really stressful.

Pat's note:

British Council 官方明确指出：IELTS 口试的评分原则之一是"A negative answer is just as good as a positive one."（只要英文正确，肯定的答案或者否定的答案都是考官愿意接受的）。如果您觉得自己很少匆忙做事，那么也不妨试试这些地道的词汇和短语：No, I don't. I'm not a person who likes to leave things to the last minute. I like to plan ahead and start early, so I usually have plenty of time to get things done.

拖延症：Procrastination

☞ ☆ Do you think sleep is important?

Pat's answer: Sure. A good night's sleep makes us feel happy and energetic. Sleeping well also helps to reduce stress and boost the brain's efficiency. People who don't get enough sleep often find it difficult to concentrate.

Pat's note:

（i）短语 feel happy and energetic 的意思是 "感到心情愉快而且精力充沛的"，短语 boost efficiency 的意思是 "提升效率"

（ii）find it difficult to do sth. 是英文口语里很常用的句型之一，意思是 "感到做某事很困难"。例如，美剧《纸牌屋》（*House of Cards*）里的男主角 Kevin Spacey 就说过，"Sometimes I find it difficult to decide between two choices. "

Sports / Outdoor Activities

What sports are most popular in your country?

Do you like swimming?

Where do you swim?

What games are popular in your country?

☞ ☆ Do you think it's important to play a sport?

注意：play a sport 是很地道的英文，不是 "中式英语"。（深入讲解请看 Day 7 的 Topic 15）

☞ ☆ Do you like swimming?

Pat's answer: Yes, I do. Swimming is a good way to relax and reduce stress. It's also a good form of exercise and helps me keep fit.

Pat's note:

（i）地道短语 reduce stress 的意思是 "减轻压力"；

（ii）地道英文里还常说 Swimming is a good way to lose weight（游泳是减肥良方）. 如果您希望练出像宁泽涛那样健美的体型，则可以说 Swimming is a great way to build up muscles.

☞ ☆ Where do you swim?

🐾 **Pat's answer:** I often swim in our community swimming pool because it's close to my home and is very clean and well managed.

🐾 **Pat's note:**

（ⅰ）地道表达 is well managed 的意思是"管理得很完善的";

（ⅱ）如果想说在湖里或者海里游泳可以"更加接近大自然",地道英文里会用 get closer to nature 这个短语

[剑桥例句] Swimming in the sea helps me get closer to nature.

☞ ☆ Do you often play games?

英语国家里的常见游戏:

tag（基本就等于国内小伙伴们玩的"捉人"游戏）,hopscotch（国内翻译成"跳房子",其实是跳在地上编有数字的方格）和 hide-and-seek（捉迷藏）。board games 在地道英语里是泛指各种"棋类游戏",具体地说在英美很流行的有 chess（象棋）,Monopoly（大富翁）和 Scrabble（Pat 自己小时候喜欢玩的一种拼字游戏,它对小朋友甚至成年人提高 spelling 都大有好处）,以及 card games（牌类游戏）,puzzles（拼图游戏）和 math games（近几年在英美特别流行的一种数学游戏叫 Sudoku）等。

▲ 在英美的玩具店里,Scrabble 和 Monopoly 经常是邻居

另外还有两种 Pat 不清楚在中文里叫什么但是在英美特别常见,一种是 scooter,就是左边这种,riding a scooter 是 Pat 住的小区里小朋友们的最爱活动之一。还有一种是 pogo stick,叫弹跳棍感觉很别扭,但总之就是右面的这种东东了。

☞ ☆ What games are popular in China?

Pat 在中国时看到的流行游戏：

Chinese chess，mahjong，puzzles（拼图游戏），riddle games（猜谜语），jumping rubber band（跳橡皮筋），playing with marbles（玩弹子球），Dota 2，GTA 5（侠盗猎车手 5），Clash of Clans（部落战争），League of Legends（英雄联盟），Hearthstone：Heroes of Warcraft（炉石传说）等等。

The Media

What types of TV programme do you like watching?

Why do we need advertisements?

What types of film do you like best?

☞ ☆ Why do we need advertisements?

最重要的原因肯定是 They give us information about new products. 而且很多广告的娱乐性很强（entertaining），更不用说还可以在广告里面看到 celebrities（名人）；而对于商家（businesses）来说，advertisements 则是 important marketing tools。

The Internet

How often do you use computers?

What are the differences between emails and letters?

☞ ☆ What are the differences between emails and letters?

在英美 letters 也经常被叫作 snail mail（蜗牛信），因为实在太耗时间（time-consuming）了。

Reading & Writing

Do you like reading?

Do you think handwriting is still an important skill for young people?

☞ ☆ Do you think handwriting is still an important skill for young people?

Pat's answer: Yes, I think it's still important. We still often take notes, answer test questions or write birthday cards by hand. Good handwriting is easy to read, while poor handwriting is confusing and annoying.

Pat's note:

confusing and annoying 是"令人困惑而且让人心烦的",如果要说"书写仍然是一种重要的沟通技能"就是 Handwriting is still an important communication skill.

☞ ☆ Do you prefer to type things or to write things on paper?

打字的好处除了更快(faster),还可以编辑(edit)和剪贴(cut and paste things)。

Language and Numbers

Would you like to learn another foreign language in the future?

Why is it important for children to learn maths?

☞ ☆ Why is it important for children to learn maths?

Pat's answer: That's because maths skills can help children better understand science and the world around them. Maths can also help them think in a more logical (有逻辑的) way.

Clothing

What kinds of clothing do you like wearing?

Do you buy clothes online?

☞ ☆ Do you buy clothes online?

Pat's answer: No, I don't, because I can't try on clothes online. It's hard to know if they would really fit me or not. It's much easier to go to a local clothing shop, try the clothes on and make sure they fit me well.

Pat's thought: 如果喜欢在网上买衣服，那么用地道英文可说的也同样很多，比如：Buying clothes online helps me save time. 以及 Prices are lower online than in physical shops（实体店）. 或者 Online clothing shops always have a wide variety of clothes to choose from. 等

Food

When do you usually eat snacks?

Do you think children should learn how to cook?

Do you like fruit and vegetables?

☞ ☆ When do you usually eat snacks?

Pat's answer: I usually eat snacks in the mid-afternoon, like 2-3 p.m., because that makes me feel more energetic and less tired. Sometimes I also eat snacks after working out.

Pat's note:

（i）短语 work out 是"健身"的意思；

（ii）在英美最常见的零食有 cookies, crackers, pretzels, ice cream, popcorn, jelly beans, cheese sticks, chocolate bars 等等，中国同学们熟悉的"MM 豆"在英文里叫 M & M's（中间的 & 符号要读成"and"）；

（iii）如果想说"在两餐之间饿了的时候就吃零食"，英文会说 I eat snacks when I feel hungry between meals. 而"当感觉压力山大的时候就吃零食"，在地道英文里则会说 I eat snacks when I feel stressed.

☞ ☆ Do you think children should learn how to cook?

"小盆友"们学做饭的好处包括 It teaches them an important life skill（生活技能）and makes them more independent（更独立），而且还可以 keeps them away from junk food（让他们远离垃圾食品）。

☞ ☆ Do you like fruit and vegetables?

Pat's answer: Yes，I like them a lot. They taste good and they're rich in vitamin C and fiber，so eating fruit and vegetables every day can improve my health.

Pat's note: 短语 be rich in ... 是"富含……"的意思，vitamin C and fiber 是指"维生素 C 和纤维"，如果要形容水果"多汁的"，请坚定地使用 very juicy 来表达

People   插入：englobe englobe

Do you prefer to have elderly people or young people as your neighbours?

What do you usually do when you are with your friends?

☞ ☆ Do you prefer to have elderly people or young people as your neighbours?

年轻邻居们的好处是 more sociable（更喜欢社交的），more open-minded（思想更开放的）并且 I find it easier to communicate with young neighbours 等；而老人做邻居的优点则可以强调 They tend to be quiet but helpful.

Pat's note: tend to be 是地道英文口语里表示"多半是"的常用短语：

［BBC 例句］Elderly people tend to be wiser and happier.

Art

Do you think it's important for children to learn to play a musical instrument?

Do you like painting and drawing?

☞ ☆ Do you think it's important for children to learn to play a musical instrument?

这里的 a musical instrument 表示"乐器"，小朋友学乐器的各种好处请看 Day 7。

Buildings

> Do you often go to museums?
>
> Do you think museums are important to young people?

☞ ☆ Do you think museums are important to young people?

Pat's answer: Yes, they're important. Museums are very educational（很有知识性的）. They can teach young people about history, art and science. Some museums are pretty entertaining（娱乐性很强的）too. They provide fun activities（有趣的活动，注意不是"搞笑的活动"）, videos and stories as part of their exhibitions（展览）.

Pat's thought: Pat 在国外看到一些中国孩子出国之后天天在宿舍里"宅"着，每天接触到的英语还没有在国内准备雅思的时候多。Pat 认识的一个北京孩子在美国生活了两年，英语丝毫没见长进，反倒熟练掌握了两种国内的方言，"留洋"变成了"留唐"。其实即使是性格内向的同学至少也应该多去 local sports centers，museums 和一些 cultural events，多感受当地人的真实生活方式。否则当你离开的时候，就真的成了"挥一挥衣袖，不带走一片云彩"。

Weather & Seasons

> What types of weather do you like best?
>
> What is your favourite season?
>
> Do you like the rain? Why?

☞ ☆ Do you like the rain? Why?

Pat's answer: I like light rain because it makes me feel calm and relaxed. Walking in light rain is fun, and I really like the sound of light rain drops（雨点儿）falling on the ground. But if the rain gets heavy, driving can be difficult or even dangerous.

Shopping

Do you like shopping?

Do you often shop online?

Collection

Why do some people like collecting things?

What do you like to collect?

☞ ☆ Why do some people like collecting things?

详解请看 Day 7 的 Topic 13。

Colours

Do any colours have special meanings in China?

Nature

Do any flowers have special meanings in your culture?

深入讲解请看 Day 7 的 Topic 19。

Pets

Do you like pets?

Why do many people keep pets?

☞ ☆ Why do many people keep pets?

Pat's answer: That's because pets can help their owners reduce stress and loneliness（减少压力和孤独的感觉）. It seems people who have pets are happier and more active. Keeping pets is also a good way for children to learn about responsibility because they need to take care of their pets.

🖊 **Pat's thought:** 人们"遛狗"叫 walk their dogs（注意：不是"走狗"），把东西扔出去让小狗捡回来的游戏叫作 play fetch with their dogs。

Travel

Do you like travelling?

Do you have a driver's license?

☞ ☆ Do you have a driver's license?

对于这种题最好不要只用 Yes ∕ No 一个词就把考官简单粗暴地顶回去，看在 1850 大洋的份上至少也必须跟他 ∕ 她多练几句口语。比如可以用在英美人人皆知的一句名言来解释自己为什么要"考本子"：Driving is not a right（权利）. It's a privilege（特权）. 或者如果您觉得 privilege 这个词太难记那就简单地说 Driving is fun and it makes life easier for me. 也很好。

如果没有 driver's license 也不必紧张，你同样可以说出让考官满意的答案，请牢记 British Council 的官方建议 —— If your answer is negative, don't worry. 比如，可以说 I don't have a driver's license because the traffic in my city is always bad and it's always hard to find a parking space. 或者说自己乘坐公共交通出行（I use public transport to get around.），喜欢玩儿深沉的还可以说家乡的司机们都严重缺乏责任感（There're a lot of dangerous drivers out there.），或者就坦白地说开车有风险（can be risky），会让自己很"怕怕"（I'm afraid of getting hurt）等也同样都是合理、地道的英文。

Festivals，Holidays & Parties

Do you like going to parties?

Do you prefer to celebrate your birthday with your family members or your friends?

How do you spend holidays?

详情请看 Day 7 的 Topic 20。

Part 2 的答案完全可以合理、合法地合并

　　仅从 2016 年 5 月 7 日至 2016 年 7 月 9 日短短两个月的时间内，在中国大陆累计出现的卡片题就超过了 70 个。现实地说，除非是有长期的备考时间，否则把 IELTS 口试卡片题库里面的每道题都准备得很熟练是不可能的（That would be out of the question.），所以才会有那么多孩子在准备 Part 2 的时候大呼"累觉不爱"。

　　恰当地"合并"卡片题答案的备考方法不仅是可行的，而且是必行的。请看：

Describe a teacher who has influenced you.	Describe a neighbor who helped you before.	Describe a person who can speak a foreign language well.
Describe someone who helped you before.	Describe an important person in your life.	Describe an old person who you admire.
Describe someone who you have studied or worked with.	Describe a family member.	Describe someone who gave you good advice.

　　很明显，通过准备 an old English teacher，我们不仅可以准备好左上角的一个题目，还可以很自然地覆盖这个表格里其他所有的 topics，甚至还可以把一部分内容借用到 Describe a subject you liked at school. / Describe the first day of a course you attended at school. / Describe an ideal job. 等看似"不搭界"的考题里。

　　又比如下面这个表格：

Describe a special meal you had recently.	Describe a difficult thing you can do well.	Describe a skill.	Describe an interesting thing you did in your spare time recently.
Describe a happy event in your childhood.	Describe a birthday party.	Describe a good cook.	Describe an exciting experience.

　　通过准备一个关于 cooking 的详细过程，会让我们对描述这些题目都有足够的信心。

　　下面请您自己感受一下合并 topics 的乐趣，练习下面的话题怎样快速搞定：

Describe an electronic device (not a computer).	Describe a gift you have received.	Describe an expensive thing you want to buy.	Describe something you lost.
Describe your favourite method of communication.	Describe something you saved money for a long time to buy.	Describe something you use every day.	*mobile phone* **?**

一个 mobile phone 的答案就可以让这么多 "闹心" 的话题都迎刃而解了。

此外，您还可以在本书的 Day 8 里看到完整的雅思 Part 2 真题库详解。

Part 3 考什么?

下面的题目都是近期在中国大陆出现的 Part 3 真题，可以帮助您领略 Part 3 的出题风格，对于 Part 3 的详解您可以在 Day 9 看到。

○ **What do you think is a healthy lifestyle?**

(思路提示：have a balanced diet / eat plenty of fruit and vegetables / drink 8 glasses of water a day "一天喝 8 杯水" 是英国国家医疗体系 NHS 提出的健康生活标准之一 / exercise regularly / early to bed and early to rise 这可不是 "中式英语"，而是很地道的英文：早睡早起)

○ **Do you think TV programmes can teach us about history?**

(思路提示：There're lots of history programmes on TV. / some of them are fun and informative / but others are not based on historical facts / they're entertaining but misleading just to attract more viewers)

○ **What are the differences between modern buildings and traditional buildings?**

(思路提示：traditional buildings are more eco-friendly 更加有益环保的 / traditional buildings look more attractive / modern buildings are taller and stronger / modern buildings lack character 缺乏个性特色)

○ **What are the differences between Chinese movies and Hollywood movies?**

(思路提示：The violence in many Hollywood movies really bothers me. / Hollywood movies tend to be more entertaining and creative. / Even in China, many box-office hits are Hollywood movies.)

○ **What are the differences between fresh food and canned food?**

（思路提示：fresh food is rich in fiber（纤维）and vitamins / fresh food tastes better / canned food takes less time to prepare and cook）

○ **How do TV programmes affect education?**

（思路提示：some TV programmes are interesting and informative / they can provide young people with lots of useful information / but on the other hand, there're also TV programmes that contain violent or sexual images / young people tend to copy what they see on TV）

○ **What do you think of giving children gifts when they behave well?**

（思路提示：That's like a reward for their good behaviour. / On the other hand, children may be spoiled if adults always do that / it would be better to reward them with words than with gifts）

○ **What's your idea of success?**

（思路提示：It can be anything I really try hard to do. / anything that can give me a sense of achievement / even as ordinary as cooking a nice meal for my family or friends can be called a success / some people are very ambitious and always try to achieve success in their studies or careers）

○ **Who can give good advice to us?**

（思路提示：our parents / our teachers / our friends who have had similar experiences / other people who really care about us）

○ **How can we solve the global warming problem?**

（思路提示：control the number of cars / make public transport more reliable / encourage people to walk or cycle to work）

○ **What are the differences between individual sports and team sports?**

（思路提示：We're more focused when we do individual sports such as jogging and swimming. / Individual sports can give us a stronger sense of achievement. / Team sports can improve our teamwork skills. / Team sports are more fun because we work closely with our teammates.）

Pat 指南

　　Part 3 的题目不管听起来多么怪异（weird），也没必要把答案想得太"深邃"（profound）了。请牢记：雅思口语里的高分答案毕竟也还是口语（spoken English），而不是写作（written English）。用 British Council 官方的建议来说就是，"Remember this is a test of English conversation."

Think hard. Speak softly.

Day 3

 雅思口语的词
IELTS Speaking Building Blocks

You think that I don't even mean a single word I said.

They're only words.

And words are all I can possibly have.

* http://www.topics-mag.com *

这个网站上的网友来自世界各地，您不妨经常上去看一看。

它的英语风格其实就很接近雅思口语高分答案的风格：不是很难，但也并不是很"痞"；有一定的描述性，但绝不是背书。

▶ *We take the test seriously, but we want to make it fun and interesting as well.*

☐ 试的时候词汇用得好会加分，这是不争的事实。可到底什么叫好词？在培训界却很有争议。

英文有句名谚，"A man travels across the world in search of what he needs and returns home to find it." 中文里叫 "舍近求远"。

其实大家准备雅思口语备考的过程，也多半如此。我经常告诉自己的学生们："老师教的 '亮点' 词句只是用来点缀（spice up）你的答案的，多数内容完全可以用简单一点的英文自己说。口语的本质是交流，而不是吓人。"

请您体会 British Council 提供的这个官方高分答案实例：

> **Which do you prefer, getting an email or a text message?**
>
> *I prefer emails. I work in front of a computer all day so this is easier for me. I'm not good at texting. I know I'm a bit old-fashioned.*

用词如此简洁的答案之所以会是 British Council 的官方高分答案，就因为它并没有 "语不惊人死不休" 的难词怪词，但却风格自然、内容清晰。

我们再来看这个官方高分实例：

> **Have you ever cooked a meal for your family?**
>
> *Well, I haven't actually. My mum tends to do all the cooking in our house. But I did bake some biscuits once. They were terrible. No one would eat them.*

整体用词非常浅显，只用少量略有难度（但也并不是很难）的单词和短语（phrases）作为 "点缀"，这就是典型的 British Council 官方高分答案的用词风格。

再来看这个《剑11》Test 1 里面的高分实例：

> **Do you agree there is a right age for young adults to stop living with their parents?**
>
> *Yes, I agree because young adults who still live with their parents tend to rely too much on their parents. Most of them don't cook for themselves or clean their rooms.*

> *That's not fair to their parents. I think after young adults find their first job, usually at around 22 years of age, they should be independent and stop living with their parents.*

清晰、自然的用词风格仍然是如此一致。

下面的高分答案同样用词平实，请时刻牢记"交流"才是口语的目的：

> **How do you think we can help our neighbours?**
>
> *There're a number of ways. For example, we can help elderly neighbours with their housework. When new neighbours move in, we can show them around the community, and give them important community service phone numbers.*

再来看下面的答案：

> **Do you think bicycles are good for all ages?**
>
> *I don't think so. Cycling is a good way to keep fit for most ages. But for people who are too young or too old to have good balance skills, cycling can be dangerous.*

这样的答案，如果能够比较流利地说出来而且发音也不错，至少会有 8 分，但它并没有刻意使用任何"霸气"的词汇，只是努力地想和考官进行一次实实在在的交流。

当然，并不是每个人都需要 8 分，再看这个回答：

> **What kinds of radio programme do you like best?**
>
> *I don't really listen to the radio very often. But it seems I tend to prefer news shows and sports shows because they are fun and helpful. They give me information about what is happening around the world and in important sports competitions.*

这样的答案之所以是高分的答案，就因为考生的目的明显是要和考官进行很真实的交流，而不是想把一堆大词和连自己都不明白的难句扔给考官之后就"闪"。

即使比较抽象的考题也仍然并不需要用所谓"高端、大气、上档次"的词汇才能拿到高分。

请再看这个常考题的高分答案：、

> **Do you think it's possible to be friends with people who you've never met in person?**
>
> *Yes, it's possible. I've heard about pen friends or "pen pals" who'd never met in person but could still communicate well with each other by letter. And these days, it's very easy to make new friends on social networking websites.*

像这样的答案，已经绝对是 IELTS 口试中的高分答案了，就因为它合理（make sense），而且它的目标是真实有效的交流（effective communication）。

今天 Pat 就跟您分享在 IELTS 口语考场上真正能打动考官的词汇和短语。它们多数貌不惊人，但当您亲身踏出国门之后就会真正明白它们在国外生活里是何等地常用了。

雅思口语中最常用的"小词"
Common Colloquial Words and Phrases

◇ 标"★"的词句表示极为常用，一定要熟练掌握。

◇ 对于没有标出"★"的词句，如果时间很紧的话那就不要记了。准备 IELTS 听说读写四项有一个真理：不要为了那些在考场里你可能想不起来的东西去牺牲（compromise）掉那些考场里你一定会用到的东西。

◇ 此表格充分考虑了英、美两国的英语习惯。对于那些只在美国和加拿大使用，但是英国人并不常用的口语词汇在本书中一律不予推荐。对于没有十分把握的词句，Pat 还专门向我的英国朋友们做了确认。

序号	英文表达	讲解	用法举例
1	★ stuff	东西，口语里面等于 things，但同时必须提醒国内的同学们：stuff 永远**不能用复数**	The **stuff** in that store is very expensive.

（续表）

序号	英文表达	讲解	用法举例
2	★ pretty	= 副词 very	My new iPhone is pretty fun.
3	★ fun	= interesting（请朋友们注意 fun 作形容词时其实并不是 funny"搞笑的"意思）	There're lots of fun things to do in Stanley Park. 注：Stanley Park 是温哥华的一个大公园，离我家很近，非常美
4	★ adore	非常喜欢	I adore that singer.
5	shortly	= soon	I'll get these things done shortly.
6	★ decent	在中国上英语课时老师可能会语重心长地告诉你这个词是"体面的"，但在国外真实生活里这个词更多的时候是表示"不错的，挺好的"意思 = quite good	This job offers a decent salary and some impressive benefits（工作的"福利"在英文里就直接用 benefits 最地道）.
7	★ hang out	休闲放松	(1) I often hang out in bars at weekends. (2) I often hang out with them at the park.
8	★ kind of = sort of	有点……, = somewhat	My boss is kind of hard to get along with.
9	★ like…	like 在英美口语里极度常用，可以表示"比如说"、"像是……"、"差不多是……样的"	(1) I bought lots of stuff, like carrots, beef and salmon. (2) That programme is like, … boring.

（续表）

序号	英文表达	讲解	用法举例
10	in a row	= one after another 连续地,这个短语在英美生活里用来描述一系列连续的事物时都已经到了无孔不入的程度,但在国内孩子们那儿却悄无声息	Patricia passed four exams in a row. (请注意:in a row 通常都是放在它所修饰的复数名词后面)
11	★ entire	= whole / complete,而且它的副词 entirely 也是在考试时替换 completely 的绝佳选择。请牢记在口语里 entire 后面跟名词,entirely 后面跟形容词	(1) Daniel ate the entire cake and made no apology for that. (2) Our situation is entirely different from theirs. (3) Jessica is not entirely sure if she can get a nice job after graduation.
12	★ ... as well.	也…… = ... too.	Beijing has exciting nightlife. And it has many historical attractions as well.
13	... is a piece of cake. =... is a snap. =... is a breeze.	小菜一碟,后面这两个国内考生普遍不熟悉,但在英美生活里也时常能听到	The IELTS speaking test is just a breeze if you know all the tricks.
14	★ know... inside out	精通……	He knows computers inside out.
15	I'm all for...	我完全支持某事物(= I strongly support ...,注意:这个句型在英美口语里很常用,但在学术写作里不要用) 反义:I'm against...	I've got nothing against change — I'm all for it.

（续表）

序号	英文表达	讲解	用法举例
16	is no picnic = is a pain in the neck	很折磨人	Getting the homework done everyday **is no picnic**.
17	★ … really bothers me.	让我很烦	The noise really **bothers me**.
18	★ kick back and relax	放松	At parties, we just **kick back and relax**.
19	★ a couple of	几个	I stayed in France for **a couple of** weeks.
20	a bunch of	= some 一些	I went there with **a bunch of** new friends.
21	★ loads of =tons of	= lots of	I've got **loads of** work to do this week.
22	★ make sense	= be reasonable 合理	The plot（剧情）of that movie didn't **make sense**.
23	★ …, you name it. = and the list goes on and on	……应有尽有(通常被放在列举出的几个名词之后表示其实还有更多,数不胜数)	Beijing has traditions, modern lifestyles, top universities, exciting night-life, … **you name it**.
24	By doing that, I kill two birds with one stone.	一举两得	When I travel around, I take photos and then sell them online. So you see, **I** just **kill two birds with one stone**.
25	★ … is the best + 名词, hands down.	……绝对是最……的	The new iPad is **the best** tablet（平板电脑）I've ever seen, **hands down**.

（续表）

序号	英文表达	讲解	用法举例
26	... would be the last thing I want to do.	……是我最不想做的事	Doing the dishes **would be the last thing I want to do.**
27	★ mess up...	把某件事给"弄糟了"，尤其是生活在节奏紧张的大城市里的人们特别爱用 mess up...这个短语	（1）There are always people who come to a party and try to **mess things up.** （2）Julia **messed up her chances of** becoming a great singer.
28	get the hang of...	基本了解怎样做某事	"I've never used a word processor before." "Don't worry — you'll **get the hang of** it shortly."
29	It's a shame!	"太可惜了"（在这里 shame 跟"羞耻"无关）	**It's a shame** that you have to leave so soon.
30	...is non-existent.	这个表达完全等于中文里"压根儿就不存在"	Some scientists believe global warming **is non-existent.** They even argue that the Earth is actually getting colder.
31	★ end up + 动词 +ing	在这个短语的后面经常接动词的 ing 形式，用来描述某人或某事物最终处于某种状态	（1）I **ended up** having to do all the work by myself. （2）There were no tickets left for that movie, so we **ended up** watching a different movie.

（续表）

序号	英文表达	讲解	用法举例
32	★ suit my needs	国内同学们普遍都爱使用 suitable,简直是"用 suitable 上瘾"。事实上,在英美日常生活里动词 suit 要比形容词 suitable 更常用。	The flat looks nice and is pretty close to my university, so it really suits my needs.

从非常喜欢到极度讨厌的地道英文表达

IELTS 口试里经常会涉及喜欢(like)或者不喜欢(dislike)的话题。下面这个表格覆盖了从非常喜欢一直到极度讨厌的全部常见地道英文表达,在 IELTS 口试的 Part 1 里你一定能用到其中的几种:

… is my biggest passion. (最喜欢) I'm fascinated by… I'm crazy about… I adore… I love… I'm a… buff (……迷, 在 buff 前填入自己特别喜欢的东东) I'm really into… I'm very fond of… I like …	I'm not keen on… I'm not very fond of… It's a drag. I totally dislike… I hate… I can't stand… I loathe… (最不喜欢) 其实口语里还有语气更强的, 不过基本就是骂人了,考试时勿用

Pat指南

☆ 注意:buff 在英美是指"粉"某种事物,比如 movie,car 或者 music。但如果是指"粉"某一个人,则还是必须用 fan 或者 admirer:

I am a movie buff. I go to the movies whenever I can find some free time.（buff 这个词的语气很像中文里的"……控"）

I am a big fan（或者 a big admirer）of Stephen Curry.（某一个人的"粉丝"就不能用 buff 了）

从最频繁到最偶然的地道英文表达

How often...? 类考题也是 IELTS 口试里的常客。下面的表达分别对应从最频繁到最少发生的各种频率，只要听到考官张嘴说 How often...的题就要条件反射地想到这个表格：

I... all the time.（总是……）

I constantly...（不间断地……）

I... daily.（daily 不止是《日报》，在地道英文中它也经常作副词，表示"每天都……"）

I... almost every day.（几乎每天都……）

I... every other day.（每隔一天就……）

I... on a weekly basis.（每周都……）

I often...（定期地……）

I ...regularly.（经常……）

I ... on a regular basis.（定期地……）

I ... every now and then.（时常…）

Sometimes I...（有时候……）

I ... once in a while...（偶尔……）

I don't... very often.（不常……）

I rarely...（中国考生极其爱用的 seldom 在英美生活里用的不如 rarely 多）

I hardly ever...（几乎不……）

I never....（从不……）

让你在 Part 1 和 Part 3 做到
"言之有物" 的 English phrases

Pat 发现很多中国同学在回答 Part 1 和 Part 3 的问题时经常是刚开了一个头儿就说不下去了，而且面部表情也相当痛苦。即使勉强说下去，答案也是一个单词一个单词地"蹦"出来的，无法形成连贯、有效的意思。同学说着揪心，Pat 听着也是"步步惊心"（skating on thin ice）的感觉。

这其中的原因，除了很多中国学生多年来学英语的方式一直都是"君子动眼不动口"之外，另一个原因就是国内同学们普遍不熟悉 native speakers 在讨论问题时经常会借助的实用短语。但使用 English phrases 的能力却是口语考官在实战评分时相当重视的一种技能。

如果您能在考前把下面的三类短语记熟、说溜，您就会发现自己回答问题的胆子开始大起来了，而且答案也立刻有了实际有效的内容（truly meaningful answers），而不再是空话连篇（a bunch of hot air）。

动 词 部

（i）下面各动词按"从易到难"的顺序排列，请在您想记的短语（phrases）前面的方块上画 √，并及时复习自己画 √ 的短语。基础一般的同学不必追求"全覆盖"，只有懂得取舍才会有重点，关键是：只要记一个 phrase 就必须真正把它记熟、记准。

（ii）本节的音频也可以帮助您记忆和复习这些短语；

（iii）本书的 Day 7 和本书附赠的《IELTS 口语高频词汇 & 短语速查手册》也是帮您复习这些 phrases 的好帮手。复习 — 实践 — 再复习，能够脱口而出才有实战意义。

feel 感觉

- ☐ **feel calm and relaxed**　感觉心情平静而且放松

- ☐ **feel happy and energetic**　感觉心情愉快、精力充沛

  　🈟 native speakers 还经常说 feel fresh and energetic

- ☐ **feel motivated**　感觉很有动力，"动力满满"

- ☐ **feel stressed**
  　感觉压力山大，英美生活里还经常说 feel stressed out

What's the difference?

　　Pat 发现很多国内同学会把 stressed 和 stressful 这两个形容词用混，其实它们并不难区分：

　　stressed 是指（人）感觉压力很大的，而 stressful 是指（事物或者生活方式）让人感觉压力很大的。

　　所以，如果您执意跟考官说 "I'm very stressful."，那么意思就是："你可要当心了，我会让你压力很大的。"

拓展延伸　… makes me feel… 是在 Part 1 解释你为什么喜欢某种事物的一个实用句型。虽然看上去"很 easy"，但只要你真的能把它流利地说出来，听起来就很自然，因为 native speakers 确实经常这么说：

- Listening to Ed Sheeran's music **makes me feel** calm and relaxed.

- Jogging（慢跑）**makes me feel** happy and energetic.

have 有

- ☐ **have more choices**　有更多的选择
- ☐ **have more freedom**　有更多的自由
- ☐ **have more job opportunities**　有更多的就业机会

do 做……

- ☐ **do housework**　做家务
- ☐ **do outdoor activities**　做室外活动

□ do voluntary work / do volunteer work
做志愿者，做义工

注 这两种说法都是地道的，前者在英国更常听到，后者美国人用得更多一些

help 帮助

□ help me relax　帮助我放松

□ help me concentrate　帮助我集中注意力

□ help us better understand...
帮助我们更好地了解……

□ help us keep fit　帮助我们保持体格强健

What's the difference

Pat 发现有相当多的国内同学都误以为 stay healthy 和 keep fit 是一样的意思，其实在地道英文里它们是有区别的：

stay healthy 是泛指保持整体的身心健康、远离疾病，而 keep fit 则是特指保持体格强健、"有形儿"的状态。

例如：慢跑（jogging）既可以帮助你 stay healthy，也可以帮助你 keep fit。但是晚上睡前听让人放松的音乐（relaxing music）虽然可以帮你 sleep well and stay healthy，但是却不能够帮助你 keep fit。

enjoy 享受

□ enjoy the fresh air　享受新鲜的空气

□ enjoy the natural beauty　享受自然的美景

注 natural beauty（自然的美景）和 natural scenery（自然风光）都不能加复数

go 去

□ go camping　去野营

□ go jogging　去慢跑

□ go sightseeing　去观光旅行

make 产生，制造，让……变得……

- ☐ make new friends　结识新朋友
- ☐ make contributions to society　为社会做贡献
- ☐ make life more convenient　让生活变得更方便
- ☐ make children more intelligent
  让儿童变得更聪明，例如演奏乐器（musical instrument）
- ☐ make children more independent
  让儿童变得更独立，例如教孩子做饭（cooking）

take 接受，乘坐

- ☐ take their advice　接受他们的建议
- ☐ take public transport　乘坐公共交通

请用 spend 或者 take 的正确形式填入下面的括号里：

1. Walking to school（ *take* ）more time but is more eco-friendly（有益于环保的）.
2. Organic food（有机食品）（ *takes* ）more time to produce.
3. Many teenagers these days（ *spend* ）too much time on mobile games（手机游戏）.

1. takes（主语一般是活动、事件或人，表示一般人来花时间） 2. takes 3. spend（主语是人、事件或活动）

give 给

- ☐ give me the opportunity to…　给我……的机会
- ☐ give them a nice surprise　给他们一个惊喜
- ☐ give them a sense of achievement　给他们一种成就感
- ☐ give money to charities　给慈善组织捐款

work 工作

- ☐ work full-time　全职地工作
- ☐ work part-time　兼职地工作
- ☐ work overtime　加班
- ☐ work closely together　一起紧密合作

  注 这个短语里面的 work 不仅可以指工作，也可以指学习、运动、国际合作等领域里面的努力，是 native speakers 说团队合作（teamwork）时的一个必用短语

☐ **work out regularly** 经常健身

• *What's the difference* ❓ •

如果你说 I work out regularly，那么 native speakers 首先会想到的就是你经常去健身房（gym）锻炼。

但如果你说 I exercise regularly，那么各种锻炼，无论是去健身房还是慢跑、游泳或者跳广场舞（practise your Square Dance routine），都是"可以有"的 ☺

keep 保持	☐ **keep a balance between work and life** 在工作和生活之间保持合理的平衡

☐ **keep a balance between work and family**
在工作和家庭之间保持合理的平衡

☐ **keep children away from unhealthy food**
让孩子远离不健康的食品

☐ **keep children away from violent images**
让孩子远离暴力的画面

☐ **keep in touch with family and friends**
和亲友们保持联系

share 分享	☐ **share ideas** 分享想法

☐ **share photos and videos online** 在网络上分享照片和视频

☐ **share interests and hobbies online** 在网络上分享兴趣和爱好

☐ **share the joy** 分享快乐

📖 **注** share the joy 虽然"无比简单"，却真心是 native speakers 在讨论 festival 和 family 话题时的常用短语之一，还有些人说 share the joy and happiness 这个短语也是一样的意思

communicate 交流	☐ **communicate with friends** 和朋友交流

☐ **communicate with family members** 和家人交流

☐ **communicate freely** 自由地交流，畅通无阻地交流

search 搜索

□ search for information 搜索信息

□ search online 在网络上搜索

在 IELTS 口试里这 8 个常考名词都<u>不能加</u> s：

| information | knowledge | advice | behaviour |
| furniture | equipment | scenery | heritage |

browse 浏览

□ browse through websites 浏览网站

□ browse through newspapers 浏览报纸

□ browse through magazines 浏览杂志

□ browse through shops 在店里浏览（但未必会买东西）

copy 模仿

□ copy what they see on TV
（青少年）模仿他们在电视上看到的内容

□ copy what they see in video games
模仿他们在电子游戏里看到的场景

play 进行某种活动，起……的作用

□ play online games 玩网络游戏

□ play sports 进行体育运动

注 play sports 不是中式英语，而是一个地道的 English phrase

□ play a key role in... 在……当中起很关键的作用

hang out 休闲放松

□ hang out with friends 和朋友一块儿休闲放松

□ hang out together 一起休闲放松

look 看起来

□ look the same 看起来一样

□ look very similar 看起来很相似

□ look unique 看起来十分独特

□ look attractive 看起来很有吸引力

☐ look unattractive 看起来毫无吸引力

🔊注 它们都很简单，但是在考场里讨论全球化、建筑、城市等话题时却真的相当实用。good phrases 的评判标准不是难度，而是听起来是不是自然、是不是确实符合 native speakers 的表达习惯

look after
照看，照顾

☐ look after their children 照看他们的孩子

☐ look after their elderly parents 照看他们的老年父母

☐ look after their grandchildren （老人）照看他们的孙辈

know
知道，了解

☐ know someone very well 非常了解某人

☐ know a place very well 非常了解某个地方

reduce 减少

☐ reduce stress 减少压力，减压

☐ reduce funding for... 减少对于……的资助

☐ reduce poverty 减少贫困，"扶贫"

☐ reduce the risk of heart disease and high blood pressure
（运动、健康的饮食等）减少患心脏病和高血压的风险

increase 增加

☐ increase funding for...
增加对于……的资助

☐ increase the burden on taxpayers
增加纳税人的负担

☐ increase the risk of heart disease and high blood pressure
增加患心脏病和高血压的风险

gain 获取

☐ gain confidence 获得自信

☐ gain new knowledge 获取新的知识

🔊注 gain new knowledge 既可以指在学校获取新知识，也可以指通过博物馆、互联网、旅行等方式来获取新知识。注意：地道英

文里不能说 learn new knowledge ✗，因为 native speakers 认为 knowledge 是不可以 "learn" 的，但你却可以说 learn new things ✓，这就是 English phrases 的可恨又可爱之处 ☺

lose 失去

- ☐ lose their jobs　失去工作
- ☐ lose their privacy　（名人）失去隐私
- ☐ lose their traditions　失去他们的传统
- ☐ lose weight　减肥

　🔵注 英美生活里也常说 lose a few pounds "掉几磅肉" ☺

get away from...
摆脱……

- ☐ get away from busy city life　摆脱繁忙的都市生活
- ☐ get away from it all　摆脱日常的各种琐事

　📝注 native speakers 特别爱用这两个短语来讨论和 travel 或者 park 有关的话题

get closer to ...
更加接近……

- ☐ get closer to nature　更加接近大自然
- ☐ get closer to my goal　更加接近我的目标

save 节约

- ☐ save time and money
　既省时间又省钱，例如：online shopping（网络购物）
- ☐ save water　节约用水
- ☐ save energy　节约能源，例如：改用太阳能（solar power），风能（wind power）

manage 管理

- ☐ manage their time well　有效地管理时间
- ☐ manage their money well　有效地管理财务

guide 指导

- ☐ guide their children　（家长）指导他们的孩子
- ☐ guide their students　（教师）指导他们的学生

contribute to...
为……做贡献

- ☐ contribute to society 为社会做贡献
- ☐ contribute to the economy 为经济做贡献
- ☐ contribute to charities 为慈善机构做贡献

  注 如果想表示"为……做出很大的贡献"，native speakers 在口语里常会说 contribute a lot to...，在写作里则常会写 contribute greatly to...或者 contribute significantly to...

concentrate on...
集中精力在……上面

- ☐ concentrate on their studies 集中精力在他们的学业上面
  注 study 的复数 studies 在地道英文里常表示"学业"
- ☐ concentrate on their tasks 集中精力在他们的任务上面

contain 含有

- ☐ contain a lot of vitamin C and fiber
  （水果、蔬菜等）含有大量的维生素 C 和纤维
- ☐ contain too much fat
  （垃圾食品等）含有过多的脂肪
- ☐ contain too much sugar 含有过多的糖

celebrate 庆祝

- ☐ celebrate a festival 庆祝节日
- ☐ celebrate a birthday 庆祝生日

receive 收到

- ☐ receive a thoughtful gift
  收到一个"贴心"的礼物
- ☐ receive good reviews
  （产品、电影、电视节目等）收到很好的评价

develop
发展，成长

- ☐ develop their... skills 发展他们的……技能
- ☐ develop into useful members of society
  （学生、青少年）成长为对社会有用的成员

IELTS 口试里最常"聊到"的 7 种技能

- life skills　生活技能
- reading and writing skills　读写技能
- computer skills　计算机技能
- communication skills　沟通技能
- teamwork skills　进行团队合作的技能
- time-management skills　时间管理技能
- cooking skills　做饭技能，"厨艺"

form 形成

- form good learning habits　形成良好的学习习惯
- form good eating habits　形成良好的饮食习惯
- form good spending habits　形成良好的消费习惯

improve
增进，改善

- improve my mood　改善我的情绪
- improve my memory　改善我的记忆力
- improve our health　增进我们的健康

experience 体验

- experience a different culture　体验一种不同的文化
- experience a different lifestyle　体验一种不同的生活方式

注 experience 作为名词也同样很常用，例如：have more experience（有更丰富的经验），an enjoyable experience（一次令人愉快的经历）等

attract 吸引

- attract many tourists　吸引很多的游客
- attract many viewers　（电影、电视节目）吸引很多的观看者
- attract many listeners　（广播节目）吸引很多的收听者
- attract many readers　（报纸、杂志）吸引很多的读者

prepare 准备
- prepare for employment （学生）为就业做准备
- prepare for future success
  （青少年）为将来的成功做准备

provide 提供
- provide a variety of information 提供多种多样的信息
- provide the opportunity to... 提供……的机会
- provide a relaxing atmosphere 提供令人放松的氛围

  注 这个短语里的 relaxing 还可以用 lively（很有活力的），friendly（很友好的）等代替

中国考生们更爱用 many kinds of 或者 many types of 表示"多种多样"的，而 native speakers 却更爱用 a variety of 这个短语：

剑桥例句
① The equipment can be used for **a variety of** purposes.
② The event provides **a variety of** outdoor activities.

---

control 控制
- control pollution 控制污染
- control the number of cars 控制汽车的数量

damage 破坏
- damage our health 破坏我们的健康
- damage the environment 破坏环境
- damage their self-confidence 打击他们的自信
- damage their self-esteem 伤害他们的自尊，"伤自尊"

face 面对
- face fierce competition （毕业生、企业）面对激烈的竞争
- face extinction （野生动物、少数语言）濒临灭绝

suffer from... 遭受……的困扰
- suffer from pollution 遭受污染的困扰
- suffer from noise 遭受噪音的困扰

□ suffer from stress and anxiety
遭受压力和焦虑的困扰

lack 缺乏

□ lack... skills　缺乏某种技能

□ lack funding　（博物馆、学校等）缺乏资助

□ lack depth　（电影、歌曲等）缺乏深度

cause 导致

□ cause health problems　导致健康问题

□ cause traffic accidents　导致交通事故

□ cause misunderstandings　导致误解

break 打破，违反

□ break the law　违反法律

□ break traffic rules　违反交通规则

punish 惩罚

□ punish criminals　惩罚罪犯

□ punish dangerous drivers
惩罚危险驾驶的司机

obey 遵守

□ obey the law　遵守法律

□ obey school rules　遵守学校的规定

need 需要

□ need repairs　需要维修

□ need help and support　需要帮助和支持

support 支持

□ support their children　支持他们的孩子

□ support their teammates　支持他们的队友

rely too much on...
过度地依赖……

□ rely too much on mobile phones　过度地依赖手机

□ rely too much on the Internet　过度地依赖互联网

□ rely too much on technology　过度地依赖科技

focus too much on... 过度地关注……	▫ focus too much on money 过度地关注金钱
	▫ focus too much on fashion 过度地关注时尚
	▫ focus too much on appearance 过度地关注外表

meet 遇到	▫ meet our needs 符合我们的需要
	▫ meet their online friends in real life "见网友"

raise 提高，养育	▫ raise people's standard of living 提高人民的生活水平
	▫ raise public health awareness 提高公众的健康意识
	▫ raise public environmental awareness 提高公众的环境意识
	▫ raise children 养育孩子

respect 尊重	▫ respect their peers 尊重他们的同龄人
	▫ respect their privacy 尊重他们的隐私

treat 对待	▫ treat... well 很好地对待……
	▫ treat... fairly 很公平地对待……

bother 让……很烦	▫ really bothers me 让我"好烦"
	▫ bother their classmates 让他们的同学们很烦

expand 扩展，开阔	▫ expand my mind 扩展我的思维
	▫ expand my vocabulary 扩展我的词汇量
	▫ expand my horizons 开阔我的视野
	注 这个短语里的 horizon 必须用复数

express 表达	▫ express their feelings 表达他们的情感
	▫ express their ideas and opinions 表达他们的想法和观点

take part in... 参与	□ take part in group activities　参与集体活动 □ take part in sports　参与体育运动 注 基础好的同学也可以用 participate in... 表示相同的意思

exchange　交换	□ exchange ideas　交换想法 □ exchange gifts　交换礼物

achieve　实现	□ achieve success　获得成功 □ achieve their goal　实现他们的目标 □ achieve sustainable development　实现可持续发展（听起来有点儿"虚伪"，其实就是指不破坏环境的发展）

overcome　克服	□ overcome the language barrier　✓. 克服由于语言不同导致的沟通障碍，"跨越"语言障碍 □ overcome the generation gap　✓. 克服代沟，"跨越"代沟

build　建设，树立	□ build self-confidence　树立自信 □ build a successful career　建设成功的事业 □ build strong family ties　建设亲人之间的关系，增强亲情

boost　提升	□ boost my mood　改善我的情绪 □ boost my efficiency　提升我的效率 □ boost my concentration　提高我的注意力 □ boost our immune system　增强我们的免疫机能，例如：运动和户外活动（outdoor activities）

create　创造	□ create jobs　创造就业 □ create opportunities for...　为……创造机会 □ create more nature reserves　创建更多的自然保护区

promote 促进
- ☐ promote tourism 促进旅游业
- ☐ promote economic growth 促进经济的增长
- ☐ promote world peace 促进世界和平

hold back...
阻碍......的发展
- ☐ hold back the economy 阻碍经济的发展 ✓
- ☐ hold back their careers 阻碍他们的事业发展

realise 实现
- ☐ realise my dream 实现我的梦想
- ☐ realise their ambitions 实现他们的志向

recycle 循环使用
- ☐ recycle waste 循环使用废弃物
- ☐ recycle used materials 循环使用被用过的材料

walk or cycle
步行或者骑自行车
- ☐ walk or cycle to work 步行或骑自行车上班
- ☐ walk or cycle to school 步行或骑自行车上学

value 重视，珍惜
- ☐ value their advice 重视他们的建议
- ☐ value our traditions 重视我们的传统
- ✓ value our cultural heritage 珍惜我们的文化遗产
- 🈺 advice 和 heritage 都不能用复数

bring back ...
（照片、童年时喜
欢的歌曲等）唤起
某种回忆
- ☐ bring back good memories 唤起愉快的回忆
- ☐ bring back fond memories 唤起美好的回忆

avoid 避免
- ☐ avoid mistakes 避免错误，例如好的建议（good advice）可以帮助我们避免错误
- ☐ avoid unhealthy food 避免不健康的食品

prevent 预防
- □ prevent crime　预防犯罪
- □ prevent heart disease and high blood pressure
  预防心脏病和高血压

spoil 溺爱
- □ spoil their children　溺爱孩子
- □ spoil the fun　"扫兴"

satisfy 满足
- □ satisfy tourists' needs　满足游客的需求
- □ satisfy our curiosity　满足我们的好奇心

distract
干扰……的注意力
- □ distract others　干扰别人的注意力，例如：noise
- □ distract drivers　干扰司机的注意力，例如：mobile phones

★　★　★

下面这几个动词的难度比较大，基础一般的读者请量力而行，如果觉得基本肯定会记不住或者想不起来那就不要勉强。把简单的短语真正记熟才是你的"第一要务"。

strengthen
增强，增进
- □ strengthen family ties　增强亲情
- □ strengthen friendships　增进友情

enrich 丰富
- □ enrich our lives　丰富我们的生活
- □ enrich our experience　丰富我们的经历

preserve
保护某种资源（但
保护某人还是必须
用 protect）
- □ preserve natural resources　保护自然资源
- □ preserve historic buildings　保护历史建筑
- □ preserve our traditions　保护我们的传统

explore 探索	☐ explore the local culture 探索当地的文化
	☐ explore space 探索太空

pose 构成（威胁）	✓ pose a threat to our health 对我们的健康构成威胁
	☐ pose a threat to the environment 对环境构成威胁
	☐ pose a threat to the local wildlife 对当地的野生生物构成威胁，例如：污染，旅游业（tourism）等

address 努力解决	☐ address the problem 努力解决问题
	☐ address the difficulties 努力解决困难

tighten 让（法律）变得更强硬，强化法律	☐ tighten the law against air pollution 强化限制空气污染的法律
	☐ tighten the law against dangerous driving 强化限制危险驾驶行为的法律

deter 震慑	☐ deter crime 震慑犯罪行为
	☐ deter dangerous driving 震慑危险的驾驶行为

capture 捕捉	☐ capture precious moments in life （照片、录像等）捕捉生活里的宝贵瞬间
	☐ capture people's attention 抓住人们的注意力，强烈地吸引人们的注意力

stimulate 激发	☐ stimulate people's imagination 激发人们的想象力
	☐ stimulate children's creativity 激发儿童的创造力

adopt 接受（某种新科技或者新的生活方式）	☐ adopt new technology 接受新科技
	☐ adopt a healthy lifestyle 接受健康的生活方式

形容词部

10 对儿 形容词

　　下面这"10 对儿"形容词能帮助您快速熟悉 IELTS 口试里的常见形容词构词法：

entertaining 很有娱乐性的 inspiring 激励人的，励志的	relaxed 放松的 dedicated 敬业的
helpful 有帮助的 useful 有用的	informative 信息量大的 attractive 很有吸引力的
energetic 精力充沛的 athletic 擅长运动的	cultural 文化的 global 全球的
reliable 可靠的，值得信赖的 portable 便于携带的	nutritious 很有营养的 precious 珍贵的
user-friendly 方便使用的 eco-friendly（生活方式或产品）有益于环保的	well-located 位置十分便利的 well-educated 受到良好教育的

形容人的短语

□ friendly and helpful 　很友好而且乐于助人的	□ polite and respectful 　有礼貌的、尊重别人的 　反义 rude and annoying 　粗鲁的、烦人的
□ confident and independent 　自信而且独立的	□ understanding and patient 　体谅别人的、有耐心的 　注 这个 understanding 是作形容词， 　"体谅别人的"
□ open-minded and creative 　思想开明的、有创造力的	□ hardworking and dedicated 　勤奋的、敬业的

□ too materialistic　过于物质化的，"拜金的" 注 selfish and unkind 自私的，不友善的	□ lonely and unhappy 孤独的、不快乐的
□ addicted to...　对于……（社交网站、电子游戏、电视等）上瘾的	

:::::::::::::::::::::::::::::: **形容事物或者活动的短语** ::::::::::::::::::::::::::::::

□ fun and enjoyable 有趣的而且令人愉快的 注 fun 作形容词时是"有趣的"，而 funny 则是"逗乐的，搞笑的"	□ fun and rewarding 有趣而且很有回报的 注 rewarding 既可以指在物质方面很有回报，也可以指在心理方面很有回报
□ interesting and informative　（电视节目、报纸、网站等）有趣而且信息量很大的	□ dull and boring 乏味的、枯燥的
□ useful and reliable （工具、网站等）有用的、可靠的	□ false and misleading　（广告、新闻报导）虚假的、有误导性的
□ moving and unforgettable （电影、歌曲等）很感人的、令人难忘的	□ disappointing and annoying 令人失望的、令人烦恼的 注 要说（人）感到失望、烦恼的，那就是 feel disappointed and annoyed，甚至 feel frustrated（感到失落、沮丧的）
□ nice and comfortable　称心的、舒适的 注 如果是特指房间、家具称心舒适，那么还可以说 nice and cosy	□ neat and tidy （房间、笔迹等）干净整洁的
□ spacious and bright 宽敞明亮的	□ quiet and peaceful （公园、夜晚等）宁静安详的
□ noisy and overcrowded 喧闹而且过于拥挤的	□ fresh and nutritious （食品）新鲜并且很有营养的
□ high-fat and high-calorie 高脂肪、高热量的	

★   ★   ★

:::::::: **好方法和好来源** ::::::::

在 IELTS 口试 Part 1 和 Part 3 里面，考生经常会被要求解释自己喜欢某一类事物的原因是什么。有两个简单地道的 phrases 在 native speakers 谈论自己喜欢的事物时特别常用：

> ❖ a good way to...   是……很好的方法
>
> ❖ a good source of... 是……很好的来源

请认真体会下面的例句：

◇ Listening to music <u>is a good way to</u> relax（是很好的放松方法）.

◇ Playing a musical instrument <u>is a good way to</u> reduce stress（是很好的"减压"方法）.

◇ Swimming <u>is a good way to</u> keep fit（是保持身强体健的好方法）.

◇ Visiting museums <u>is a good way to</u> gain new knowledge（是获取新知识的好方法）.

◇ Travelling <u>is a good way to</u> make new friends（结识新朋友的好方法）.

◇ The Internet <u>is a good source of</u> information（是很好的信息来源）.

◇ Television <u>is a good source of</u> fun（是很好的乐趣来源）.

◇ Apples <u>are a good source of</u> vitamin C（是很好的维生素 C 来源）.

在英美生活里，a good way to...前面的主语用**动名词**（动词 + ing）更常听到，而 a good source of 前面的主语用**名词**更常听到。

无论您在何时何地参加 IELTS 口试，都至少有机会用到上面例句里的 1~2 个短语结构，虽然简单，但真心实用。

名 词 部

□ the pace of life	生活节奏
□ the cost of living	生活成本，生活开支
□ a waste of...	对……（时间、钱、精力等）的浪费
□ standard of living	生活水平
□ economic growth	经济增长，经济发展 注 native speakers 不说 economy growth ✗
□ consumer culture	崇尚消费的文化
□ designer clothes	这个简单的 phrase 就是英文里"名牌服装"最地道而且也最常用的表达 ❓ 错在哪里　Pat 注意到有很多中国同学都会说错 clothes 的发音，其实 clothes 里面的 e 是不发音的，没把握的同学请注意听音频跟读
✓□ a tight budget	紧张的预算
□ bad spending habits	不良的消费习惯 反义 good spending habits
□ a wide variety of courses	多种多样的课程
□ life skills	生活技能
□ behaviour problems	（儿童、青少年的）行为问题 注 日常生活里也经常就直接说 bad behaviour，注意：behaviour 不可数

□ useful members of society	有用的社会成员，能够为社会做贡献的社会成员
□ a successful career	成功的事业
□ family members	家庭成员
□ community members	社区成员
□ team members	团队成员
□ members of society	社会成员 ⚠ 英文里的 society members 是指某个协会的成员，而不是泛指社会成员，"社会成员"在地道英文里必须要说 members of society √ [剑桥例句] It is very rewarding for teachers to see their students develop into useful **members of society**.
□ common goal	共同的目标 注 common interests 共同的兴趣爱好
□ family ties	亲人之间的情感联系，亲情 注 也可以说 family bonds
□ nuclear family	只有父母和孩子生活在一起的小家庭，"核子家庭" 反义 extended family 三代人甚至四代人生活在一起的大家庭
□ generation gap	代沟
□ elderly people	老年人 注 很多 native speakers 认为它比 old people 听起来更有礼貌
□ population ageing	人口老龄化

□ equal opportunities	平等的机会
□ the gap between the rich and the poor	贫富差距
□ low-income families	低收入家庭 注 英文口语里也常把穷人委婉地称为 people in need
□ fierce competition	激烈的竞争 注 "面对"激烈的竞争动词就用 face 最地道
□ social networking website	社交网站 注 口语里也可以更简单地说 social networking site
□ online forum / Internet forum	网络论坛
□ a useful tool	有用的工具

? 错在哪里

经常有学生"质问"Pat 为什么不说 an useful tool ✗。

这其中的原因是：到底用 a 还是用 an，其实应该看读音，而不是看拼写。

虽然 useful 的第一个字母是 u，但这个 u 在 useful 里面的读音是 /juː/，所以 useful 的读音是辅音 /j/ 开头，它前面应该用 a，而不能用 an。

这也就是为什么你可以说 a university，但你绝不能说 an university ✗。

[剑桥例句]

① Email is **a useful tool** for exchanging ideas and information.

② The Royal Agricultural University is **a university** located in Cirencester.

□ online community	网络社区
□ the virtual world	虚拟的世界 反义 the real world 真实的世界

□ special effects	（电影或电视节目里面的）特技效果
□ sound advice	它不是"出声音的建议" ✗ ，而是指"中肯、务实的建议" 注 advice 不能加 s
□ a thoughtful gift	一个"贴心"的礼物
□ a friendly and relaxing atmosphere	友好、轻松的氛围
□ natural beauty	自然的美景
□ outdoor activities	户外活动 □ community activities　社区活动 □ group activities　集体活动 □ leisure activities　休闲活动　短语家族
□ a healthy lifestyle	健康的生活方式 注 native speakers 在 a... lifestyle 前面一般用动词 lead 或者 have
□ an active lifestyle	经常运动锻炼的生活方式
□ a good form of exercise	（游泳、慢跑、打篮球等）一种很好的锻炼方式
□ sports facilities	运动设施，例如：stadium （体育场），basketball court （篮球场），tennis court （网球场），swimming pool （游泳池）等 注 sports equipment 则是指具体的"运动器械"
□ fond memories	美好的回忆
□ casual clothes	休闲服装

a sense of achievement	成就感
a sense of belonging	归属感
a sense of responsibility	责任感
the greenhouse effect	温室效应
global warming	全球变暖
extreme weather	极端的天气
electric cars	电动汽车，例如：著名的 Tesla Model S
clean energy	清洁能源 注 例如：wind energy 风能，solar energy 太阳能
an eco-friendly lifestyle	有益于环保的生活方式
a long-term solution	一个长期有效的解决办法 反义 It's short-sighted to... 某种做法是短视的
sustainable development	可持续发展，不破坏环境的发展
natural resources	自然资源
under threat	受到威胁
endangered animals	濒危动物
nature reserves	自然保护区
animal rights	动物权益
work of art	艺术品 注 它的复数是 works of art
art gallery	美术馆 注 地道英文里当谈到博物馆和美术馆时，collection 就是指"馆藏"

□ hand-made products	手工制作的产品 反义 mass-produced products　大批量生产的产品
□ live performance	现场的表演 注 这个短语里面的 live 正确读音是/laɪv/
□ cultural heritage	文化遗产 注 heritage 不能用复数
□ cultural diversity	文化的多样性 注 bio-diversity　就是生物的多样性
□ a symbol of...	……的象征

雅思口试里最常涉及的 7 类象征意义

wealth	财富
good health	良好的健康状况
long life	长寿
romantic love	浪漫的爱情
happiness	幸福
good fortune	好运
peace	和平

□ **tourist attractions**	旅游景点

IELTS 口语里最常考的 3 类景点

□ cultural attractions　文化景点

□ historical attractions　历史景点

□ natural attractions　自然景点

剑桥例句 London has many **cultural attractions**, such as the British Museum and the National Gallery.

☐ rush hour	上下班的高峰期 **注** 地道英文里还经常更具体地说 the morning rush hour 或者 the evening rush hour
☐ traffic volume	交通量，车流量
☐ car fumes / exhaust fumes	汽车尾气
☐ public transport	公共交通
☐ transport facilities	交通设施
☐ the hustle and bustle	喧闹拥挤 **注** 地道英文里说 city 时的必用短语之一
☐ high-rise building	高楼，高层建筑

    Pat 注意到很多中国同学有一种倾向就是只要说"高楼"就必用 skyscraper。

    其实 skyscraper 在英美只能用来指近百米甚至更高的"摩天楼"，而 high-rise building 这个短语才是泛指各种高楼。如果您非要说自己住在一个六层的 skyscraper 里面，考官就只能说"我 get 不到"。☺

    "一栋六层高的公寓楼"在地道英文里叫作 a six-storey flat block，"一栋八层高的办公楼"叫作 an eight-storey office building。您可以把它们称为 high-rise building，但是却不能浑水摸鱼地把它们叫作 skyscraper…

☐ fresh air	新鲜的空气
☐ air pollution	空气污染
☐ thick smog	严重的雾霾
☐ health problems	健康问题
☐ health care	医疗
☐ a healthy diet	健康的饮食结构 **反义** an unhealthy diet

☐ vitamin C and fiber	维生素 C 和纤维 注 需要跟考官讨论水果、蔬菜的时候您就会感到这个短语有多么"可口"了 ☺
☐ organic food	有机食品
☐ genetically-modified food 	转基因食品 注 如果感觉"舌头绕不过来",那么可以直接说 GM food,因为 native speakers 在生活里甚至写论文时也经常这么简称
☐ an indispensable part of...	不可缺少的一部分,不可或缺的一部分
☐ current events	时事
☐ the latest news	最及时的新闻
☐ in-depth reports	深度的报导
☐ a flexible schedule	灵活的时间安排

考前时间充裕的同学还可以在本书 Day 7,Day 9 和本书附赠的《IELTS 口语高频词汇 & 短语速查手册》里看到更多在 Part 1 和 Part 3 实用的 good phrases。

★ ★ ★

以上这些短语已经可以让您在回答任何 Part 1 和 Part 3 的问题时都做到言之有物了。但同时应该注意的是:也不要用 good phrases 把你自己的每一句话都"武装到牙齿"。口语里的多数句子完全可以用普通的基础词汇来表达,这样的答案听起来才会是真正自然、流畅的。请牢记:native speakers 说英文的一个明显特点就是 native speakers 其实并不会让每句话都"语不惊人死不休"。

★　　★　　★

● 能让考官"身临其境"的 **4** 个形容词 ●

即使你并不是"外貌协会会员"或者"视觉动物",也请记住下面这 4 个形容词,因为它们都是 native speakers 描述自然美景（natural beauty）和城市风光（cityscape）的常用词：

spectacular
壮观的

  □ a spectacular view　壮观的景象
  □ a spectacular building　壮观的建筑

sparkling
闪烁的

  □ sparkling stars　闪烁的星星
  □ sparkling water　闪烁的水面

crystal-clear
纯净透明的

  □ crystal-clear water　清澈见底的水
  □ crystal-clear air　纯净透明的空气

rolling
起伏的

  □ rolling hills　起伏的小山
  □ rolling waves　起伏的波浪

怎样用地道英文说"走路 **5** 分钟就到"和"全年无休"？

描述 Part 2 经常会涉及到距离和时间。Pat 发现中国孩子们普遍很熟悉 near，close to 和 far away from 这 3 种表示距离的说法,也普遍很熟悉 always，often，sometimes 这 3 种表示时间的说法。

您在 IELTS 口试里用这些说法是完全可以的,因为它们确实都是地道的英文。但下面这几个短语同样也是 native speakers 介绍距离和时间的"必杀技"（essential phrases）,Pat 却极少会听到中国同学们使用这几个短语,这种"歧视"不能不说是一种遗憾：

紧挨着……

right beside...

注 这个 right 不是指右边，而是"正好儿"的意思

[剑桥例句] Our school is right beside a busy street, which makes it very noisy when window are open.

距离……步行 5 分钟就到

is just a 5-minute walk from....

[剑桥例句] The hotel was just a 5-minute walk from the beach.

距离……20 分钟车程

is a 20-minute drive from...

[剑桥例句] My office is a 20-minute drive from the airport.

定期地，经常性地

regularly / on a regular basis

[剑桥例句] They have a healthy diet and exercise regularly.

有时

from time to time（sometimes but not very often, occasionally）

[剑桥例句] We go to the beach from time to time.

整年如此，全年无休

all year round

[剑桥例句] Cambridge is not just a university town. It's also a tourist destination （大量游客的目的地） all year round.

除了上面这几个含义很具体的形容词，gorgeous（非常美的），amazing（令人惊叹的），is dotted with...（点缀着……）也都是 native speakers 描述视觉享受时的"口头禅"。此外，您还可以在 Day 8 每一个话题后面的"轮到你了"和本书附赠的《IELTS 口语高频词汇 & 短语速查手册》里看到各类话题所需的单词和短语完整版。

让你的描述变得更具体的 **33** 个 **phrases**
33 Building Blocks in Part 2

Part 2 的话题库总数可以用"庞大"（enormous）来形容，如果把所有话题全都准备一遍很容易让人产生悲观甚至厌世的思想。但下面的 33 个 phrases 却可以帮助您迅速把握"趴吐"的话题范围，而且我们在上一节学习的"趴1"和"趴3"常用 phrases 有很多在 Part 2 里也仍然有机会用到。

我们的弹药还是很多的，关键就是一个字：熟。

描述人的 English phrases

_01_	kind and patient	友善的而且很有耐心的
_02_	friendly and sociable	友好的而且外向的

> 注 在英美，sociable（外向的、喜欢社交的）这个词是和 outgoing 一样很常用的，但中国同学们却总是只说 outgoing, outgoing, outgoing… ☺

_03_	responsible and reliable	很有责任感而且值得信赖的
_04_	open-minded and creative	思想开明、很有创造力的
_05_	young and talented	年轻又有才华的
_06_	hale and hearty √	（特指老年人）身体健康的，"老当益壮的"
_07_	humble and modest ✓	谦虚低调的
_08_	is a team player	很善于团队合作
_09_	always has a smile on his / her face	总是面带微笑
_10_	has a good sense of humour	很幽默（在英美生活里远比"humorous"更常听到）
_11_	is of average build	中等身材的

> 注 is of athletic build 则是指身材很健美的

描述物的 English phrases

_12_   is easy to carry = is portable   便于携带的

_13_   is easy to use = is user-friendly   便于使用的

_14_   is thin and light   很薄而且很轻的

_15_   is simple and practical   简单实用的

> 何以舍近求远
>
> 一个产品的"性价比很高"用地道英文应该怎么表达？
>
> 当您还在对 proportion，ratio 等"大词"进行排列组合的时候，native speakers 已经轻松地说出了下面这两种说法里面的一种：
>
> It's good value for money. 或者
>
> It offers good value for money. 性价比.
>
> 这才是 native speakers 说一个产品的"性价比很高"真正常用的英文表达。

_16_   is well laid-out   （建筑、城市、网站、报纸杂志的版面等）布局非常合理的

_17_   is well-designed   设计得很完善的

_18_   is well-managed   管理得很完善的

_19_   is always packed   （旅游景点、餐馆、商店）总是挤满了人

_20_   provides a wide variety of...   （餐馆、商店、图书馆等）提供多种多样的食品、商品、书籍等

_21_   is good for all ages   （博物馆、体育运动、电影）适合各个年龄段的人们，"老少皆宜"

_22_   an economic powerhouse   （城市或者区域）经济中心

_23_   a cultural hub   文化中心

_24_   four distinct seasons   分明的四季

_25_   an oasis in the city   城市里的一片"绿洲",例如一个公园或者一个花园

描述人或者物都可以的 English phrases ✔

_26_   lively and energetic   很有活力的(描述人、活动、城市、音乐等都行)

_27_   is well-organised   (形容人)很有条理的;(形容事物)很有秩序的,"井然有序的"

_28_   elegant and classy   优雅的、有品位的(描述人、建筑、服装都可以,classy 这个词在英文里和上课一点儿关系也没有,而是完全等于中文的"有品位的")

_29_   has a good reputation   有很好的声誉(描述有名的人、餐馆、商店、学校等都很实用)

描述经历的 English phrases ✔

_30_   a memorable experience   一次值得回忆的经历

_31_   an enjoyable experience   一次令人愉快的经历

_32_   a rewarding experience   一次很有回报的经历(物质上或者心理上的回报都可以用这个短语表达)

_33_   a disappointing experience   一次令人失望的经历

★   ★   ★

今天的必备词汇学习结束之前,Pat 想再次认真地提醒各位:英语从来都不是"贵族语言",它其实是一种极为看重实效(pragmatism)的语言。在欧洲,它不如法语那么"有格调"(classy),也没有德语严谨(rigid),但最后英语还是靠着自己的实用性(utility)征服了世界。实用、自然永远是英文口语的最高标准。

潜水去也。

Sleep tight.
Don't let the bed bugs bite.

Day

说好雅思口语的句子
*Convoluted Sentences
Won't Work*

Pat's Guide
To The IELTS Speaking Test

I try to take a breath but I'm already choking
because everywhere I look, I can see
how you hold back.
How long till this goes away?

不知您是否熟悉 podcast 这种在国外已经相当流行的学习手段，比如在 google 上搜索一下 English as a second language（ESL）podcast，就会有上千个学习资源供你选择，而且都是标准的发音和地道的英文，真的该试一下了。

► *We take the test seriously, but we want to make it fun and interesting as well.*

词汇是砖，句子是墙。

如果墙太长，就变成了长城，会把你封闭起来，让人感觉你很 closed-off。

很多培训老师推荐学生说长难句。其实长难句有两层意思，一是要长，二是要难。因为这样可以迅速让学生产生"仰视老师"的崇拜心理。但问题是，是否有必要在考口语的时候让考官"仰视"考生呢？

任何一个有英语国家生活经历的人都会知道和 native speakers 交流时"处心积虑"地说长难句是多么不靠谱。考雅思口语的时候，如果您想让自己的语言听起来不那么机械和怪异，就请尽量少用难、怪的畸形句子。

﹨ 怎样说出不"难"的长句？

长期在国外学习和工作，Pat 可以很坦诚地告诉您：真实生活里的英语句子有一个明显的特点，就是虽然使用的动词、名词和形容词千变万化，但是最常用的连词却只有十几个。即使已经在国外住了很多年，积累了大量的动词、名词、形容词，但每天用到的连词也还是这十几个。对于雅思口试而言，考生 Coherence 部分的分数很大程度上就取决于是否能够把这十几个连词准确、自然地运用好。

WARNING 很多中国考生在口语考试里把像 Moreover, ...这样非常正式的连接词用到"也是醉了"。但 Pat 必须提醒您：在您的口试过程中请不要使用 Moreover, ... 否则将会导致考官感觉你是一个拘谨、较难接近的人。事实上，"其次"在国外日常生活里通常会使用 also / as well 等自然的形式，或者就更简洁地直接使用 and 来表达。

我们现在就来看看地道英文口语里真正常用的连接词到底是哪些：

Pat 总结的英文口语里最常用的连接词

类别	内容	用法说明与例句
因果	... because ... so... therefore As a result	☆ 一句话里用了 because，就不要再用 so，它们在同一个句子里 "互不兼容" ☆ therefore 在地道口语交谈里用得并不多，如果在 IELTS 口试里使用，最多也就是在 Part 3 里出现 1 ~ 2 次，过多会让考官产生压迫感 ☆ As a result, ...（因此）也是更适合 Part 3 的深入讨论
让步	Although..., ... as long as...	☆ Although..., ...是 "尽管" 的意思 例：Although I only spent one night at this hotel, I was really impressed by the room and the service. ☆ as long as 是 "只要……" 的意思，比如 Backstreet Boys 的歌词 "I don't care who you are, where you're from or what you did, as long as you love me." 例：My parents don't care what job I do, as long as I'm happy.
转折	But... However, ...	☆ 表示转折，这两个说法都可以，在口语里 But 要比 However 更常用
补充	Besides, ... ★ ... also ... ★ ... too. ★ ... as well. ★	例：I don't really want to go. Besides, it's too late now.（Besides, ...常用于句首） 例：Olivia is very fluent in Chinese and English. She also speaks a little French. ☆ ... too. 和 ... as well. 常用于句子结尾 例：The new system is more efficient, and it's cheaper too. 例：I need a ticket for *Star Wars*, and one for *X-Men* as well.

类别	内容	用法说明与例句
对比	On the other hand, …★ … while … By contrast…	☆ On the other hand, … （另一方面，……） 例：My job is boring. On the other hand, it pays well. ☆ while 表示两种人或物之间的对比，日常生活里用得并不算多，但在口试中，特别是在 Part 3 里面用 1~2次完全可以，而且效果也挺自然： 例：I do most of the housework while Amanda only does the dishes. ☆ By contrast…在生活口语里用得也不算多，但可以用它在 Part 3 的深入讨论部分里引出两种人或两种事物之间的对比： 例：Men think of shopping as a task. By contrast, women think of shopping as a hobby.
举例	like… ★ such as… ★ For example, … ★ … and stuff like that. … and things like that.	☆ 除了 For example, … / such as 这两个实用的举例方式之外，"like… + 名词"也是英美生活口语里常用的"举例神器"： 例：I'm into fantasy novels like *Harry Potter* and *The Hunger Games*. （这里改用 such as 也可以） 例：There can be a wide variety of ways to help others. For example, we can do voluntary work in our community. We can also give money to charities. Even just giving others advice when they need it would be a good way to help them.
替代	rather than ★	☆ rather than 和 instead of 都表示"而不是……"，中国孩子们普遍都很熟悉这两个地道短语，却很少能想到在口语里面使用它们： 例：These days, most people drive to work rather than taking public transport. 例：Developed countries should help developing countries improve their education system instead of just giving them money.

也许你不愿意相信，上面表格中的这些连词，不仅仅是对付雅思口语考试的长句子足够了，甚至对付您今后几年的国外校园生活里的长句子也足够了。英语日常口语里的动词、名词、形容词极为丰富，但是连词却真的是相当有限的。

仍然请牢记：口语里的长句子是对短句子的使用得非常熟练之后，再对这些最高频的连接词自然运用而形成的，而不是刻意去堆砌出来的（Don't just cram them into your sentences）。

可以用来攒人品的句型

攒人品（RP）对于雅思考分的重要性已经越来越高。在一些城市的烤鸭当中正悄然兴起用业余时间帮助公园里老奶奶回收农夫山泉塑料瓶的风潮，据说对提高分数很有效。

下面的这些考试时躲不掉的句型，对于考前攒 RP 也有着不可忽视的作用。

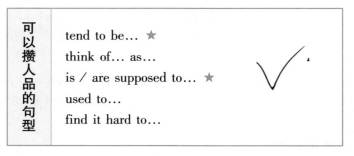

可以攒人品的句型	tend to be... ★ think of... as... is / are supposed to... ★ used to... find it hard to...	✓

☆ tend to be ...　　多半是……

这个句型的语气听起来很客气，但意思又很明确，是 native speakers 在口语里表达自己观点时的常用句型之一。

例 1：Children tend to be more active than adults.

例 2：Young people tend to be more open-minded than their parents.

例 3：The winter in Beijing tends to be cold and snowy.

而且这个句型里面的 be 还可以换成别的动词：

例 1：People who lead a healthy lifestyle tend to live longer.

例 2：People who have good communication skills tend to have more job opportunities.

☆ think of... as...　把……看作是……

例1：I think of photography as a good way to express my feelings.

例2：Some people think of collecting stamps as a good investment.

☆ is / are supposed to...　= should

在口语里代替 should 非它莫属（但在写作里仍然要用 should）。

例1：Students are supposed to follow the school rules and be polite and respectful to their teachers.

例2：I was supposed to be there by 9：30，but I got stuck in the traffic.

☆ used to...

常用来表示过去的某种习惯或者状态，当需要把过去的情况和现在的情况进行对比时这个句型很实用：

My hometown used to be a nice place for young people. But these days, it's not very attractive to young people because the air pollution is really bad. It's also very difficult for young people to find jobs there, and the nightlife there is quite dull and boring.

［注］有的朋友把英文名曲"Somebody I Used to Know"翻译成"一些身体我用过才知道"是严重的翻译错误。

☆ find it hard to ...　感到做某事很难　　*decent*

在这个句型里，find 并不是找到，而是"感到"的意思。

例1：I find it hard to improve my IELTS speaking score.（That's exactly why you'll find this book helpful. ☺）

例2：Many dropouts（辍学者）found it hard to get decent jobs without a degree.（decent 这个词在真实的英美生活里就是"还不错的"意思，但国内的孩子们宁可舍近求远地说 quite good 或者 fairly good，也不愿意用 decent 这个既省事又拿分的说法）

同类句型 find it helpful, find it interesting, find it attractive 等也都是轻松说口语的有用工具。

　思考：下面这个《剑11》例句里的 find 是什么意思？　*think.*

Children may find it rather frightening.

雅思口语考试中到底有没有很特殊的句子？

Yes and No.

为什么这么说呢？因为口语的本质就是用来进行实时交流的工具，如果"处心积虑"地搞特殊那就一定不是正常人说的语言了。但是另一方面，下面两种句子确实有点特殊，如果恰当使用，在考试里还是会有明显拿分的作用的。

❶ 定语从句

用 that，who，which 引导的定语从句其实是中国同学们很熟悉的一种句式，但是对于以有效的沟通和交流为高分标准的 IELTS 口语来说，定语从句已经是一种很好的特殊句式了。而且《剑11》的 Speaking 部分和 Listening 部分里就出现了不少定语从句，您完全可以放心使用：

Describe a house / apartment that someone you know lives in.

There are two large rooms that will be decorated next month.

The website provides live chat，which is very helpful.

❷ 虚拟语气

听起来很神奇，其实说白了就是用过去的时态表示现在或者将来的事情，表示比较客气的假设或者建议。虚拟语气是受过良好教育的 native speakers 在口语对话时很常用的一种特殊句式，而且也是《剑11》的 Speaking 部分和 Listening 部分里的常客之一：

If you could change your name，would you?（很客气地假设）

They might try to find people who all use a particular product.（也是很客气地假设）

Maybe you could give each of them a scarf, as well.（很客气地提出建议）

★　　★　　★

定语从句和虚拟语气虽好，但也请您注意不要使用过度，因为在短短的 11~14分钟口试里用得太多那它们也就不"特殊"了。

超短线
The Ultra-Short Track

关于雅思备考，Pat 一直坚信而且确实被大量 7 分或以上的高分考生证明的真谛就是备考必须紧密地围绕剑桥官方所喜爱的英语风格进行。深刻领会剑桥官方提供的《剑 4》~《剑 11》就是体会"剑桥风格"的最好武器。

对于备考时间已经彻底不够，甚至连书都已经看不下去了的"烤鸭"来说，其实不妨试试通过练习剑桥听力题来提高口语语感的方法：多听剑 4 ~ 剑 11 每套题里面的听力段子，并且把剑 4 ~ 剑 11 后面的听力文本（audioscripts）也看上几遍，耳濡目染也能学到不少地道的口语句子。退一步说，即使这样做之后你的口语还是一点儿进步都没有，那么至少也熟悉了听力的常考词汇和句型，并没有浪费时间。

比如，《剑 9》里的这个听力段子就用到了不少我们已经学到的地道英文连词，有力地证明了这些内容的实用性：

Recycled materials have been used whenever possible. For example, the floors are made of reclaimed floor. And the owners haven't bought a single item of new furniture. So the occupants of the house won't pollute the land or use any damaging chemicals. It is true that the construction of the house was harmful to the environment, mainly because they had to use large amounts of concrete. And, as you know, this is very damaging to the environment.

像这样的剑桥"段子"，就远比一些艰深晦涩的口语答案更接近于当代英美 native speakers 的真实口语交流风格。

Day

 雅思口语的段
Bricks versus Concrete

Pat's Guide
To The IELTS Speaking Test

Are you listening?
We write a thousand pages
They're torn and on the floor
Headlights hammer the windows
We're locked behind these doors
And we are never leaving
because this place is part of us
And all these scenes repeating are just so cold to the touch

这个相当酷的辩论网站几乎覆盖了所有的常考口语讨论话题。在页面中部选择 Education，Culture，Environment & Animal Welfare 等主题后，您就可以在 This house believes that 的后面看到各种各样的辩论话题。点击辩论话题之后，您就可以立刻找到自己需要的各种支持和反对理由(points for & points against)。

► *We take the test seriously, but we want to make it fun and interesting as well.*

怎样才能说出长段落？

（本章推荐给备考时间比较充裕的同学）

如果您上过培训课，那么口语老师一定给自己的方法起了一个新奇有趣的（fancy）名字，通过它来使自己的方法在学生的心目中产生一种神秘感和敬畏感（get you mystified and put you in awe）。这种做法确实可以增强教师授课的综合效果，但其实如果看穿了，雅思口语 Part 1 和 Part 3 的答案不管多么有创意，却一定是沿着两条思路展开的：顺承与对比。

中国艺术讲究"起承转合"四个字，咱们就用这四个字来形象地分析一下顺承和对比的区别。

结构1 "起—承—（合）"

这种结构的特点是：

（1）先直接回答考官提出的问题（起），（2）具体展开自己的回答（承），（3）如果愿意还可以在答案的结尾总结一句（合），但这句话并不是必需的，如果感觉不自然那就不要说。

具体展开的方式有：

• 使用 because，so，For example，such as，like（比如……），if，and，also，even 等逻辑关系词

• 使用 they，I，we，it，that 等代词

• 正常人其实不会说每句话都是"金句"，有些时候就把前一句话用更"直白"的语言解释一下也是展开的好方法。IELTS 口试是面对面的交流，答案如果过于机械反而会让考官感觉不是"人人对话"，而像"人机对话"了。☺

以上三种方法并不互相排斥，它们既可以确保你说出的答案完全扣题，又可以让你的句子之间产生自然的承接。

请看这个常考问题：

Do you enjoy travelling?

下面的 7 分答案就是很典型的 "起—承—合" 结构。

（起：回答考官提出的问题）Yes，I do.（承：具体展开）Travelling is fun. It helps me relax and I can **make new friends** during my trips. Travelling can also expand **my** mind. It helps **me** learn about other places and cultures（就用简单的话把前一句解释一下也同样是展开的好方法，你不必每句话都是 "金句" 甚至 "警句"）.（合：总结，这句话不是必需的）I guess that's exactly why **I** enjoy travelling.

再来看这个问题：

At what times of day do you like to listen to music?

下面这个 7 分答案同样是典型的 "起—承" 结构：

（起：回答考官提出的问题）I like to listen to music in the late afternoon <u>and</u> at night.（承：具体展开）**I** tend to feel tired in the late afternoon. Music can make **me** feel more energetic. Listening to music at night before bedtime makes **me** feel relaxed <u>so</u> I can sleep well.

再来看这道常考题：

Why do some people like collecting things?

下面这个 7 分答案还是标准的 "起—承" 结构。

（起：回答考官提出的问题）Different people may collect things for different reasons.（承：具体展开）<u>For example</u>，some people collect things <u>**because they**</u> have too much spare time and need personal pleasure. Others may think of collecting as a good investment. **They** think the things will go up in value（用 "直白" 的语言解释前一句话也会让答案听起来更充实）. Some people <u>even</u> just collect things to show **them** off to friends.

再看这道常考题：

Do you like shopping?

一个 6 分水平的 "起—承" 结构答案就是这样的：

（起：回答考官提出的问题）Yes，I like it.（承：具体展开）I have lots of free time, so when I feel bored, I go shopping with friends.

"起—承—(合)"式的**优点**:逻辑简单明白,就是向着同一个方向展开回答就可以了。

"起—承—(合)"式的**缺点**:口语不太好的同学有可能会说不长。但平心而论,如果您的口语目标只是 6 ~6.5 分,答案本来也不需要很长,平均起来 2 ~3 句话已经足够(当然答案的长度只是一个方面,更重要的还是要看内容是不是地道)。

结构 2 "起—承—转—(合)"

"起—承—转—(合)"结构就是先回答考官提出的问题,然后开始展开说其中一方面,接下来再说另一方面。每方面说多少其实是比较随意的,没必要太机械。最后的"合"部分如果感觉不自然也可以选择省略。

请看下面这个 Part 3 常考问题:

How do large shopping malls affect small local businesses?

下面这个 7 分答案就是典型的"起—承—转"结构:

(起:回答考官提出的问题) They can have both positive and negative effects. (承:展开其中的一个方面) The competition between shopping malls and local businesses can make local businesses improve their service. (转:展开另一个方面) On the other hand, large shopping malls can usually provide consumers with lower prices, so they can take customers away from local businesses.

"起—承—转—(合)"式的优缺点和"起—承—(合)"式正好相反:它的内容比较容易说得更多。但是相应地,它的结构也要更复杂一些。

雅思口语的 Part 1 对于答案长度的要求是 2 ~3 句话就很好,所以在 Part 1 里面"起—承—(合)"结构更加常用。而对于口语 Part 3 的深入讨论,则是"起—承—(合)"和"起—承—转—(合)"这两种结构都很常用,详见 Day 9。

Part 2 结构的 4 种选择

Scenario 1：对于"牛人"，Pat 建议您不要太担心卡片答案的结构，只要确保自己的答案能够覆盖卡片上的每一个提示要点，并适当补充确实与话题相关的内容即可。

Scenario 2：对于有一定的英语表述能力的考生，Pat 建议您看到卡片之后有一个大致（rough-and-ready）的顺序安排就好了，同样不必过于机械（mechanical）。

Scenario 3：对于完全没有口语功底但是又有"野心"想考高分的苦孩子们，也可以考虑背一些结构性的句子。下面是一些还不算太呆板的结构性句子，每组知道一句就够了：

❶ I'm going to talk about…

I'd like to talk about…

Let me talk about…

I'd like to describe…

省略号里填入你要描述的话题，比如 my favourite sport, a film I like…

❷ I'll start off by talking about…

To begin with, I'll talk about…

省略号里填入卡片上面第一个提示的问题。

❸ Moving on to…
As for…, …

省略号里填入卡片上面第二个提示的问题。

❹ Now let's look at…

省略号里填入卡片上第三个提示的问题。

❺ Now I'm going to explain to you…

省略号里填入卡片上 Explain…后面的第四个提示的问题。

Scenario 4 : 下面的几个词组，适合从"大牛"到"菜鸟"（rookies / newbies）的全部考生，因为它们可以帮助你在不同话题之间快速转换，或者从一个话题引申出一些内容。而且最重要的是，这个表格里的词组听起来是自然的。

▶ **in terms of...** （谈到……，关于……）

= regarding = concerning = when it comes to

e. g. In terms of price, this car would be a great choice.

▶ **What I need to emphasise here is that...** （我需要特别强调的是……）

= What I need to stress here is that...

e. g. What I need to emphasise here is that he did it all by himself.

▶ **By the way, ...** 常用在答案快要结束的位置,表示"顺便说"

e. g. By the way, some parrots can be used as alarm clocks.

▶ **In other words, ...** （换句话说，换言之……）

= I mean...

e. g. It's an office building. In other words, people go there not for pleasure, but for business.

Day 6

练出 **decent** 的发音
Pronunciation Counts.

I take it you already know.

Of tough and bough and cough and dough.

And now you wish, perhaps,

To learn of less familiar traps.

* *http://www.bbc.co.uk/worldservice/learningenglish/grammar/pron*

要练出不错的发音，除了积极模仿音频里的英国 SG 和 MM，还
可以登录上面的这个 BBC 官方网站，里面的发音部分相当酷。

* *www.howjsay.com* 与 *www.inogolo.com*

如果你遇到即使通过词典还是拿不准发音的单词，请立刻登
录左边这个网站，它会带你朗读所有的英语常用词。而右边这个
网站则专门提供对人名、地名等专有名词的朗读。

► *We take the test seriously, but we want*
to make it fun and interesting as well.

前文已述，地道英文口语里有个相当实用的单词，意思与中文里的"不错"极为接近：decent。native 的发音需要长期积累，attractive 的发音需要专业训练，但 decent 的发音还是有可能在短时间内就练成的。

多短呢？也许，一天……

三大纪律

☆ 少看理论 ☆

关于英语发音的书面理论不管听起来多么玄妙，它们其实只会让你的中文 reading 能力越来越强，靠研究书面理论去提高英语发音要比让老外分清张馨予、张予曦、张雨绮的名字更难。

☆ 集中精力 ☆

只要开始练习你就必须把 TV set，PC，laptop，tablet，PSP，smartphone 等干扰源全部关掉，完全投入到战斗中（Throw yourself into it.），唯一允许留在你身边的电子产品是一个录音设备（a recording device）。

☆ 听自己说 ☆

身边放一个录音笔，这样进步更快。实在不好意思就把你身边的人都赶走，并且规定一个小时之后才能回来，"no zuo no die"。

适合国内同学的英文单词发音测验
A Pop Quiz on Pronunciation

请您先做三个小测验，都是 Pat 总结的中国考生常见发音错误，看看现在你属于哪种水平。测试的时候请随时对照音频里的录音。

☆ TEST 1 — EASY

If your English is every bit as good as the average English learner in China, you will have no difficulty pronouncing the following words correctly.

这个测试很简单，是看你能不能达到中国学生发音的平均水平，如果错了 5 个以上，那你的英语现在就肯定处在中国人能听懂你的意思，但是外国人完全听不明白你在说什么的状态。测试的时候请随时对照音频里的录音。

❶ beach   ❷ because   ❸ yesterday   ❹ famous

❺ invite   ❻ library   ❼ night — light   ❽ slow — snow

❾ thick — sick   ❿ said — sad

☆ TEST 2 — HARDER

Your English pronunciation skill is distinctly above average in China if you can pronounce the following words properly.

这个测试难度大一些，如果这些单词你的发音都正确，你的发音就处在 native English speakers 能轻松听懂的状态。测试的时候请随时对照音频里的录音。

❶ newspaper   ❷ industry   ❸ quite — quiet   ❹ temperature

❺ sandwich   ❻ thought   ❼ clothes   ❽ kind

❾ comfortable   ❿ loose — lose

☆ TEST 3 — HARDEST

Now you can discover how close you are to native English speakers in pronunciation. The next ten words are no cinch — you will be acquitting yourself creditably if you pronounce eight of them correctly.

这个测试最难，是看你英语发音的可爱指数。如果这 10 个词你都能正确发音，不用我说，肯定有老外夸过你发音好。测试的时候请随时对照音频里的录音。

❶ atmosphere   ❷ celebrity   ❸ affluent   ❹ synthesize

❺ photography   ❻ economic   ❼ gorgeous   ❽ unique

❾ resources   ❿ sunbathing

单词发音的七宗罪

听来听去，国内的考生发音其实只有 7 种常见错误。如果 7 种错误都能改掉（您不是要告诉我刚才的测试里 7 种错误您全都犯了吧？），发音虽然还不完美，但是已经完全可以让老外轻松听懂你的英语了。

1. 应该是长音还是短音?

Pat 经常听到学生会把 meal 说成 mill,把 sheet 读成 shit,甚至还有人把 beach 说成 bitch,真不知是故意还是误伤。请您一定仔细跟音频朗读下面的单词:

heat   hit   peak   pick   team   Tim

2. 力度够不够?

北京话讲究的是轻快,所以很多北京考生在说英语的时候发音力度不够,把 because 发成"笔铐子",sorry 说成"骚瑞",apple 说成"挨剖",都是因为发音的力度不够。请来自北京方向的读者仔细听 native speakers 怎样朗读下面的单词:

net   Patrick(有无数北京孩子把 Pat 英文名字里的 Pa 轻轻松松地发成了"拍"的音)

family   kind   easily   because   sorry   apply

3. 有没有儿化音?

北方话,特别是北京话,儿化音超多。像"公主坟儿",如果说成"公主坟",或者把"冰棍儿"说成"冰棍",就会让人不寒而栗。但是来自中国北方的同学一定要注意:对于不含 r 这个字母的单词,即使在美国,也是不会有儿化音的。

请来自北方的读者仔细跟音频朗读下面的单词:

famous   panda   grandpa   gorgeous   difficult

4. th 音到底怎么说?

中文里面没有 th 这个音,所以要发好这个音还真要好好练一练。关键是舌尖儿要伸到上牙的外面一点点(不要太多,否则很难看),轻轻地碰到上牙,然后轻轻吹口气,效果就出来了。如果是 these 里面的 th,就把舌尖伸出来一点点,轻轻地在上牙上摩擦一下,就可以了。请您放下面子,虚心跟音频朗读下面的单词:

thought   threat   throw   although   those

5. l 和 n 怎么区分?

这两个音在中国南方的一些地区经常有考生分不清,因为一些方言里面没有 n 这个音。另外我还发现一些说粤语的同学，有时候把 fat 里面的 t 省掉了，把 report 里面的 t 也省掉了，也请务必注意改正。请南方的读者仔细跟音频模仿下面单词的发音：

night   light   slow   snow   money（有些南方同学会把这个词说得像英文里的女孩名字 Molly，如果您也有这个问题请一定注意跟着录音积极模仿）

6. 重音究竟在哪儿?

把重音位置发正确是比较高端的要求了。重音的位置发错，小则会听起来别扭，大则会导致考官难以理解你的意思。请读者仔细跟音频模仿下面单词的发音：

comfortable   newspaper   atmosphere   celebrity   photography
yesterday   temperature

7. v 和 w 的区别

这两个音区分的关键是牢记发 v 的音牙齿会碰到下嘴唇，但是发 w 的音牙齿不碰下嘴唇。请大家仔细跟音频模仿下列单词的发音：

invite   wife   swim   win   visit

☆ TEST 4 — TONGUE TWISTER PRACTICE

下面的三个绕口令都是帮助你巩固今天学习的效果的，请跟录音好好练习朗读一下。

❶ If Peter Piper picked a peck of pickled peppers, where's the peck of pickled peppers Peter Piper picked?

❷ We will wish to visit their wives.

❸ I think this thin thread will go through the eye of this thick needle.

★   ★   ★

好，单词的发音我们先练习到这里，您可以打开手机刷一会儿朋友圈了。

★   ★   ★

练好句子的发音

现在我们再前进一步，突破句子的发音。还是强调我们练习的三大纪律：

★ 少看理论

★ 集中精力

★ 听自己说

高分考生的发音凭什么拿高分？

经常有学生跟我抱怨，为什么看 *Gossip Girl* 或者 *The Big Bang Theory* 的时候没有几句话能听懂。其实除了很多国内同学所习惯的词汇与当代真实英语的常用词汇严重脱节外，另一个重要原因就是不熟悉连读、弱化这些发音规则，所以导致很多你认识的单词说出来却听不懂。

不信您试试这个：

http://www.oprah.com/oprahs-lifeclass/What-Oprah-Learned-from-Randy-Pauschs-Last-Lecture-Video

这个 Randy 教授在英美可是鼎鼎大名的，号召力甚至超过 Obama 和 David Cameron，您能听懂 Oprah Winfrey 对他的最后一次演讲的思考吗？

几年来的教学实践告诉我，发音能真正接近 native English speakers 的中国考生，一定会注意下面四个方面：

★ 连读	★ 弱化
★ 句子重音	★ 语调

A 弱化与连读 Weak form and Liaison

弱化与连读是区分发音高手和菜鸟的重要依据。这两个技巧效果相似，都是让你的句子更流利更连贯，所以我们把这两项放在一起练习。请仔细听音频的朗读，认真模仿下面的发音。

part-time

but now

105

I'll

He'll

what's

Where is she?

Do you want a beer?

Want to go shopping?

give me an answer

three hundred years

but that word is hard

it used to be

You should take care of them.

kick back and relax

the gap between the urban area and the rural area

B　句子的重音 Sentence Stress

一般来说，名词、动词和形容词会倾向于重读，而介词、连词和代词会倾向于轻读。但是要注意别太机械地使用这个规则，其实很多时候最重要的是看你的句子要强调哪一个单词。比如下面的句子，强调的内容不一样，重读的单词就不同。

I don't know where he is now.（Maybe someone else does.）

I don't know where he is now.（So don't keep asking me.）

I don't know where he is now.（But I know where Nancy is.）

I don't know where he is now.（But I saw him last week.）

C　句子的语调 Sentence Intonation

大家都知道，一般来说，疑问句用升调，陈述句用降调。但实际上可没那么简单，native English speakers 说话，每句话里面都会有几次升降调的变化。只是陈述句一般句尾落在降调，而疑问句句尾落在升调。请仔细听录音，体会下面一段话每个句子的升降调，并注意模仿。（放心，这个段落一定不会白模仿的，里面的很多句子在雅思口语 Part 1 和 Part 2 我们都可以用的）

（Please pay close attention to the word stress sentence intonation. ）

Three Great Reasons to Learn a Foreign Language

☆ Improve your Chinese

As a person who speaks only one language，you have no basis for comparison；all you know is Chinese. In different languages the same idea is often expressed in different ways. There is a reason most great writers and poets are students of many languages.

☆ Enhance your travel experiences

Traveling is one of the great joys of life and also one of the most expensive. Why not get the most out of your experience? As a person who doesn't know the native tongue you are completely excluded from the culture. Knowing even a few phrases of the language will make a huge difference. You will meet many more people and find it much easier to get around.

☆ Languages are beautiful

Language is what makes us human. It is the medium we use to share our thoughts with the world. Could you imagine thought without language? Great language also has a wonderful musical quality. Learning a new language is like learning a new way to think and a new way to sing.

超短线
The Ultra-Short Track

对于备考时间紧但又对自己的单词发音没有信心的同学，如果你对某个词甚至句子的发音不确定，也许你会选择查字典。其实可以试试 www. oddcast. com/home/demos/tts/tts_ example. php。它甚至允许你自己选择英音还是美音、男声还是女声，而且屏幕上的大脑袋盯着你也特有考试的感觉☺。

Day 7

Part 1：短兵相接
Giving Short and Direct Answers

Pat's Guide
To The IELTS Speaking Test

Modern designs can be amazing,
with just being simple and plain.

☞ **口语 Part 1 话题库索引**

Part 1 素材工具箱
Pat's Idea Pool for Part 1

作为 IELTS 口试的开场白，口语 Part 1 的话题都是生活里常见的（您可以在 Pat 的博客 blog. sina. com. cn ∕ ieltsguru 上看到本月最新的口语预测题）。从答案长度来看，British Council 官方明确指出：Remember to keep your Part 1 answers short and direct（简短的，直接的）. In general, your answers in Part 1 should be 2 or 3 sentences. 也就是说：Part 1 的答案不需要"迂回曲折"，准备起来并不难。

如果您在准备 Part 1 预测题的过程当中遇到实在想不出 ideas 的"危急情况"（emergency），那也不必紧张，本章里的素材将是您的"锦囊秘笈"（your reliable go-to resource）。为了扩展您的思路，Pat 对每一个 Topic 都同时提供了正、反两方面的 ideas，请您根据自己的实际需要选择正方或者选择反方来回答（注意：只要英文正确，一个肯定的答案或者一个否定的答案都是你的考官愿意接受的，而且答案不要说得太长，请把深入交谈的能量留给你的 Part 3）。

请牢记 British Council 对于 Part 1 的官方提示：Your examiner may interrupt（打断）you if you give a very long answer in Part 1.

Studies（including learning English）
学 习（含学习英语）

★ **I'm sure all my hard work will pay off**（会有回报）.

FOR（正方）	AGAINST（反方）
My university **has a good reputation**. 注 a good reputation 是"良好的声誉"	It's not a **well-known** university（它的知名度并不高）.
It has an **attractive** campus. 注 attractive 是"有吸引力的"	The **campus**（校园）is too small and **crowded**（拥挤的）.
★ Most of my professors are **friendly and helpful**. 近义 kind and helpful	Many students are not really **motivated** to learn. 注 motivated 是指"很有动力的"

111

FOR （正方）	AGAINST （反方）
★ They encourage us to **think independently**（独立地思考）.	★ We're not encouraged to **share ideas**. 注 share ideas 是"分享想法"
★ We can choose from **a wide variety of**（多种多样的） courses.	Some of the courses are too **hard** for me.
★ The university provides **a friendly learning environment**（友好的学习氛围）.	There're too many **classroom rules**. 注 "课堂规定"就叫 classroom rules
★ There are a variety of **extracurricular activities**（课外活动）we can enjoy, like the debate club, the chess club, the university newspaper, the **choir**（合唱团） and even a rock band. 注 "学校的社团"在地道英文里就叫某某 **club**，这里并非指俱乐部	But extracurricular activities can be **time-consuming**（很耗时间的）. 注1 **time-consuming** 是"很耗时间的"意思，它在地道英文里的反义词有两个：一个是 **efficient**（高效率的），另一个是 **rewarding**（很有回报的） 注2 如果想说"纯属浪费时间"，那么英文就是"It's just **a waste of time**."
I **do voluntary work** at the university library. 注 其实做 voluntary work 是英美考官们相当希望听到的一种经历，而且他们从小到大自己也都做过很多次 volunteers（志愿者）	I have **a heavy class load** this term. 我这学期的课业负担很重。 注 在大学里当您听到别人说 **workload** 的时候其实也是指课业负担
The **canteen** / **cafeteria** serves **good food** at **reasonable** prices. 注 大学和中学的"食堂"叫 **cafeteria** 或者 **canteen** 都可以，**reasonable prices** 就是"合理的价格"	The canteen / cafeteria food is **gross**（差得出奇的）. 注 雅思口试时不能说 yucky ✗
We're **well prepared for employment**（为就业做好充分的准备）.	We're not well prepared for **the job market**（就业市场）. 注 在地道英文里 **the job market** 是泛指整个就业市场，而中文所说的"人才交流会"在英文里是叫作 a job fair

scrambling 争先恐后.

Studies 学习

Learning English 学英语

It's important to be bilingual（双语的）today.

FOR（正方）	AGAINST（反方）
Understanding English **helps** me **better understand** English-speaking cultures. 注 "双语的" **bilingual** 有很多考生认识，但口试时却往往会忘记你自己其实就是 **bilingual**	You **are considered** "**left behind**" if you can't speak English. 注 听说技能 **listening and speaking skills**，读写技能 **reading and writing skills**，"发展"某种技能最地道的动词就是 **develop**
★ Learning a foreign language helps us become **more open-minded**（思维更开放的）.	★ Learning a foreign language **takes time and energy**. 注 **takes time and energy** 是 "需要投入时间和精力"
★ People who are bilingual tend to **have more job opportunities**.	Learning a foreign language can be very **challenging**. 注 **challenging** "有挑战的"
★ **Singing along to** English songs is a good way to improve my English **pronunciation**（发音）. 注 **sing along to**...就是 "跟着一起唱"	There're plenty of **test-taking techniques**（应试技巧）. But as a matter of fact, there're no **shortcuts**（捷径）to learning a foreign language.
★ Reading English novels and magazines is a good way to **expand my vocabulary**（扩展词汇量）.	English **grammar**（语法）is very different from Chinese grammar.
I can understand English movies without reading **the Chinese subtitles**.	中文字幕叫作 **Chinese subtitles**，用中文配音的电影叫 **films dubbed in Chinese**

Pat 指南

☆ 良好的英语技能无疑会在就业市场中给我们带来明显的竞争优势，那么"竞争优势"怎样用地道英文表达呢? native speakers 不说 a competition advantage ╳，而会说 a competitive advantage √ 或者 a competitive edge √

Good English skills can give us a competitive advantage / a competitive edge in the job market.

Topic 02 **Work 工作**

FOR（正方）	AGAINST（反方）
★ I have an **fun and rewarding**（很有回报的）job. 注 **rewarding** 既可以指物质上很有回报，也可以指心理上面很有回报	My job is **dull and boring**（乏味的，枯燥的）.
The **salary**（工资）is good. 注 同义表达是 The **pay is good**. 请注意这句话里的 **pay** 不要说成 payment	I'm really tired of **working for peanuts**（挣钱少）. 注 native speakers 经常把挣钱少叫作"为了花生而工作"
My job provides me with a variety of **benefits**, like **health insurance**（医疗保险）, **paid holidays**（带薪休假）and a **pension**（养老金）**plan**. 注 native speakers 常用 **benefits** 来指"工作福利"	We don't have **equal opportunities** for promotion（提职）.

FOR（正方）	AGAINST（反方）
★ My boss **treats everyone fairly**	My boss is a **slave driver**（真不把员工当人）.
★ My **colleagues**（同事）are **friendly and helpful** （注）native speakers 也经常把同事称为 co-workers	Some of my co-workers are **rude and selfish**（自私的）.
I have **a nine-to-five job** （注）一份"朝九晚五"的工作在地道英文里就叫 a nine-to-five job	★ I often have to **work overtime**（加班）.
★ My job provides the opportunity to **develop new skills**（发展新的技能）.	It's **a dead-end job**（没前途的工作）。
Employees are paid **time-and-a-half**（150%）if they work at weekends. （注）在英美，员工在周末或者公共假日（public holidays）上班一般能获得150%或者 double time（200%）的酬劳	I've never been paid for the **extra work**（额外的工作）.

Pat指南

My job gives me a sense of satisfaction.（我的工作给我一种满足感）是英美人说很喜欢自己的工作时特别爱说的一句话。

如果对自己的工作并不满意呢？不管是工作的原因还是自己的原因，native speakers 常说的一句话都是：I don't feel motivated at work（我上班的时候完全没动力），然后就是一脸无辜的表情……

Topic
03

Hometown (Including Traffic & Pollution)
家 乡 (含交通和污染)

FOR (正方)	AGAINST (反方)
It's a city **in the northeast** (东北部) of China. 注 **northwest** (西北部), **southwest** (西南部), **southeast** (东南部), 如果要说中国的中部地区, 那就是 **central China**	★ The **cost of living** (生活成本) there is pretty high.
It's a **coastal city** (沿海城市) and has **gorgeous** (非常美的) beaches.	It has long and **windy** winters.
It's an **inland** (内陆的) city and is surrounded by beautiful **rolling hills** . 注 **rolling hills** 是起伏的小山丘, 而 **high mountains** 则是高山	It's **hot and dry** (又热又干燥的) in the summer. 注 "又热又潮湿的" 是 **hot and humid**
★ The city is well-known for its **cultural attractions** (文化景点). 注 **attraction** 在英文里经常表示 "景点"	Many historical buildings have been **replaced** by modern **high-rise buildings** (高层建筑).
★ The city **attracts** (吸引) many tourists each year.	The locals have become **too materialistic** (过于物质化的, 只在乎金钱和物质享受的). 注 英文里常用 **the locals** 来指 "当地人"
★ It has a long and **rich history** . 注 **a rich history** 并不是 "富裕的历史", 而是指 "丰富的历史"	Many **traditions** have been lost. (很多传统被遗忘了)
Most people there lead a simple and **laid-back** lifestyle. 注 形容词 **laid-back** 是 "心态平和、与世无争的"	★ The **pace of life** (生活节奏) is fast and **stressful** (让人感觉压力很大的).

FOR（正方）	AGAINST（反方）
★ Most people are **friendly and helpful**. 注 **a strong sense of community**（很强的"社区感"，很强的社区凝聚力）	I don't even know my neighbours（甚至不认识自己的邻居）.
It has lots of things for young people, such as cinemas, **karaoke bars** and sports centers. 注 卡拉 OK 厅叫 **karaoke lounge** 或者 **karaoke bar** 都可以，第一次"考察"北京的卡拉 OK 厅时 Pat 真的感觉被震撼了（I was totally amazed.），相比之下英美城市里面的卡拉 OK 厅都实在太"低调"（humble and modest）了 ☺	It's not a good place for young people because there aren't many **leisure facilities** there, and the nightlife is **dull and boring**. 注 There aren't many **job opportunities** for young people. "年轻人的就业机会不多"

城市里常见的 **leisure facilities**（休闲设施）:

cinemas, concert halls, museums, art galleries, parks, restaurants, coffee shops, shopping centers, sports centers

---

⌐ **Hometown** 家乡
└ **Traffic & Pollution 交通和污染**

FOR（正方）	AGAINST（反方）
More and more people can **afford**（买得起）a car. 注 **car owners** 有车的人，"车主"	There are tooooooooo many cars on the road.
★ Driving is an important **life skill**（生活技能）.	I often **get stuck in** heavy traffic. 注 **get stuck in**…是国外生活中相当常用的一个短语：被……困住

117

FOR（正方）	AGAINST（反方）
★ It's important to learn how to **drive safely** and be **a polite driver** . 注 **drive safely** 安全行车，**polite driver** 有礼貌的驾驶员	★ There're lots of **dangerous drivers**（不考虑后果的司机）out there. They just don't **follow traffic rules**（不遵守交通规则）. 注 **dangerous drivers** 当然应该受到惩罚（should be punished），不过今年年初在美国最新公布的一项民意调查显示公众一致认为最可怕的司机其实是 slow drivers ☺
★ We should use **public transport**（公共交通）more often. Using public transport is more **eco-friendly** than driving a car. 注 **eco-friendly** 有益于环保的	Public transport in my hometown is **not reliable**（不可靠的）. 注 The buses never arrive on time（公车从来都不准时到）.
★ Many people **walk or cycle to work** . 注 地道短语 walk or cycle to work 的意思是"步行或骑自行车上班"	★ The buses are **overcrowded**（过于拥挤的）.
The city is very **walkable** . It's easy to **get around on foot** . 注 **walkable**（适合步行的）是西方国家评价城市生活（urban living）的重要标准之一，也可以说 pedestrian-friendly，人行道在英国叫作 pavement，斑马线在英国叫 zebra crossing	The traffic is always bumper-to-bumper during the evening **rush hour** . 注 **bumper-to-bumper traffic** 就是车行缓慢、"让马路变成停车场"的拥挤交通
★ It's **quiet and peaceful**（宁静安详的）.	The traffic noise really **bothers** me（很烦人）.

When I'm **in a hurry** , I take **the subway**（美国的说法）/ **the underground**（英国的说法）/ **the Tube**（伦敦人 Londoners 特有的说法）

Pat指南 🔊

☆ 比较拿分的交通工具（即使您可能从来没有乘坐过也可以放心说）：

minibus（中巴）；shuttle bus（班车或机场巴士）；ferry（轮渡）；light rail（轻轨）；motorcycle taxi（"摩的"）

☆ 很重的雾霾英文叫作 thick smog，雾霾很重的形容词则是 very smoggy

☆ 同学们都熟悉名词 pollution，其实动词 pollute 也是地道英文口语里的高频词：

Car fumes（汽车尾气）pollute the air and damage our health.

☆ 汽车尾气也可以叫作 exhaust fumes，而工厂排出的浓烟则是 factory fumes

Topic 04 Films & TV
影视

FOR（正方）	AGAINST（反方）
I'm really into **animated films**（动画片）. 注 **I'm really into...** 在地道英文里就是说自己非常喜欢某类事物、对某类事物很"投入"	Going to the cinema **is a waste of time and money**（又花时间又花钱）.
★ I prefer films with good **acting**（演技）.	The **special effects**（特效）in this film are **amazing**（令人惊叹的）. 注 "大片儿"叫 **blockbuster**
He's **well-known for his acting skills**（他是个"演技派"）.	He **relies too much on his looks**（过度依赖外表，"靠脸吃饭"）.
★ I like films with **a happy ending**（有圆满的结局）.	The **soundtrack**（电影原声音乐）of this film is just okay — nothing special（"一般般"，并不是很出色）.
★ This film **is based on a true story**（取材于一个真实的故事）.	The **storyline** of this film is too **far-fetched**.（故事情节太牵强了） 注 电影的"故事情节"就是 **storyline**，也有些 native speakers 把它叫作 **plot**

FOR（正方）	AGAINST（反方）
★ Some films are **fun and entertaining**（有趣而且娱乐性很强的）. ☆ 上座率很高的电影叫作 **a box-office hit**	★ I don't like films that are too **predictable**（看了开头就知道结尾的那种）.
Some films are **thought-provoking**（发人深思的）.	This film is **too serious**（过于严肃的）.
Sci-fi films **stimulate our imagination**（激发我们的想象力）.	注 **sci-fi films** 是科幻片，外星人就叫 **aliens**
Some films can **bring back good memories**（带来美好的回忆）.	Some **action films**（动作片）are too **violent**（暴力的）. 注 英雄当然就是 **heroes**，反派则是 **villains**
★ This film is **moving and unforgettable**（很感人的、令人难忘的）.	★ It's **dull and boring**（乏味、枯燥的）.
★ This film **has a strong cast**.（演员的阵容很强大） 注 **cast** 就是指"演员的阵容"	My favourite star had **a bit part**（客串的小角色）in it.
Leonardo DiCaprio **played the lead**（演主角儿）in this film.	Margot Robbie **played opposite him**.（和他演对手戏）

Pat 指南

☆ 高成本电影叫 big-budget film，相应地小成本电影就叫 small-budget film

☆ 以下这些闪光的人名都是 Pat 发现国内同学们最容易念错的明星名字，请仔细听音频：

- *Leonardo DiCaprio* 环保主义者（environmentalist）莱昂纳多·迪卡普里奥的名字一直稳居读错榜榜首，这比说"岁月是一把杀猪刀"还要让他痛心

- *Beyoncé Knowles* 其实这位美女的名字正确发音并不是"碧昂斯"

- *Anne Hathaway*　她演的《公主日记》很多同学应该都看过

- *Nicole Kidman*　妮可·基德曼这么简单的名字其实也很容易读错

- *Brie Larson*　2016 年奥斯卡最佳女主角奖得主的名字同样常被念错

- *Cameron Diaz*　连影坛大姐大的名字都有人敢不敬

- *Keanu Reeves*　基努·里维斯有 1/8 的印第安人血统，所以有一个原住民的名字

- *Robert Downey Jr.*　连钢铁侠（*Iron Man*）和复仇者联盟 2（*Avengers：Age of Ultron*）里面的硬汉也经常惨遭误读

- *Matt Damon*　《拯救大兵瑞恩》里的男主角，他在 *The Martian*（《火星救援》）里面的演技也受到很高的评价（received good reviews）

- *David Beckham*　小贝虽然不是影星，但他的姓却总是被国内同学念错，也一起放进来吧

说来说去，最不容易发错音的还是超模 *Kate Moss* 和成功地摆脱了"单身男神"称号的 *George Clooney*，所以他俩必须红 ☺

In The Cinema（在电影院看电影）	At Home（在家看电影）
★ Cinemas can provide a more **fun and enjoyable viewing experience**.（提供更有趣、更令人愉快的观赏体验）	It's more **convenient**（更方便）to watch a film at home.
A cinema **screen**（屏幕）is much larger than a TV screen.	I have a large **collection**（收藏）of DVDs.
The colours also look **more vivid**（更鲜明的）.	★ Watching a film at home helps me **save time and money**（既省时间又省钱）. 注 请不要说你有看"盗版碟"（pirated DVDs）的习惯
The **sound quality**（音质）in the cinema is better than at home.	I have a **home cinema system** at home. 注 家庭影院系统叫 home cinema system 或者 home theater system

Pat 指南

☆ 还可以说 Cinemas offer a wide variety of snacks（零食）.

☆ 三维立体电影就是 3-D film

Watching a 3-D film in the cinema can be really exciting.

Films & TV 影视
Television 电视

FOR（正方）	AGAINST（反方）
Watching TV **is fun**.	Watching TV is **a waste of time**（浪费时间）.
★ This show is **informative**. It provides lots of **useful information**. ⊞ 形容词 informative 是"信息量很大的"	看电视的人叫作 **a TV viewer** 或者 **TV viewers**，看电视的观众群可以总称为 **audience**
★ This TV show is **entertaining**（娱乐性强的）. It helps me relax. ⊞ entertaining 是"娱乐性很强的"	地道英文里常把能够让人放松的事物称为 **a stress-reliever**
It's a very **creative**（有创意的）TV show.	The **storyline** is too **predictable**（剧情毫无悬念）.
Travel shows can **expand our horizons**（开阔我们的眼界）. They help us learn about other places and other cultures.	On the other hand, the information they provide is **not always reliable**（并不总是可靠的）.
★ Sometimes I just **surf through the channels**（不停换台寻找自己喜欢的频道，"频道冲浪"）.	People who watch too much TV tend to **lead an unhealthy lifestyle**. ⊞ **lead an unhealthy lifestyle** 生活方式很不健康

FOR（正方）	AGAINST（反方）
People enjoy **conversations**（谈话）about the TV shows that they like.	Watching too much TV gives you **square eyes**.（在英美有一种说法：看电视太多眼睛会变成方形）
Watching TV together helps us **build strong family ties**. 注 build strong family ties 是"增进亲情"的意思，也可以说 strengthen family ties	★ Watching too much TV **increases the risk of heart disease and high blood pressure**（增加患高血压和心脏病的风险）.
Watching TV can help children **expand their vocabulary**. 注 expand their vocabulary 是"扩大词汇量"	★ Young viewers tend to **copy**（模仿）the violence they see on TV.
Some **TV commercials**（电视广告）**are a good source of fun**. 注 a good source of fun 很好的生活乐趣来源	There're too many commercials during **prime-time hours**（黄金时段），which really **bothers me**（让我很烦）.

Pat 指南

☆ TV programmes 的常见种类：

TV series（系列剧），sitcoms（情景喜剧），reality show（真人秀），quiz show（问答节目），variety show（综艺节目），news show（新闻节目），game show（有奖竞赛节目），travel show（旅游节目），documentaries（纪录片，例如 Discovery Channel 和 National Geographic Channel 播放的节目），脱口秀（这个太简单，自己说吧）☺

☆ 系列剧的"一集"叫 an episode，"一季"叫 a season。

123

Topic 05 **Advertising**

广　告

FOR（正方）	AGAINST（反方）
★ Some TV commercials are **very entertaining**（娱乐性很强的）. 🔵 **advertisement** 可以泛指任何形式的广告，**commercial** 则是特指电视、收音机或者互联网上面播放的广告	★ They **interrupt TV programmes**（中断电视节目）. That really **bothers me**（让我很烦）.
Some advertisements are fun and **creative**（有创意的）, while others are dull and boring.	**a memorable slogan** 很容易记住的广告词，比如 Reebok 的 "I am what I am.", LG 的 "Life's good.", Nike 的 "Just do it." 和蚂蚁金服的 "每个认真生活的人，都值得被认真对待。"
They **help me better understand** new products.	Advertising **encourages**（鼓励）us to buy things we don't really need.
★ Good advertisements are **informative**（信息量很大的）.	★ Many advertisements **are aimed at** children and teenagers. 🔵 **are aimed at...** 针对……这个群体
They really **attract our attention**（吸引我们的注意力）. 🔵 **advertising campaign** 大规模的广告系列宣传活动	Some advertisements provide **false and misleading**（虚假的、有误导性的）information.
Advertising **makes products more attractive** to consumers.	Children often **put pressure on** their parents to buy the toys advertised on TV.
The advertising industry **creates many jobs**（创造很多就业机会）and **contributes to the economy**. 🔵 **contribute to the economy** 为经济做出贡献	Advertising is just a **marketing tool**（营销手段）for companies.

Pat指南

☆ 公益广告叫 public service advertisements

Public service advertisements educate people about health，safety or the environment.

Topic 06

Reading
读书、报纸和杂志

FOR（正方）	AGAINST（反方）
★ I'm **an avid reader**（特别爱读书的人）.	注 只要考到和 reading 有关的题你就必须想到 **an avid** /ˈævid/ **reader** 这个说法，因为在 native speakers 谈读书时它实在是太常用了
★ Reading **expands our horizons**（开阔我们的眼界）.	Watching TV and playing video games can be **more entertaining**（更有娱乐性的）.
★ This book is **fun and enjoyable**（有趣而且令人愉快的）.	This book is **dull and boring**（乏味、枯燥的）.
I liked the book so much that I **couldn't put it down**（爱不释手）.	地道英文里还有一种说法是 **read a book from cover to cover**（从封面一直看到封底，一页也不舍得错过）
★ Reading English books is a good way to **expand my English vocabulary**（扩展英语的词汇量）.	Our university library doesn't provide many English books.
Electronic books **take up less space**（占的空间更小）and **are easier to carry**（更便于携带）. 注 **electronic books** 电子书，也可以叫 **e-books**	I find it harder to **concentrate**（集中精力）when I read on **a screen**（屏幕）.

FOR（正方）	AGAINST（反方）
E-books are **more eco-friendly**（更有益于环保的）. They help to **save trees**（保护树木）.	Reading e-books for too long really **hurts my eyes**（伤视力）.

Pat指南

☆ 说"一本书好看"在地道英文里有个说法叫 It's a good read. 语法貌似是错的，但其实它是英文口语里经常听到的一句话。话说 Pat 上学时曾在图书馆找到了一本 On the Road（在路上），拿给图书管理员正准备 check out 时，librarian 突然就来了句：It's a good read.

☆ 有几种书值得一说（虽然并不一定值得一看）：

literary classics（文学经典），suspense novels（悬念小说），cookery books（教你做菜的书），travel guides（旅行指南）

Reading 读书、报纸和杂志
Newpapers & Magazines 报纸和杂志

FOR（正方）	AGAINST（反方）
★ Newspapers are **a good source of information**（是很好的信息来源）.	注 information 不能加复数，IELTS 口试里同样不能加复数的名词还有 **knowledge**，**advice**，**behaviour**，**equipment** 和 **scenery**
Local newspapers tend to **focus on** things that affect the local area.	Some local newspapers **are full of ads**（广告太多）.
International newspapers **cover a wide variety of topics**.	注 "时事" 叫作 **current events**
★ The **articles**（文章）are **well-written**.	"页面布局很合理的" 英文是 The pages are well laid-out.

FOR（正方）	AGAINST（反方）
Browsing through fashion magazines is a good way to relax.  browse though magazines 是 "翻阅杂志"	This magazine is **not very informative**（信息量并不是很大）.
This magazine **is aimed at** young readers.	 This magazine **is aimed at** …（某类人）的意思是 "这本杂志的目标读者群是……"

Pat 指南

☆ 报纸常见的版块（sections）：business section（商务版块），financial section（金融版块），entertainment section（娱乐版块），sports section（体育版块），classified ads（分类广告）

☆ 在地道英文里特指报纸或者杂志的销量有一个专门的词叫作 circulation。

This newspaper has a good reputation（声誉好）and a large circulation（销量大）.

Topic 07

Computers & The Internet
计算机和互联网

FOR（正方）	AGAINST（反方）
Computers **make our lives more convenient**（更方便）.	★ It's important **not to rely too much on**（不过度地依赖）computers.
★ There are many **educational games** on the Internet, such as maths games and language games.  educational games 有教育作用的游戏	Looking at a computer screen for too long **hurts my eyes**（伤视力）.
The Internet has become **an indispensable part of our lives**（我们生活里不可或缺的一个部分）.	★ Many children **are addicted to**（对……上瘾）computer games.

127

FOR（正方）	AGAINST（反方）
★ People who have good **computer skills** tend to **have more job opportunities**（有更多的就业机会）.	People who spend too much time on the Internet tend to **lead an unhealthy lifestyle**（过着不健康的生活方式）.
The Internet is **a good source of information**（是很好的信息来源）. 📵 **search engine** 搜索引擎，**find information easily** 轻松地找到信息	Some websites **contain violent images**（含有暴力的画面）.
★ Online shopping helps us **save time and money**. 📵 **save time and money** 既省钱又省时间	**Online crime**（网络犯罪）is increasing. 📵 网络安全叫作 **online security**，计算机病毒是 **computer virus**，恶意软件是 **malware**

Pat 指南

☆ 电子邮件（email）的好处是 free，easy to send 而且 can be delivered very quickly

☆ 书信的好处是 can better express our feelings（更好地表达我们的感受），而且 Business letters are more formal than business emails.

Computers & The Internet 计算机和互联网
Handwriting 笔迹

FOR（正方）	AGAINST（反方）
★ Good handwriting is easy to read. 📵 **neat and tidy** 干净整洁的	**Messy**（混乱的，潦草的）**handwriting** can be **confusing and annoying**. 📵 **confusing** 令人困惑的，**annoying** 让人很烦的，**embarrassing** 令人羞愧的，让人很"囧"的
Handwriting needs to **be practised regularly**（经常练习，经常实践）.	★ Children shouldn't **rely** too much on **typing**（打字）.

Topic 08

Mobile Phones
手 机

FOR（正方）	AGAINST（反方）
★ Mobile phones help us **keep in touch with**（保持联系）family and friends. ㊟ "保持联系" 的另一种地道说法是 **stay connected with…**	★ These days, people have fewer **face-to-face conversations** . ㊟ face-to-face conversations 面对面的谈话
We can also **surf the Internet** , **listen to music** and **take photos** with our mobile phones. ㊟ 上网在英美生活里也可以叫 **browse the Web**	★ Many people **rely too much on**（过度地依赖）mobile phones.
Smartphones are **fun and enertaining**（娱乐性很强的）. ㊟ smartphone 智能手机	Playing **mobile games**（手机游戏）can be an **expensive hobby** .
Text messages are **less expensive** than phone calls.	I call my friends when I need to have real **conversations**（谈话）with them.
★ Text messages work better in a **public place**（公共场所）.	Making phone calls is more likely to **distract** other people around me. ㊟ more likely to… 更有可能会…… distract others 干扰别人的注意力
★ We have more time to think before **responding to**（回应）a text message.	Using **emoticons**（表情符号，也可以叫 **emojis** ）in text messages is fun, but they may cost extra money.

ANDROID PHONE	iPhone
★ **Android phones** are very **user-friendly** (便于使用的). 注 Android phones 基于安卓系统的手机，也可以叫 **Android-based phones**	It seems iPhones are **more reliable** (更可靠的). 注 如果您觉得安卓手机更可靠考官也同样没脾气，他／她的任务是判断你的英文口语是否地道，而不是鉴定你到底是"果粉"还是"果黑" ☺
They are less expensive.	My iPhone is very **thin and light** (很薄很轻的).
There're more free **apps** (应用程序) available for Android phones.	The screen is **gorgeous** (特别"靓"的).

Topic 09 Clothing & Shopping
服装和购物

FOR (正方)	AGAINST (反方)
★ I like **casual clothes**, such as T-shirts and jeans (牛仔裤). 注 casual clothes 休闲服装，"帽衫儿"叫作 **hoodie**，休闲短裤当然就是 **shorts**	★ People are supposed to wear **formal clothes**, like **white shirts** (白衬衣) and **trousers** (长裤) in the office. 注 suit 就是套装，比如 **business suit** 就是"西装"，着装规定叫作 **dress code**
★ Casual clothes make us feel more **comfortable and relaxed**.	Formal clothes make us look **serious and professional** (职业的).
★ Clothing is a good way to **express ourselves** (表达自己的一种方式).	Many people are **fashion victims**. They choose fashion over comfort (宁可不舒服也要看起来"潮"). 注 fashion victim 过度追逐时尚的人

FOR（正方）	AGAINST（反方）
These days, fashion is very **diverse**（多样化的）.	Some people have **bad spending habits**（不良的消费习惯）. 注 buy things on an impulse（冲动地购物）.
Designer clothes are often considered **status symbols**.（身份和地位的象征） 注 designer clothes 是地道英文里对"名牌服装"最常用的说法	These days, people have become too **materialistic**（过于物质化的，只在乎金钱和物质享受的）.
I **shop till I drop**（生命不息，购物不止，"买买买"）. 注 这是喜欢"血拼"的 native speakers 特别爱说的一句话，也可以说 I'm **a real shopaholic**（如假包换的"购物狂"）.	**Consumer culture** encourages people to buy more than they need. 注 consumer culture 崇尚消费的文化 consumer society 崇尚消费的社会
Many people **follow** the **latest trends** because they want to look "cool" or popular.	I just **stick to**（坚持）my own style.
★ Online shopping helps us **save time and money**. It's also more **eco-friendly**（更环保）.	I can't **try on clothes**（试穿）online.

Pat指南 🔊

☆ 卖服装和饰品的精品店叫作什么？在英美最常用的一个词是 boutique（请仔细听音频里对这个词的正确发音）

☆ "忠实的顾客"叫 loyal customers

131

Weather & Seasons
天气与季节

FOR (正方)	AGAINST (反方)
★ I like **sunny and bright**(阳光灿烂的)weather.	**Overcast weather**(阴天)**affects my mood**(影响我的心情). 注 "阴天" 并不一定非要用 cloudy weather
★ Sunny and warm weather is perfect for **outdoor activities**, such as jogging(慢跑), camping(宿营)and hiking(徒步旅行，远足).	**sunny and breezy weather** 是 "风和日丽的天气"
I feel comfortable when it **drizzles**. The sound of **raindrops**(雨点儿)falling on the ground is very relaxing. 注 drizzle 下小雨，pour 下大雨	But I feel **upset** when it **pours**. 注 描述心情不好时 upset 极为常用，就像中文里说 "郁闷的"
★ I like walking in light rain. It makes me **feel fresh and energetic**. 注 短语 feel fresh and energetic 的意思是 "感觉很有活力"	Heavy rain can make the road **muddy** and **slippery** and cause traffic jams. It may even cause **flooding**(洪水). 注 muddy 泥泞的, slippery 很滑的
★ This city has **four distinct seasons**(分明的四季).	常见的恶劣天气（bad weather）：**thunderstorm**（暴风雨），**snowstorm**（暴风雪）和 **thick fog**（浓雾）
The spring is **warm and pleasant**(令人愉快的). Everything feels so fresh and most plants **bloom** in the spring. 注 bloom 开花儿	The spring is very short.

FOR（正方）	AGAINST（反方）
The summer is **mild**（温和的） and enjoyable.	The summer is **hot and humid**（又热又潮湿的）.
The city looks so beautiful with the **autumn foliage** . 注 短语 autumn foliage 是指秋叶，foliage 不能加复数，"观赏秋叶" 的英文是 **view the autumn foliage**	It gets **chilly** in the autumn. 注 Pat 在中国时注意到有的老师教学生用 **chilly** 这个词表示 "很冷的"，其实在地道英文里chilly 只是 "凉嗖嗖的"，而 cold 或者 freezing 才是表示 "很冷的"
It's a perfect place for **winter sports**（冬季运动）. 注 **skating** 滑冰，**skiing** 滑雪	The winter is cold, **windy**（风很大的）and **snowy**（连续下雪的）.

Pat 指南

☆ 中文里的 "雪花" 在地道英语里不能说 snowflower ✗ ，而要说 snowflakes ✓；"堆雪人儿" 不能说 pile a snowman ✗ ，而要说 build a snowman ✓

☆ 说自己喜欢某个季节的原因也可以是 My birthday is in the spring / summer/ autumn / winter. ☺

Topic 11 The Arts
音乐、绘画和摄影

FOR（正方）	AGAINST（反方）
★ Listening to music is a good way to **relax** .	I've never been to a **live concert**（现场音乐会）. 注 live 作形容词时的发音是/laiv/
This song makes me feel **happy and energetic** .	Loud music can **distract drivers**（干扰司机的注意力）.

FOR （正方）	AGAINST （反方）
Classical music （古典音乐） makes me feel calm and relaxed .	Some people think classical music is dull and boring .
This is a memorable （很容易记住的） song.	Some country songs sound similar to （听起来很相似） others. 注 country music 是特指美国的乡村音乐，而 folk music 则可以指中国、英国等任何国家的传统民族音乐，也就是"民乐"
★ Playing musical instruments （乐器） can make children more intelligent . 注 make children more intelligent 让儿童变得更聪明	Learning to play a musical instrument takes time and energy （需要投入时间和精力）.
Playing musical instruments can boost children's concentration （提高儿童的注意力）.	Learning to play an instrument takes a lot of patience （耐心） and practice （练习）.
★ Playing musical instruments is a good way to express ourselves （表达自己的一种方式）.	These days, learning to play an instrument can be very expensive .
This song is moving and unforgettable （感人的、令人难忘的）.	This song lacks depth （缺乏深度）.
Many people go to live concerts （现场音乐会） to see their favourite musicians in person . 注 see... in person 看到……本人，看到"活的" ☺	Concert tickets can be pricey . 注 英美生活里常用 pricey 表示 expensive 的意思
We can make new friends at rock concerts.	Too many people scream （尖叫） at rock concerts.

The Arts 音乐、绘画和摄影
Drawing & Painting 绘画

FOR（正方）	AGAINST（反方）
★ Painting is a good way to **reduce stress** .	I can't paint well. I just paint for fun.
Drawing and painting skills can help us better **appreciate**（欣赏）works of art. 🈺 works of art 艺术品	It **takes time and energy** to learn to paint well.
★ Drawing and painting can make children **more creative**（更有创造力的）.	Students should spend more time on **core subjects**（核心课程）, such as language, maths and science.
Some paintings are **thought-provoking**（发人深思的）.	I can't understand **abstract paintings**（抽象画）. 🈺 realistic paintings 写实的画，具象画

The Arts 音乐、绘画和摄影
Photography 摄影

FOR（正方）	AGAINST（反方）
★ Taking photos is a good way to **express ourselves**（表达自己感受的一种好方法）	We need to make sure we don't **invade other people's privacy**（侵犯别人的隐私）when we take photos. 🈺 bother others 让别人很烦

135

FOR （正方）	AGAINST （反方）
★ Photos can **bring back fond memories** （带来美好的回忆）.	Photos and videos **take up a lot of space** （占用很多空间） on my mobile phone.
My mobile phone has a **built-in camera** （内置相机）.	I can easily **slip it into my pocket** （轻松地放进口袋）.
Taking selfies is fun. 🈲 take selfies 玩儿自拍	★ Many people **are addicted to** （对……上瘾） taking selfies.
Good photos **capture precious moments in life** . 🈲 capture precious moments in life "捕捉人生里的宝贵瞬间"，它是 native speakers 谈摄影时特别爱用的一个 good phrase	**Lighting** （光线） is important to taking good pictures.
Many people **share photos online** （在网络上分享照片）. 🈲 photo-sharing website 照片分享网站，例如 Instagram	Some people use **Photoshop** to make their photos look better. 🈲 profile photo "头像" 照片

Pat 指南 🔈

☆ portrait 和 landscape photo 分别是人像和风景照片

☆ 随时随地 "抓拍" 叫作 snap some shots

Topic 12 People
家人、朋友、邻居、团队成员

FAMILY（家人）	FRIENDS（朋友）
My parents **are in their 40s / 50s / 60s…** 我的家长40多岁（或者50多岁、60多岁……）	Most of my friends **are around my age**（和我年龄相仿）.
They **work full-time**（全职工作）. ㊟ **work part-time** 兼职工作 **have retired** 已经退休了	★ My friends and I **share the same interests**（有共同的兴趣爱好）. ㊟ 也可以说 **have common interests**
My parents **are my role models**（是我的榜样）. ㊟ 英美的年轻人说自己很敬佩父母时都爱这么说	★ We **get on very well**（关系非常好，"合得来"）.
My parents are always **understanding and patient** with me（很体谅我而且很有耐心）.	My friends can always **cheer me up**（让我开心、振作起来）when I'm **upset**（郁闷的）.
My parents are very **strict**（要求很严格的）.	★ Most of my friends are very **sociable**（喜欢社交的、外向的）.
★ I use the Internet to **keep in touch with** my parents. ㊟ **keep in touch** 是"保持联系"，网络摄像头叫作 **webcam**	Hanging out with my friends makes me happy. ㊟ **hang out** 休闲放松
I have no **siblings**. ㊟ **siblings** 是泛指"兄弟姐妹"，**cousins** 是泛指"表兄弟或者表姐妹"	It's easy to **make new friends**（结交新朋友）online. ㊟ **online forum** 在线论坛，**chatroom** 聊天室，**social networking websites** 社交网站，**online community** 网络社区

FAMILY（家人）	FRIENDS（朋友）
★ Having meals together as a family can **strengthen family ties**（增进亲情）.	Some people choose to **meet their online friends in person**（"见网友"）.
My parents give me good advice about my **education and career choices**.	My friends often give me advice about **food, shopping and entertainment**.
I help my parents with **housework**（家务）. 注 **do the dishes**（洗碗刷盘子） **do the laundry**（洗衣服） **do the cleaning**（打扫房间）	We shouldn't **take our parents or friends for granted**（我们不应该把家长或朋友为我们做的事看成是理所应当的）.
These days, people tend to live in small **nuclear families** rather than large **extended families**. 注 **nuclear family** 只有父母和孩子一起住的小家庭, **extended family** 三代人甚至四代人一起住的大家庭	I live alone（独自生活）because I like being **independent**（独立的）. But sometimes I **feel lonely and unhappy**. 注 只要英文地道, 考官就会很愿意和你交流, 虽然你不是黄致列☺
The **one-child policy**（独生子女政策）has been changed.	Now **married couples** are allowed to have two children.

Pat 指南 🔊

☆ "忠实的朋友" 叫作 loyal friends, 如果你觉得自己的朋友总是很可靠, 那就说 I can always count on them.

□ **People** 家人、朋友、邻居、团队成员
└ **Neighbours 邻居**

FOR（正方）	AGAINST（反方）
★ My neighbours are very **friendly and helpful**（很友好而且乐于助人的）.	My neighbours are **unfriendly and unhelpful**. They don't even return things they've borrowed from me. 注 如果这么说，那就要满腔悲愤的 ☺
★ They are **polite and respectful**（有礼貌、尊重别人的）.	They are **rude and noisy**.
They never ask questions that are **too personal**. 注 英美人普遍重视隐私（value their privacy），所以 **nosy neighbours**（喜欢"打听事儿"的邻居）和 **noisy neighbours**（吵闹的邻居）一样都不受欢迎	They often have **noisy parties**（吵闹的聚会）.
★ We **get on well**（关系好，"合得来"）.	They often **play loud music** and their dog **barks**（狗叫）at night. That really **bothers me**（让我很烦）.
I see them at least **a few times a week**.	I **rarely** see my neighbours（很少见到）although they live next door.

Pat 指南 🔊

☆ 就住在"隔壁"的邻居叫作 my next-door neighbours，也可以说 They live next door.

139

People 家人、朋友、邻居、团队成员

Team Members 团队成员

FOR（正方）	AGAINST（反方）
★ Teamwork（团队合作）can **boost our efficiency**. 🈯 **boost our efficiency** 提升我们的效率	Some team members may **lack teamwork skills**（缺乏团队合作的技能）。
★ Team members need to **work closely together**（紧密地协作）. 🈯 **work closely together** 里面的 work 不仅可以指工作，也可以指学习、运动等需要努力才能完成的事情	Some team members **don't feel motivated**（感觉没动力）。
We need to work closely with our **teammates**（队友）to **achieve our common goal**（实现共同的目标）.	★ Some of them are **selfish**（自私的）and **unkind**（不友善的）。
A strong team spirit（很强的团队精神）can help the team **achieve success**（获得成功）.	They **don't care about** their teammates.

Pat指南 🔊

☆ "团队运动"就是 team sport，例如：basketball，football 和 volleyball（排球）：

Team sports help children develop their communication skills（沟通能力）.

Collection

收　藏

FOR（正方）	AGAINST（反方）
Collecting stamps can be **a lifetime hobby**（终生的爱好）.	★ **I used to** collect stamps **as a child. But now I** collect music CDs. ㊟ I used to… as a child. But now I…是 native speakers 对比自己童年曾经有过的习惯和现在的习惯有什么不同的时候特别常用的一个句型
Collecting stuff is **fun and enjoyable**（有趣而且令人愉快的）.	It can be **an expensive hobby**.
Some people think of collecting **works of art as a good investment**（很好的投资）. ㊟ works of art 艺术品	Many people collect things for **pleasure**（乐趣），not for **profit**（利润）.
Collecting things is a good way to **gain new knowledge**（获取新的知识）.	Some people collect **rare things** just to **show them off**（炫耀）. ㊟ rare 稀有的

Pat指南 🔊

☆ 几种常见收藏品：stamps（邮票），music CDs（音乐光盘）coins（硬币），antiques（古董），souvenirs（旅游纪念品）

☆ 要说自己收藏了很多的……，native speakers 会说 I have a large（或者 big）collection of…：

I have a large collection of DVDs.

Topic
14

Buildings
住所，博物馆，图书馆，老建筑

FOR（正方）	AGAINST（反方）
My flat **is just a five-minute-walk** from my university campus. ㊟ 也可以说 is just a short walk from...	It's very far from where I work.
I live near a convenient **bus route**（公车线）.	It's in a friendly **neighbourhood**（居民区），but the location is not convenient at all.
The living room is **spacious and bright**（宽敞明亮的）and it has **a nice view of** the city. ㊟ 客厅里常见的装饰（decorations）有： **potted plants**（盆栽植物） **family photos**（家庭合影） **paintings**（绘画） **posters**（海报）	The living room is a bit dark because the windows are small.
★ The bedroom is **nice and comfortable**. ㊟ 房间很舒适也可以说 It's **nice and cosy**.	The bedroom is only big enough for a bed.
My favourite room is the kitchen because I really **enjoy cooking** for my family and friends.	There's not enough **storage space**（储存物品的空间）in the kitchen.

□ **Buildings** 住所，博物馆，图书馆，老建筑
└ **Museums 博物馆**

FOR（正方）	AGAINST（反方）
Good museums are both **informative**（信息量很大的）and **entertaining**（很有娱乐性的）. Visitors can **gain new knowledge**（获取新知识）and have fun at the same time.	Some museums focus too much on **making a profit**（营利）.
Visiting museums is a good way to **expand our horizons**（开阔眼界）.	Some museums don't provide **hands-on activities**（可以实际动手操作的活动）.
★ Some museums **provide free admission**（提供免费参观）.	Most museums **charge admission fees**（收取参观费）.
★ Popular museums can **contribute to tourism**（为旅游业做贡献）.	Local visitors have already paid money to the museums through the tax system. They should **get free admission**（获得免费参观）.
★ This museum has **a large collection**（大量的馆藏）of interesting objects.	Many museums **lack funding**（缺乏资金）.
It provides a wide variety of **exhibitions**（展览）.	Some museum are boring and don't **attract many visitors**.
History museums **bring history to life**（让历史变得鲜明生动）.	如果是科技博物馆，那就可以说 It **brings science and technology to life**.

Pat 指南 🔊

☆ 英美最常见的博物馆类型有：history museum（历史博物馆），natural history museum（自然史博物馆，里面有很多的 fossils），science and technology museums（科技博物馆），space museums（航天博物馆），art gallery（艺术博物馆，例如伦敦的 the National Gallery），children's museums（儿童博物馆），wax museum（蜡像馆）和 military museum（军事博物馆）

Buildings 住所，博物馆，图书馆，老建筑
图书馆 Libraries

FOR（正方）	AGAINST（反方）
Public libraries are an important **source of information**（信息来源）.	Many public libraries **lack funding**（缺乏资金）.
★ This library provides **a friendly atmosphere**（友好的氛围）. 注 a ´quiet atmosphere 安静的氛围	I only go there **before exams**.
★ It has **a large collection**（大量的馆藏）of books and magazines.	It only has **a small collection of** English books.
It also has an area with large tables for **group discussions**（小组讨论）.	The librarians（图书管理员）are not very **helpful**.
The library has a **computer lab**（计算机房）where users can **search for information** on the Internet. 注 一个设备齐全的图书馆叫作 a well-equipped library	The **Internet connection** is too slow.

Buildings 住所，博物馆，图书馆，老建筑
Old Buildings 老建筑

FOR（正方）	AGAINST（反方）
Old buildings show us how people **lived or worked in the past**. 注 任何历史悠久的建筑都可以称为 old building，但是只有曾经有过重要历史意义的老建筑才可以叫 historic building	★ New buildings can **better meet our needs**（更好地满足我们的需要）.

FOR（正方）	AGAINST（反方）
★ Historic buildings are an important part of our cultural heritage（文化遗产）. 　注 heritage 不能加 s，historic site 历史遗址	Some of them are unsafe（不安全的）.
They make cities more attractive（更吸引人的）.	★ They need regular repairs（定期的维修）.
★ Historic buildings can attract many tourists（吸引很多的游客）.	Repairing them is very expensive.

Topic 15

Sports & Outdoor Activities
运动和户外活动

FOR（正方）	AGAINST（反方）
★ Sports are fun and enjoyable（有趣而且令人愉快的）.	Many people surf the Internet or watch TV to relax. 　注 "上网" 在英美生活里也经常叫 browse the Web
Playing badminton（打羽毛球）is a good way to keep fit and have fun at the same time . 　注 is a good form of exercise：是一种很好的锻炼方式	Many children spend too much time in front of a computer or TV screen（屏幕）.
★ Playing sports can reduce the risk of heart disease and high blood pressure（减少患心脏病和高血压的风险）.	More and more people are overweight and find it hard to lose weight（减肥）. 　注 overweight 的语气要比 fat 客气一点，但现实是一样的残酷

FOR（正方）	AGAINST（反方）
★ Playing sports is **a good way to make new friends**（结识新朋友的好方法）.	Many people prefer to **make friends online**（在网上交友）.
Parents should encourage their children to **lead an active lifestyle**（经常运动锻炼的生活方式）.	Governments have not done enough to **promote healthy lifestyles**（促进健康的生活方式）. ㊟ **exercise regularly** 经常锻炼，**have a healthy diet** 保持健康的饮食结构
★ Team sports（团队运动），such as football, basketball and volleyball（排球），can help us develop our **teamwork skills**（团队合作的能力）and **communication skills**（沟通能力）.	Individual sports（个人运动），such as **jogging**（慢跑），swimming and **skiing**（滑雪），can **boost our concentration** and **self-discipline**（提高我们的注意力和自制力）.
Extreme sports, such as **bungee jumping**（蹦极），**rock climbing**（攀岩）and **rafting**（漂流），can **give people a great sense of achievement**（极大的成就感）.	They are **very challenging**（很有挑战的）and can be **dangerous**（危险的）.
Televised（电视播放的）sports events **attract many viewers**（吸引很多观众）. ㊟ 看电视的人叫 **TV viewers**，而去现场看体育比赛的人叫 **spectators**	Some sports stars **earn too much money**.
Professional athletes（职业运动员）need many years of **training**（训练）to develop the skills that lead to success in their sports.	We should **value** scientists, teachers and nurses more highly because they contribute more to society. ㊟ **value** 当动词时是"重视、珍视"的意思

Pat 指南

☆ 关于运动，您如果能再记住这两个名词就更好了：strength（力量）和 endurance（耐力）

Sports & Outdoor Activities 运动和户外活动
户外活动 Outdoor Activities

FOR（正方）	AGAINST（反方）
Outdoor activities，such as **hiking**（徒步旅行，远足），**camping**（宿营）and **fishing**（钓鱼），help us **get closer to nature**（更加接近大自然）.	Outdoor activities **depend on**（取决于……）the weather.
★ I can **enjoy the sun** and the **fresh air**.	Sometimes I have to change my plan because of **bad weather**.
Outdoor activities help me **recharge my batteries**. 注 在英文口语里说 **recharge my batteries** 的意思是"让身心恢复良好的状态"，而跟"周末上补习班"无关 ☺	Outdoor activities can be very **tiring**（让人疲惫的）.
Doing outdoor activities as a family is a good way to **strengthen family ties**（增进亲情）.	Many parents find it hard to **keep a work-family balance**（保持工作和家庭之间的合理平衡）.
★ Outdoor activities can help children **learn about nature**（了解大自然）.	These days, many children **spend too much time in front of** a computer or TV screen.
★ I feel **fresh and energetic** when I'm outdoors. 注 **feel fresh and energetic** 感觉很有活力	Some outdoor activities, like rock **climbing**（攀岩）and **rafting**（漂流），are very **challenging**（有挑战的）and can be dangerous.
Outdoor activities can **boost our immune system**（增强我们的免疫机能）.	We may **get wet in the rain** and **catch a cold**（感冒）.

FOR（正方）	AGAINST（反方）
Cycling is a great way to **keep fit**.	I would have to **share the road** with cars and buses.
Bicycles don't **pollute the air**（不污染空气）.	I would have to **breathe in**（吸入）lots of **car fumes**（汽车尾气）.

Pat 指南

☆ 3 种中外小朋友都喜欢的户外活动：

kite-flying（放风筝），hide-and-seek（捉迷藏），tag（基本就等于国内小朋友们玩的"捉人"）

☆ native speakers 在谈论户外活动时特别爱说的一句话是 I can soak up some vitamin D （吸收一些维生素 D）. 因为据说阳光可以促进皮肤生成维生素 D ☺

Topic 16 **Travel**
旅 行

FOR（正方）	AGAINST（反方）
Travelling helps me **get away from it all**（摆脱日常的各种琐事）.	Travelling abroad is expensive.
★ We can **explore**（探索）new places and **meet new people**. 注 英文里的 new people 可不是"刚结婚的人"，而是指"以前不认识的人，新认识的人"	Many tourists don't have the **opportunity**（机会）to talk with **the locals**（当地人）. 注 跟团旅行叫 group tour 或者 guided tour，自助游叫作 independent travel

FOR （正方）	AGAINST （反方）
Travelling alone **gives me more freedom** （给我更多的自由）. I can have **more flexible** （更灵活的） travel plans.	Travelling alone can be **boring** .
Travelling with friends **is more fun than** travelling alone.	Sometimes we **argue** （争论） about what to do.
★ Travelling with friends is a good way to **strengthen friendships** （增进友情）. 注 增进亲情是 **strengthen family ties**	My friends are always too busy to travel.
We can **share the experience** together.	We spend too much time talking to each other.
★ Tourism **contributes to** （做贡献） the economy.	Tourism may **damage the environment** （破坏环境）.
Tourists spend money on hotels, transport, food, entertainment and **souvenirs** （旅行纪念品）.	Some tourists don't respect （尊重） the local traditions （当地的传统）.

Pat指南 🔊

☆ 在英美，年轻人谈论旅行时很爱说的一句话是：I prefer to travel light （轻装旅行，只带很少的行李）.

☆ native speakers 说旅行的好处时经常会用到一个短语叫 recharge my batteries （"充电"）。但请注意：这个 phrase 在地道英文里是指"让疲劳的身心恢复良好的状态"，而不是"周末上补习班" ☺

I'm going to spend the weekend on the beach to recharge my batteries.

Topic 17 Food & Cooking
饮食和做饭

FOR（正方）	AGAINST（反方）
★ It's important to have **a healthy and balanced diet**（健康的、均衡的饮食结构）.	Many people have busy careers and **rely on**（依赖于……）**fast food** for their meals.
★ Fruit and vegetables are **rich in**（富含……）vitamin C and fiber（维生素 C 和纤维）. 注 英文里说水果时还常会用到 juicy（多汁的）这个词	★ Eating too much fast food **damages children's health**（破坏儿童的健康）.
Seafood is high in **protein**（蛋白质）and low in **fat**（脂肪）.	Fast food **contains**（含有）too much **fat**, **salt**（盐）or **sugar**（糖）.
I like to start my day with a **hearty**（丰盛的）breakfast.	I often **skip**（不吃，"跳过去"）breakfast.
I always try to **eat three square meals**（吃好三餐，每顿饭都"不对付"）a day.	I'm often too busy to cook.
People **eat out** to **socialise**（社交）. 注 eat out 在餐馆儿吃，"在外面吃"	**Eating out** is more expensive than eating at home.
Some restaurants provide a **relaxing and comfortable** atmosphere, while others are **overcrowded and noisy**.	注 relaxing and comfortable 轻松舒适的，overcrowded and noisy 过于拥挤而且很吵闹的
The food at this restaurant is very **well-priced**. 注 native speakers 经常用 well-priced 来形容餐馆的食品"定价合理的"	Restaurant food tends to be **unhealthy**（不健康的）.

FOR（正方）	AGAINST（反方）
Restaurants provide **a wide variety of food**.	Good restaurants **are always packed**（总是挤满了人）.
★ **Locally-produced food**（本地生产的食品）**is more nutritious** and tastes better. 注 **more nutritious** 更有营养的	These days, food is often **transported**（运输）over long distances.
Organic food（有机食品）is produced without **chemicals**（化学药品）.	Organic food is expensive.
Genetically-modified crops（转基因的庄稼）grow faster. 注 如果觉得太长，就说 **GM crops** 也同样地道	Many people **don't trust**（不信任）GM food.
★ **GM food looks more attractive**（更吸引人的）.	GM food could **damage our health**（有可能破坏健康）. 注 提出假设时，could 语气比 can 更客气

□ **Food & Cooking 饮食和做饭**
└ **Cooking 做饭**

FOR（正方）	AGAINST（反方）
★ Cooking is an important **life skill**（生活技能）. ★ Teaching children cooking skills can make them **more independent**（更独立的）.	Many parents don't know how to **cook healthy meals**.
Cooking helps children **build self-confidence**（树立自信）.	Cooking can be **risky**（有风险的）for young children.

FOR (正方)	AGAINST (反方)
★ Children who can cook tend to **eat less junk food** (比较少吃垃圾食品).	Many children **are addicted to** (对……上瘾) junk food.
Cookery classes are **fun and helpful** (有趣而且有帮助的). ⊞ cookery classes / cookery courses 厨艺课	Parents can teach their children how to cook **for free** (免费地).
Food is always **beautifully cooked** on **cookery shows** (厨艺节目). ⊞ ★ It's almost like an art form. 简直就像是一种艺术形式。	I don't really follow the **cooking tips** from **TV chefs**. ⊞ tips 小窍门，"小贴士"，TV chefs 厨艺节目里面的"大厨"，请注意 chef 的正确读音是 /ʃef/ √，而不是 /tʃef/ ✗

Pat指南 🔊

☆ 白面包是 white bread，全麦面包是 whole-wheat bread，虽然不太好吃，但是却更有营养（more nutritious）

☆ recipe 是指一个菜的做法：

Many people have secret recipes that they don't share with others.

☆ ingredients 是做菜的"原料"

Fresh ingredients make meals healthier.

☆ native speakers 常用下面这三种说法来形容食物"好吃的"，它们的语气依次增强：tasty（味道不错的）< delicious（非常好吃的）< out of this world（已经不是一般人类所能吃到的了），您现在应该明白为什么英语里最常用的是 delicious 了 ☺

Colours & Numbers
颜色和数字

Colours can **affect our mood**（影响我们的情绪）.

★ **Bright colours**（鲜艳的颜色）, such as orange and red, make me feel **energetic**（很有活力的）.

★ **Dark colours**（比较暗的颜色）, such as purple and brown, make me feel **calm and peaceful**（平静安详的）.

Soft colours（柔和的颜色）, like cream（淡黄色）and grey（灰色）, look **elegant**（优雅的）and **classy**（很有品位的，很有"格调"的，在地道英文里这个形容词跟上课无关）.

Pat 指南

☆ 有 3 种颜色很少有国内同学会说起，但是却经常被 native speakers 提到：一个是 lilac（淡紫色），另一个是 maroon（一种比较暗的红色，您肯定听说过 Maroon 5，虽然那个乐队现在已经不止 5 个人了），第三个是 navy blue（深蓝色，"海军蓝"）

Colours & Numbers 颜色和数字
Numbers & Maths 数字和数学

We think of 6, 8 and 9 as lucky numbers. They sound **similar to**（相似的）some Chinese **characters**（中文字，汉字）with **positive meanings**（积极的含义）.

★ My lucky number is… It's the day I was born on. ☺

Long numbers are difficult to remember.

I try to **think of a sentence**（想出一个句子）that sounds **similar to** the number. That can help me remember the number.

FOR（正方）	AGAINST（反方）
★ Maths skills can help children better **manage**（管理）their time and money.	Many children **find maths difficult**（感到数学很难）.
★ Maths skills can help children **better understand** the world around them.	They think maths is boring.
Getting **good grades**（好成绩）in maths can help children **build self-confidence**（树立自信）.	★ Learning math **takes a lot of practice**（需要很多的练习）.

Topic 19   Parks, Plants, Animals & Birds

公园，植物，动物，鸟类

FOR（正方）	AGAINST（反方）
★ Parks are **quiet and peaceful**（宁静安详的）.	Some parks are **noisy and overcrowded**（喧闹而且过于拥挤的）at weekends. 注 英国人更常说 at weekends，美国人则更常说 on weekends
★ Parks help us **reduce stress**（减轻压力）.	There are not enough parks in this city.
This park is a good place to **hang out**（休闲放松）**with friends** and **meet new people**.	注 地道英文里的 new people 跟"刚结婚"没关系，而是指"以前不认识的人，新认识的人"
★ Parks help children **learn about nature**（了解大自然）.	Some parks are not safe at night.

FOR（正方）	AGAINST（反方）
This park is a great place for **having a picnic**（野餐）or a relaxing walk.	The picnic tables are **worn-out**（破旧的）.
★ We can **get away from busy city life**（摆脱繁忙的都市生活）and relax for a couple of hours.	Big cities are **concrete jungles**. 🈁 中文里经常把大城市叫作"钢筋水泥的丛林"，英文里则把大城市叫作 concrete jungles "混凝土的丛林"，有空的时候您不妨听听 Alicia Keys 版的 *Empire State of Mind* 来感受一下纽约的"混凝土丛林" ☺
We can enjoy the sun and **fresh air**（新鲜的空气）.	The park **equipment**（设备）is old and some **has been damaged**（被破坏了）. 🈁 equipment 不能加 s
Cities need more **green space**（绿化空间）.	Very few people are interested in **planting trees**（种树，植树）.
Neighbourhood parks（居民区里的公园）help people develop **a sense of community**. 🈁 a sense of community 社区感，社区凝聚力	Many neighbourhood parks **lack funding**（缺乏资金）.
I like to **watch the plants grow**. 🈁 英美人谈论自己的 garden 时经常这么说	I have to **water the plants**（给植物浇水）by myself.

Pat 指南 🔊

☆ native speakers 谈到自己喜欢的公园或花园时特别爱说的一句话是 This park / garden is an oasis from city life. oasis 的意思是"绿洲"，请注意听音频里的正确读音

☆ 公园里面常见的景物有 flowerbeds（花坛），lawns（绿地），fountains（喷泉），benches（长椅），sculptures（雕塑），gazebos（亭子），paths（公园里的小路），以及小朋友们玩的 swings（秋千），slides（滑梯），see-saws（跷跷板）等

☆ 如果要说公园里"点缀着"一些池塘和湖泊，地道英文会说 The park is dotted with ponds and lakes.

Parks, Plants, Animals & Birds 公园，植物，动物，鸟类
Plants 植物

FOR（正方）	AGAINST（反方）
Trees **produce oxygen**（制造氧气）and **absorb carbon dioxide**（吸收二氧化碳）.	**Global warming**（全球变暖）is a very serious problem.
★ Trees can help to **reduce pollution**（减少污染）and **clean the air**（净化空气）.	There are more cars on the road, which means more **car fumes**（汽车尾气）in the air.
★ They **provide shade**（提供树荫）in the summer.	There are not enough trees in this city.
Trees are **the main source of**（主要的来源）wood and **contribute to the economy**（为经济做贡献）.	Millions of trees are **cut down** each year.
★ Trees make streets **more attractive**.	Very few people are interested in **planting trees**（植树）in their **neighbourhood**（居民区）.

花的作用	
★ Many plants **bloom**（开花）in the spring.	★ We can enjoy the colours and **fragrance**（香气）of the flowers.
Many people like to **decorate**（装饰）their **living room**（客厅）with **fresh flowers**（鲜花）.	Fresh flowers are more expensive than **plastic flowers**（塑料花）or **silk flowers**（丝花）.
Fresh flowers are beautiful.	They **don't last long**（不耐用）.
★ Flowers are **simple but thoughtful**（简单但是很"贴心"的）gifts. ★ They can help us **express our feelings**（表达我们的情感）.	Flowers can help to **cheer up patients**（帮助病人振作起来）. 注 native speakers 把送给病人的花叫作 **get-well flowers**

一些花的象征意义

❖ The **lotus**（莲花）is a symbol of **purity**（纯洁）.

　　注 **is a symbol of...** 是……的象征

❖ The red rose（红玫瑰）is a symbol of **romantic love**.

❖ The carnation（康乃馨）**means** love and respect.

❖ The peony（牡丹花）**represents**（象征着）wealth and prosperity（财富和兴旺）.

❖ The plum flower（梅花）represents **hard work and courage**（勤奋和勇气）.

Pat指南

☆ 您还可以在 p. 228 页看到很多好记又好说的植物名称

Parks, Plants, Animals & Birds 公园，植物，动物，鸟类

Animals & Birds 动物和鸟类

FOR（正方）	AGAINST（反方）
I like to hear birds **chirping**（鸟叫）in the morning.	**Wild**（野生的）animals are leaving this area because of **noise and pollution**.
Birds are an important part of the **ecosystem**（生态系统）. ❀ **wild species** 野生物种, **endangered species** 濒危物种	Not all wild species **are protected by law**. ❀ **are protected by law** 受到法律的保护
There used to be（过去曾经有）a wide variety of wild animals and birds living in this area. ❀ **protect biodiversity** 保护生物的多样性	★ Now their **habitats** are being polluted and destroyed. ❀ **habitat** 栖息地
Governments should **spend more money on** the protection of wild species.	Many wildlife reserves **lack funding**（缺乏资金）. ❀ **wildlife reserves** 野生动植物保护区, **nature reserves** 自然保护区
Some birds have **gorgeous feathers**（非常漂亮的羽毛）.	Some birds **look plain**（看起来平淡无奇的）.
Some people tend to believe seeing a **magpie**（喜鹊）brings good luck.	Some people believe seeing a **crow**（乌鸦）brings bad luck. ❀ That's just an old **superstition**（迷信）.
★ Pets can help to **reduce loneliness**（减少孤独感）.	Some pets make a lot of **noise**.
★ Pets can help children develop **a sense of responsibility**（责任感）.	Some pet owners（宠物的主人）are not **responsible owners**. They don't take good care of their pets.

Pat 指南

☆ native speakers 在描述小朋友或者小动物可爱的时候除了用 cute 之外，还常会用短语 cute and adorable 来说明"可耐"的程度 ☺

Celebration & Rest
节日，聚会，礼物，跳舞和睡眠

FOR（正方）	AGAINST（反方）
★ Celebrating festivals is **fun and enjoyable**（有趣而且令人心情愉快的）.	Festivals are noisy, but that's part of the fun.
★ Festivals **contribute a lot to the economy**（为经济做出很大的贡献）.	Celebrating festivals can be expensive.
Festivals help to **strengthen family ties**（增进亲情）.	More and more people choose to **live alone**.
★ Family members **get together**（聚在一起）and **share the joy**（分享喜悦）.	Trains are **overcrowded**（过于拥挤的）, with many **passengers**（乘客）standing.
Traditional festivals are an important part of our **cultural heritage**（文化遗产）. 注 heritage 不能加 s	Many young people think Western festivals, like **Christmas**（圣诞节）and **Valentine's Day**（情人节）, are more **fun and exciting**. 注 Thanksgiving Day 感恩节，give thanks for what we have 对我们所拥有的表示感谢
★ Traditional festivals help children **better understand**（更好地理解）their culture.	Traditional festival food tends to delicious but unhealthy.
On New Year's Eve, many people watch the **TV specials**. 注 这里 special 是名词"特别节目"的意思	"看焰火"叫作 **see the fireworks**，"放鞭炮"则叫 **set off firecrackers**，给小朋友红包儿是 **give children red envelopes with money inside**。如果非要跟考官说"春晚"，下面这个表达会让他/她听得很舒服，尽管你自己会说得比较累：the TV gala broadcast on the eve of Chinese New Year

Pat 指南

☆ native speakers 在新年时特别重视的一件事情是 make a New Year's resolution（做新年决定），通常是决定对自己以前有的某种不良生活方式做出重要的改变。不过，BBC 去年年底做的 survey 显示：只有8%的人能真正坚持自己的新年决定（Only 8 percent of people stick to their New Year's resolutions.），而高达92%的英国人其实都没实现自己在新年时决定的目标（92 percent of people fail to achieve their New Year's resolutions.）☺

Celebration & Rest 节日，聚会，礼物，跳舞和睡眠

假期 Holidays

FOR（正方）	AGAINST（反方）
★ Holidays help us **take a break**, **have a good rest**（充分地休息）and **recharge our batteries**（让疲劳的身心恢复良好的状态）.	Most shops are **overcrowded**（过于拥挤的）on public holidays. 🈯 但英美的大多数商店在公共假期时却会关门（Most shops are closed on public holidays.）
Many people **go abroad** on holidays.	**Travelling abroad** is expensive and can be **challenging**（有挑战的）. 🈯 overcome the language barrier 克服语言障碍

Pat 指南

☆ 每到假期，native speakers 爱说的一句话是：I use holidays to catch up on sleep（我用假期追回睡眠，也就是中文说的"补觉"☺)

☆ 中国的 public holidays（公共假期）的英文说法：

the New Year holiday，the Spring Festival holiday（也可以说 the Lunar New Year holiday），the Qingming Festival holiday（也可以说 the Tomb Sweeping Day holiday），the Labour Day holiday，the Duanwu Festival holiday（也可以叫 the Dragon Boat Festival holiday），the Mid-Autumn Festival holiday，the National Day holiday

▯ **Celebration & Rest** 节日，聚会，礼物，跳舞和睡眠
Parties 聚会

FOR（正方）	AGAINST（反方）
★ Going to parties is a good way to **have fun with friends** and **meet new people**. ⊞ **catch up with old friends** 和老朋友"叙旧"	Some parties are too **noisy**. ⊞ **play party games** 聚会的时候玩游戏
★ People **socialise**（社交）at parties. ⊞ 地道英文里把只要一听说有 party 必去的人叫作 **party animal**	Some parties are too **wild**（疯狂的）. Some people even **get drunk**（喝醉）and do crazy things.
Most of my friends are very **sociable**（很外向的，喜欢社交的）.	My parents are too **strict**（过于严厉的）. We don't **communicate** well.

Pat指南 ◀))

☆ The more, the merrier.（人越多越好玩儿）是在英美生活里说要开 party 时一句很常用的话，而 We had a blast!（玩得非常开心!）则是开完 party 之后人们常说的一句话

Celebration & Rest 节日，聚会，礼物，跳舞和睡眠
Birthdays 生日

My birthday **reminds me**（提醒我）of how much my parents **love and support** me.

★ Celebrating my birthday with friends **makes me feel special**.

🈁 **light the candles on the cake** 点生日蜡烛，sing "Happy Birthday" 唱"祝你生日快乐"，**make a wish** 许愿，**blow out the candles** 吹蜡烛，**cut the cake** 切蛋糕，**open the gifts** 开礼物

I really **appreciate** how much they **care about** me.

★ They give me **thoughtful gifts**（"贴心"的礼物），like my favourite snacks, books or **gift cards**（礼品卡）for my favourite shops.

I particularly like the **gifts hand-made by my friends**（我的朋友们亲手制作的礼物）.

Every birthday is **a fresh start**（全新的开始）.

🈁 也可以说 **a new beginning**
We can have **new dreams**（新的梦想）and **new goals**（新的目标）.

We'll try to do things better and **achieve** more.

★ The 18th birthday is very important because it's when a young person is considered to become an **adult**（成年人）.

Pat指南 🔊

☆ 在生日聚会上，native speakers 常用 the birthday boy / the birthday girl 来称呼过生日的男孩或者女孩，而且在英美用这两个 phrases 来指过生日的成年男性或者成年女性也同样很常见 ☺

☆ "唱卡拉 OK"的英文就叫 sing karaoke，请认真听音频（英语里的日文词最后一个字母 e 通常都是要发音的)

Celebration & Rest 节日，聚会，礼物，跳舞和睡眠
Gifts 礼物

★ My friends and I **exchange gifts**（交换礼物）on New Year's Day.	Exchanging gifts is a good way to celebrate **special occasions**.
I **spend a lot of time** choosing **the right gift** for my friends' birthday. 注 **thoughtful gifts** "贴心" 的礼物	★ Giving friends gifts shows that we really **care about** them.
On Chinese New Year, children receive gifts and **red envelopes with money inside**（红包）.	On Valentine's Day, lovers give each other romantic gifts, like flowers, chocolate or **jewellery**（首饰）, to **express their feelings**（表达他们的情感）.
Some people give their friends **expensive gifts**, like **mobile phones** or **tablets**（平板电脑）.	Some people give their boss expensive gifts to develop *guanxi*. 注 *guanxi* 其实已经是地道的英文词了，而且还形成了一个短语 develop guanxi，也就是 "搞关系"，请听音频里这个词的 "正确发音" ☺
★ **Hand-made gifts** are more creative（更有创意的）and **more memorable**（给人印象更深的）.	★ It's the thought that counts. 注 这是 native speakers 谈到礼物时最常用的句子之一：真正重要的是心意。

Celebration & Rest 节日，聚会，礼物，跳舞和睡眠
Dancing 跳舞

★ Dancing is a good way to **socialise**（社交）. 🈂 **go to a dance** 参加舞会	**I have two left feet**, so I can't dance well. 🈂 native speakers 说自己不擅长跳舞时会用"我长了两只左脚"这句话给自己解围（make it less embarrassing）
★ Dancing is a good way to **keep fit**. 🈂 **a good form of exercise** 很好的锻炼形式	Learning to dance well **takes time and energy**（需要时间和精力）.
The **moves**（动作）and **steps**（舞步）of traditional dances are more **complicated**（复杂的）. They take a lot of practice to learn. 🈂 **traditional dances** 传统舞蹈，比如 **tango**（探戈）	The moves and steps of modern dances are more **fun and creative**. They are a good way to **express ourselves**（表达自己）. 🈂 **modern dances** 现代舞蹈，比如 **hip-hop dance**（嘻哈舞）
Ballet（芭蕾舞）is an **elegant**（优雅的）dance style.	I like dancing to **energetic**（很有活力的）music.

Pat 指南 🔊

☆ 国内的一些中年女士（middle-aged ladies）"跳广场舞"的英文叫 practise their Square Dance routine

☆ 鸟叔 PSY 的江南 Style（Gangnam Style）虽然能让人上瘾（very addictive），但说舞蹈时您还是别说"骑马舞"（horse-riding dance）了 ☺

164

Celebration & Rest 节日，聚会，礼物，跳舞和睡眠
Sleeping Habits 睡眠习惯

FOR（正方）	AGAINST（反方）
I always try to **keep a regular sleep schedule**（保持有规律的作息时间）.	★ **If I stay up late**（很晚才睡），then I feel tired and **find it hard to concentrate**（很难集中注意力）the next morning.
★ **A good night's sleep**（好好地睡一晚）makes me **feel fresh and energetic**（感觉很有活力）.	Lack of sleep **increases the risk of heart disease and high blood pressure**（导致患心脏病和高血压的风险上升）.
★ Getting enough sleep helps me **reduce stress**（减轻压力）and can really **boost my efficiency**（提高我的效率）.	Lack of sleep makes people **feel stressed**（感觉压力很大）.
Listening to some **relaxing music**，taking **a hot shower**（洗个热水澡）and doing some **light exercise**（做轻度的锻炼）can all help me get a good night's sleep.	I often play video games before going to bed.

Pat 指南

☆ native speakers 经常把一个爱早起的人叫作 an early bird，而把一个喜欢晚睡，越晚越精神的人称为 an night owl。有趣的是：这个短语和中文里说的"夜猫子"正好是 100% 的契合度 ☺

★　　★　　★

对于备考时间有限的同学来说，先集中准备好本次考试最可能出现的题目仍然是重中之重。您可以到 Pat 博客 blog. sina. com. cn/ieltsguru 上看本月口语预测的 Part 1 考题，同时结合我们在 Day 3 和 Day 7 讲解的语言点来进行高效的准备。

Day

8

Part 2: 清晰度 > 难度
Clear and Natural

Pat's Guide
To The IELTS Speaking Test

How many roads must a man walk down
Before they call him a man
How many seas must a white dove sail
Before she sleeps in the sand
How many times must the cannon balls fly
Before they're forever banned

IELTS 口试 Part 2 真题库全集索引

口语 Part 2 话题指南

　　对于考试当月最新出现的话题，您还可以在 Pat 的博客 blog. sina. com. cn/ieltsguru 的本月口语预测里看到。

对于考试当月最新出现的话题，您还可以在 Pat 的博客 blog. sina. com. cn/ieltsguru 的本月口语预测里看到。

╲ **Part 2** 的一分钟思考时间里你应该做的事

好消息是：在 Part 2 考官将会给你纸和笔（如果他/她居然很不敬业地忘了，你就说 Could I have a pen and a sheet of paper?）。在 1 分钟的思考时间里，考官是允许你在纸上写一些 notes 的。

☆ 卡片题必须注意时态，如果说过去的内容一定一定要记得用过去时。

如果看到题目涉及过去的内容，在思考的一分钟里你可以在纸上写上 -ed 这个符号，以确保自己不会忘记时态。

☆ 名词的复数和谓语动词的单数一定不能忘记加 -s。

你也可以在纸上写一个"大 S"来提示自己不要说错单复数。

☆ 在纸上记录 ideas 和 key words 时，字可以写得大一点。

在这方面考官完全管不着你，但如果你在描述时因为看不清楚自己在纸上写的 ideas 和 key words 而一再地停顿下来，把口语考试变成"阅读"考试，就很可能会导致悲剧。

★　　★　　★

╲ 作为 **Native speakers**，考官们喜欢什么样的答案？

对于大多数中国考生来说，口语卡片题是 IELTS 口试里最"凶险"的一关，因为 Part 2 是"独白"，一旦开始描述，全程都要自己说，而且还必须面向考官，不能扭着脸儿说。

让问题变得更复杂的是：中国考生和 IELTS 考官对于 Part 2 答案的"审美观"也是不同的。考生往往希望自己的答案成为有震撼力的"大杀器"，所以热衷于卖弄高难度的单词和可以"绕梁三圈儿"的长句。但考官作为 native speakers，却更看重描述（description）的清晰度。所以，当考官听完考生的"趴吐"之后对于描述对象往往仍然是"一头雾水"。

IELTS 考官们真正希望听到的 Part 2 答案到底有多难？我们来看看由主办方 British Council 提供的高分答案实例就真相大白了：

> Describe a time when you had to work very hard to achieve a goal.
>
> You should say:
>
> what the goal was
>
> when this happened
>
> what you did to achieve the goal
>
> and talk about why the goal was important to you.

British Council 提供的真实高分答案官方范例：

One of my recent goals was to go on a 4-day walk in the moutains in the South Island.

It's a famous walk in my country, a beautiful walk around some bays by the ocean. We planned to stay at hotels each night, so it was going to be a great holiday for my husband and me. But I needed to get fit enough to enjoy it.

I did lots of exercise and training to prepare for this goal. When I started, I knew I needed to get a lot fitter, so I did a lot of walking. At first, the 8 km circle route near my house was really hard for me. It took about 2 hours. But in the end I could do it easily in a much shorter time.

I also went for longer walks with my husband on weekends. We used to walk to the Botanical Garden, which was a long way. But we got to have lunch in a café when we got there. That was fun, and I found that I had more energy as I got fitter. But then my feet and legs started to hurt, so I went to swimming classes three times a week. I had to get up at 6 am for this, but it was worth it, and it really improved my balance.

This goal was important to me because I really wanted to go on this holiday with my husband. Reaching it also gave me a great sense of achievement. I was very proud of myself. And of course I was a lot fitter by the end of the training.

没有 "卖弄" 的痕迹，也毫无 "炫技" 的影子，除了少数略有难度的词汇和短语之外，90％的用词都是同学们几乎不屑一用的 "基础词汇"。但是这位考生确实得到了 British Council 给出的高分，原因很简单：因为她的描述（description）符合 native speaker 考官对于 Part 2 的 "审美观"。

事实上，你在口语 Part 2 里需要做的既不是安于 "眼前的苟且"，也不是追求 "诗和远方"，speaking examiner 在 Part 2 里真正希望听到你说的是：

01　一个清晰的答案，也就是通过你的英语描述考官可以比较容易地听明白你描述的人物、事物或者事件是 "什么样儿的"；

02　一个扣题的答案，也就是你应该积极地参考卡片上面列出的四个提示问题（cue questions），同时你还可以在四个提示里面选择 1~2 个自己 "最有感觉" 的提示重点展开，并适当给出合理的细节（例如：上面这个 British Council 给出的官方实例就选择了对第 1 个和第 2 个提示问题只是简要地一带而过，而对第 3 个和第 4 个提示问题进行深入的展开，并适当给出了合理的细节）。Pat 还将为您列出的 Mind Maps（思维导图）也是 native speakers 进行描述（description）的时候确保扣题、充实的常用工具；

03　一个自然的答案，你当然可以在考前针对每类话题准备一些相关词汇和短语，但请牢记：只有你能自然地说出来的词汇和短语才是真正适合你自己的，让你 "卡壳儿" 的难词在考场实战里只会是你的负担。

我们再来看《剑 10》Test 2 里面的官方卡片题实例：

Describe a shop near where you live that you sometimes use.

You should say:

　　where it is

　　what the shop looks like

　　what sorts of product or service it sells

and explain why you use this shop.

高分答案实例：

I'm going to describe a convenience store in my neighbourhood.

The store is on the south side of an old brick building. The store has large windows, and there's a sign with the name of the store, Kevin's Convenience, on top of the front entrance. There're three parking spots at the front of the store.

The store is small, but it offers a wide variety of goods, from snacks to magazines to birthday cards. It even has some stuff that I can't find in bigger stores, like baked sweet potatoes.

The owners of this store are a middle-aged couple. The store is small but tidy, with friendly and helpful employees. The shelves are always clean and well-organised, and the prices are reasonable.

I often buy things from this store because it's just a 2-minute walk from my flat, so it's really convenient for me to get to. I often shop there also because it's open 24 hours a day, all year round, and the service is always good.

这个高分实例同样也很简单，但它清晰、扣题、自然，并且有合理的细节，完全体现了主办方对于 Part 2 高分答案的真实要求。

我们再来看一个被很多考生认为比较"变态"的卡片题是不是也可以有"不变态"的高分答案：

> Describe a rule in your school（that you agree or disagree with）.
>
> You should say:
>
> what the rule was
>
> whether you followed it
>
> whether your classmates followed it
>
> and explain why you think it was good（or bad）.

学校规定？这道题真让很多"烤鸭"还没出国就已经明显感受到了国外和国内教育的不同：国内考试通常并不鼓励考生对学校教育"吐槽"，如果"吐"得太狠甚至还可能遭到高考作文零分之类的重罚。但这道卡片题却明明白白地告诉你不管是你赞同的还是反对的，只要是一条学校的规定你就可以放心地说。

高分答案实例：

I'm going to talk about the "hands-up" rule in the high school I attended. We were asked to put our hands up in class to answer questions.

I always followed this rule. But sometimes when I was chosen by the teacher to answer a question, I couldn't remember what I wanted to say. That was a bit embarrassing.

This rule made us feel that we could make our own choice to answer a question or not. And we were encouraged to put our ideas forward in a polite way instead of talking over each other. We put up our hands only when we had an answer ready, so the rule also helped us gain confidence.

But some of my classmates were too shy to put up their hands. They were afraid they would get the answer wrong and get laughed at. And some teachers always picked the same people to answer their questions.

Anyway, I think this rule helped us a lot. Without it, we would have just shouted out our answers and ended up learning nothing at all.

显然，虽然话题比较"变态"，但考官也还是更愿意接受一个"不变态"、清晰、自然，并且有合理细节的答案。

本章的真题请您充分结合 Pat 在博客里贴出的本月预测来准备，提前想想每个话题的思路、关键词和短语即可，而且同类话题的答案完全可以自然合并（p.33），把卡片题库在考前全都看一遍没有可能也没有必要。

◥ **A** 建筑

Pat 解题 **Pat's Thought**

建筑师（architects）在西方社会里的地位从历史上到今天一直是比较高的，比如 Frank Gehry 就是其中的一个，右面这张照片是 Pat 本人在世界顶级的 MIT 校园拍摄的 Frank Gehry 作品，够另类（funky）的吧？

关于 建筑 ，有两个单词中国同学们经常会用混：即 building 和 architecture。building 是可数名词，指的是一栋一栋的房子，而 architecture 是不可数名词，它其实是一个地区或者一种风格的所有建筑的总称，而不是特指一栋具体的房子。

关于 城市 ，也有两个词经常被中国同学们用混：即 city 和 urban。其实 urban 不是名词"城市"，而是形容词"城市的"，如果想用 urban 表示城市，就一定要说 the urban area。

本类最有代表性的方向 **Typical Topics**

❋ Describe an old building.

❋ Describe a house you like.

❋ Describe a place that makes you feel relaxed.

❋ Describe a tourist attraction.

❋ Describe an educational trip.

展开本类话题的思维导图　Mind Maps

（如果卡片上的 4 个提示问题仍然不能让你说出充实的答案，那么下面的思维导图可以帮助你继续扩展出扣题、充实的 ideas）

您无需记忆 Part 2 的任何一个答案，但你应该认真思考高分答案是怎样用简单、自然的英文进行扣题、清晰的描述（description），并适当给出细节的。请坚信：练出扣题、清晰的描述能力其实要比机械记忆答案更容易、也更有意义。

建　筑

分级演示 Sample Answers

☆ 一个有水的地方

Pat 指南

我们在本节里都是讨论人工的地方，如果您想描述自然界里有水的地方，还可以参考 C 类话题里的第 1，2 题

> Describe a place where there is water.
>
> You should say:
>
>   where the place is
>
>   when people go there
>
>   what people do there
>
> and explain whether you like this place or not.

难度指数：★ ★ ★ ☆ ☆

Pat 的答案

I'm going to talk about our community swimming pool. It's located behind our community center. The pool is not very big, but is clean and well-managed.

Lots of people go there on hot summer days. Some people just go there to hang out and cool off. Others go there to exercise and get in shape. Those who're good at swimming tend to stay in the deep end.

The shallow end is often packed with children who just splash water around and have fun. Sometimes there're also instructors giving them swimming lessons. Enjoying the sun and getting paid is a pretty good deal, huh?

I usually go to the pool a couple of times a week in the summer. Swimming is a really good way to relax and keep fit at the same time. And it's always fun to meet and chat with other people who also enjoy swimming. I've made lots of new friends there.

And... I don't have a girlfriend (for girls: boyfriend). So who knows? Maybe I could meet someone special there.

加分词汇和短语的作用只是"点缀"你的答案，而不是"充斥"你的答案。在真实的 British Council 官方高分范例里面，多数内容其实都是用浅显易懂的词汇表达的，也只有这样的描述（description）才能真正听起来清晰、自然。

轮到你了   It's Your Turn.

▶ Word Bank on This Topic

社区中心	community center	管理得很好的	well-managed
休闲放松	hang out	感觉更凉爽，给身体"降温"	cool off
深水区	the deep end	浅水区	the shallow end
挤满了……	is packed with…	溅起水花儿	splash water around
游泳教练	swimming instructor	几次	a couple of times
保持体格强健	keep fit	聊天	chat

扩展词汇

减轻压力，"减压"	reduce stress	社交	socialise
减肥	lose weight	增强肌肉	build muscles
室外泳池	outdoor swimming pool	室内泳池	indoor swimming pool
温水	warm water	冷水	cold water
很清澈的	crystal-clear	泳道	lanes
泳镜	goggles	蛙泳	breast-stroke
仰泳	back-stroke	蝶泳	butterfly-stroke

请参考Pat的思路，并适当借鉴这个词汇表里的单词，思考如果是您将会怎么说

自由泳　freestyle	热身运动　warm-up exercises
水性很好　swim like a fish	
彻底不会游泳，"游得像砖头一样"　swim like a brick	
初学者　beginners	狗刨　doggy-paddle
救生员　lifeguard	男式游泳裤　swim trunks
女式游泳衣　swimsuit / bikini	

请参考Pat的思路，并适当借鉴这个词汇表里的单词，思考如果是您将会怎么说

　　此外，备考时间充裕的同学还可以从这个网站了解伦敦的 Aquatics Centre 是什么样的：www. londonaquaticscentre. org

Pat 的海外生活英语实录

　　上面这个工具箱里的词都挺不错的，但也没必要全搬。可下面的这个词要是考到这个话题您还存着不用那就是"一不说成千古恨"的结果—— spot。这个名词在英文口语里经常用来表示"地点"。例如：

　　[剑桥例句] This park looks like a nice spot for a picnic.

　　相应地，下次说到"有水的地方"，您就可以理直气壮地对考官说：It's a nice spot for swimming and playing water games.

☆ 一个现代建筑

（A）宾　馆

Describe a hotel you have stayed in or visited.

You should say:

　　where the hotel is located

　　when you stayed there

　　why you went there

and explain what you liked about it.

难度指数：★ ★ ★ ★ ☆

Pat 的答案

I stayed at the Yong-Fan Hotel while visiting Shanghai last July.

It's located at the southeast corner of the city and is well-known for its guests. I was told many celebrities stayed there before, like Daniel Wu and Stephen Chow.

The hotel really provides comfort and convenience. The room I stayed in was very spacious. The bed was nice and comfortable. The TV had many channels, and the air conditioning was quiet and easy to control.

The hotel has a wide variety of rooms, from single rooms equipped with coffee maker and fridge to Presidential Suites which are on the top floor. All rooms have free Wi-Fi.

The hotel employees were friendly and helpful, and the room prices were very reasonable for the area. I really enjoyed my stay there.

轮到你了

It's Your Turn.

► **Word Bank on This Topic**

住宾馆　stay at a hotel（地道英文里"住宾馆"的动词不能用 live）

著名的　well-known　　　　　　名人　celebrities

吴彦祖　Daniel Wu　　　　　　周星驰　Stephen Chow

舒适与方便（名词短语）　comfort and convenience

舒适方便的（形容词短语）　comfortable and convenient

请参考Pat的思路，并适当借鉴这个词汇表里的单词，思考如果是您将会怎么说

宽敞的　spacious　　　　　　空调　air-conditioning

咖啡机　coffee maker　　　　　电冰箱　fridge

建　筑

平板电视 flat-screen TV	总统套房 presidential suite
免费无线上网 free Wi-Fi	员工 employees
员工（统称） staff	宾馆的房价 room prices / room rates
合理的 reasonable	

扩展词汇

豪华的 luxurious	舞厅（不是"球房"） ballroom
很有品位的 classy	入口大厅，"大堂" lobby
装饰 decorations	（服务）无可挑剔的 impeccable

恒温器（英美建筑里调节温度用的常见设备） thermostat

标志性的建筑 landmark	外观 appearance
扶梯 escalators	口碑好 has a good reputation

它给人"宾至如归"的感觉 It's a home away from home.（地道英文里的固定说法）

位于 be located at... / be situated at...

客房服务员 room attendants

　　时间充裕的同学还可以从这个网站了解英国的一个典型酒店里的客房到底是什么样儿的：ihg. com/holidayinn/hotels/gb/en/london/lonuk/hoteldetail/hotel-room-rates

Pat 的海外生活英语实录

　　如果要用英语说"宾馆的服务设施"，基础不错的同学可能会想到 hotel facilities。但在地道英文里还有个更地道的 hotel amenities 才是表达这个意思的最佳选择：

[剑桥例句] The hotel has a wide variety of amenities, such as a swimming pool, restaurants and a fitness center.

Time to Branch Out.
推而广之

Describe a modern building in your city.

building   182

补充弹药

Extra Ammo

office building　写字楼

high-rise building　高层建筑

energy-efficient　节能的

well laid-out　布局合理的

（B）购物中心

> Describe a shopping center that you like.
>
> You should say:
>
>   where it is
>
>   what it is like
>
>   how often you visit this shopping center
>
> and explain why you like this shopping center.

难度指数：★★★★☆

Pat 的答案

My favourite shopping center is Oriental Plaza. It's just a short walk from Tian'an Men Square.

The center is pretty big，and it's wrapped in glass on all sides.

The inside of the building is amazing: very spacious，clean and well-organised — not like many other shopping centers where you can easily get lost.

This shopping center is a landmark in Beijing，not just because of it's size and location，but also because of the enjoyable shopping experience it provides.

My friends and I like this shopping center because it has a wide variety of shops，and all the stuff they sell is good-quality and well-priced. And the service is good too. The shop assistants are always friendly and helpful.

The center also has a large food court，with lots of food choices，from traditional food to Western food.

轮到你了

It's Your Turn.

▶ Word Bank on This Topic

离……走一小段路就到了　is just a short walk from…

（建筑）外表面都是玻璃的　is wrapped in glass

（建筑）内部　the inside / the interior

非常好的　amazing	宽敞的　spacious
井然有序的　well-organised	标志性建筑　landmark
令人愉快的购物体验　enjoyable shopping experience	
优质的　good-quality	定价合理的　well-priced
售货员　shop assistants	友好的而且很有帮助的　friendly and helpful
购物中心的美食街　food court	

🔍 扩展词汇

位置极佳的　is well-located	巨大的　huge / enormous
……层高的建筑　a… - storey building	顶级的　top-notch
顾客　customers	问候某人　greet sb.
优惠券　coupon	电梯　lift（BrE）/ elevator（AmE）
扶梯　escalators	灯光，照明　lighting
壮观的　spectacular	装饰　decorations
很有品位的　classy	全额退款　full refund

请参考Pat的思路，并适当借鉴这个词汇表里的单词，思考如果是您将会怎么说

口碑很好　has a good reputation　　精品服饰店　boutiques

化妆品专柜　cosmetics section　　打折，促销　sales / special offers

花店　florist's shop　　面包房　bakery

电影院　cinema（BrE）/ movie theater（AmE）

收据　receipt（这个单词里的字母 p 不发音）

　　时间充裕的同学还可以在去英国之前就先逛逛伦敦著名的 Westfield ☺：
uk. westfield. com/london

Pat 的海外生活英语实录

　　只是在店里"浏览商品"（但不见得买）的英文表达是：browse through the shops，而如果只想在商场里随便逛逛放松一下，甚至都不一定会看商品，那就是 hang out in the shopping center 了。

Time to Branch Out.
推而广之

Describe a famous building in your city.

补充弹药

flock to　大量地涌向

celebrity　名人

packed　挤满了人的

建筑

（C）别 墅

> Describe your idea of an ideal house（理想的别墅）.
>
> You should say:
>
> what kind of house it would be
>
> why you would like to live there
>
> what special features it would have
>
> and explain whether you think you will ever live in a house like this.

Pat指南

这个卡片题要求你谈的是"理想的别墅"，所以您可以向考官尽情地展示你会用虚拟语气这种貌似高深、其实没什么的句式 ☺

难度指数：★ ★ ★ ☆ ☆

Pat 的答案

My ideal house would be just an average house, nothing too fancy.

It would be close to public transport, have two or three comfortable bedrooms, a spacious living room, a nice kitchen, some bathrooms and a garage. Most importantly, it must have a garden. I would love the feeling of watching my plants grow.

There should be plenty of appliances in the kitchen, like a gas stove, a fridge and a dishwasher. Beside the kitchen there would be a dining area, with a dining table and some chairs.

The living room must have large windows, a sofa, a coffee table and a flat-screen TV.

What else? Oh，the bathrooms！There must be a bathtub so I could relax in warm water after a busy day. The garage would be for my car，bicycle and tools.

Such a house would cost like 10 million *yuan* in a city like Beijing or Shanghai. So I guess it's nothing more than just a dream for me…

轮到你了   It's Your Turn.

▶ **Word Bank on This Topic**

普通的　average（在这里它不是"平均"的意思）

新奇有趣的　fancy   公共交通　public transport

宽敞的　spacious   车库　garage

后院　backyard   家用电器　home appliances

    英美家庭里最常见的家用电器有：

    fridge 电冰箱   dishwasher 洗碗机

    vacuum cleaner（生活里常简称为 vacuum）吸尘器

    microwave oven（生活里常简称为 microwave）微波炉

    washing machine 洗衣机   dryer 烘干机

平板电视　flat-screen TV   浴缸　bathtub（生活里常会直接说 tub）

（房间或者家具）很舒适的　comfortable / cozy

扩展词汇

很高的天花板　high ceiling   长沙发　sofa / couch

单人沙发或单人座椅　armchair   花瓶　vase

摇椅　rocking chair   壁炉　fireplace

高清电视　HD TV   衣橱　wardrobe

厨房里的橱柜　cupboard（注意听音频里的发音）

请参考Pat的思路，并适当借鉴这个词汇表里的单词，思考如果是您将会怎么说

187

建筑

储藏室 closet   还房贷 pay a mortgage

郊区 the suburbs   乡村 the countryside

市中心 downtown   居民区 neighbourhood

郊区 the suburbs   乡村 the countryside

装饰 decorations   草坪 lawn

生活和休闲设施 amenities（such as shops，parks and sports centers）

硬木地板 hardwood flooring（flooring 在地道英文里是指地板的材料）

它只是个幻想而已 It's just a fantasy.

一栋只含一户的别墅，独栋别墅 detached house

一栋含有左右两户的别墅 semi-detached house

一栋含三户或以上的别墅，联排别墅 terraced house

　　有时间的话您还可以登录这个网站，看看普通英国人购买最多的别墅是上面三种里的哪一种：www. dailymail. co. uk/news/article-2611281

Pat 的海外生活英语实录

　　地板上的大地毯叫 carpet，小方毯叫 rug，床上盖的毛毯叫 blanket，但墙上挂的挂毯 native speakers 叫什么呢？跟考官说 a tapestry/ˈtæpistri/，他/她就会对你刮目相看（He / She will be amazed.）。

　　[剑桥例句] It was hard to hang the tapestry on this curved wall.

Pat 指南

Describe a room that you use a lot.

　　IELTS 口试题库里有一道考题是描述你自己经常使用的一个房间。uktv. co. uk/home/dgiped/kw/236 这个网站上有各种房间的布置思路（点击页面上方的 Rooms 可以看到各种房间名称），而且都配有图片，只要"看图说话"再适当描述自己的活动答案就足够了。

building

（D） 博物馆

> Describe a museum.
>
> You should say:
>
> what kind of museum it is
>
> where it is
>
> what it is like
>
> and explain whether you like it or not.

Pat指南

Part 2 里还有一道卡片题是 Describe an art gallery. 如果准备一个现代艺术馆，就能把这两道题一起准备好了。

很多同学觉得像这样的话题只有艺术系的学生才能说好，但 IELTS 口试的出题原则之一就是不考查专业知识（The test does not require specialised knowledge.）。考官需要你说的只是一个扣题、清晰、英文自然的答案。

难度指数：★ ★ ★ ☆ ☆

Pat 的答案

I'd like to talk about my favourite museum — the Modern Art Museum in… (*put the city's name here*)

The museum is near the city center, and is close to public transport. It's a large building and looks very modern, with lots of steel and glass.

The inside of the building is very spacious. It's divided into different sections, like the Asian Art section, the European Art section and the North American Art section. The museum also provides a wide variety of art activities for children, so it's good for all ages.

I like this museum because it has a large collection of modern works of art, and it always has some interesting exhibitions going on. For example, last week it held an exhibition of works by some French artists, which attracted a lot of visitors.

建 筑

And unlike many other museums，the staff there encourage visitors to take non-flash pictures. This makes the museum even more fun.

My favourite part of the museum is the sculpture garden where there are always hundreds of sculptures on display.

The admission fee to the museum is 20 yuan for adults and 5 yuan for children. I think it's pretty reasonable.

轮到你了

It's Your Turn.

► Word Bank on This Topic

公共交通　public transport

钢和玻璃　steel and glass（地道英文常用这个短语来泛指现代建筑的材料）

石头和木头　stone and wood（地道英文常用这个短语来泛指历史建筑的材料）

宽敞的　spacious　　　　　　　　井井有条的　is well-organised

布局合理的　is well laid-out　　　被分成　is divided into…

部分　section　　　　　　　　　　艺术活动　art activities

适合各个年龄段的人们　is good for all ages（是的，出国以后您就会发现 native speakers 表达这个意思最自然的方式就是这么浅显易懂）

大量的馆藏　a large collection of…　　艺术品　works of art

展览　exhibition　　　　　　　　　吸引　attract

拍摄不用闪光灯的照片　take non-flash pictures

雕塑　sculpture　　　　　　　　　　展出　on display

参观费　admission fee　　　　　　　合理的　reasonable

扩展词汇

迷人的　fascinating　　　　　　　展品　exhibit

构图　composition　　　　　　　　色彩的搭配　colour scheme

笔触　strokes　　　　　　　　　　人像画　portrait

请参考Pat的思路，并适当借鉴这个词汇表里的单词，思考如果是您将会怎么说

风景画　landscape painting　　　静物画　still life

娱乐性很强的　entertaining　　　信息量很大的　informative

在……漫步　wander around…

　　在 Part 2 描述好一个现代艺术馆只要英文自然、思路清晰就已经很好了。但如果你真的对 modern art 有兴趣，英国著名的 Tate Modern 官方网站 www. tate. org. uk/ visit/tate-modern 会让你明白什么是 fun and enjoyable ☺

Pat 的海外生活英语实录

　　美术馆里照在艺术品上面的光线一般不是天然光线，所以不可以叫 sun，而是要叫作 lighting（照明）。

☆ 一个历史建筑

寺　庙

难度指数：★ ★ ★ ★ ☆

Pat 的答案

I'm going to talk about a temple in my hometown.

The temple dates back to the 15th century. Today, lots of people still go there to pray for good luck and good health. Interestingly, although it's a holy place, it's located on the busiest street in my hometown.

But from the moment you enter the temple, you start to feel calm and peaceful. Like most historic buildings in the area, the temple faces south, and the front gate is guarded by two stone lions. As you enter the front hall, you'll see four wood sculptures, which are called "the Four Heavenly Kings".

建筑

The Great Hall is separated from the front hall with a courtyard where you can see lots of trees and plants. The roof of the Great Hall is supported by tall, thick columns. Inside the Great Hall, you can see a Buddha statue and the statues of some of his students. On the east and west walls of the Great Hall, you can also find some Buddhist works of art.

This temple is not only a holy place. It also attracts thousands of tourists each year. And it provides cultural activities as well, including traditional art classes. So besides being a place of worship, it's also educational and fun.

轮到你了　　　　　　　　　　　　　　　　　It's Your Turn.

▶ **Word Bank on This Topic**

它的历史可以追溯到……　It dates back to…

[剑桥例句] This building dates back to the 17th century.

神圣的地方	a holy place	祈祷	pray
平静安详的	calm and peaceful	用……守护	is guarded by…
雕塑	sculpture	雕像	statue
与……隔开	is separated from…	庭院	courtyard
屋顶	roof	柱子	column
佛祖	Buddha	艺术品	works of art
从事宗教活动的场所	a place of worship	文化活动	cultural activities
有教育作用而且很有趣的	educational and fun		
佛教徒	Buddhist		

请参考Pat的思路，并适当借鉴这个词汇表里的单词，思考如果是您将会怎么说

扩展词汇

巨大的	enormous	塔	pagoda
许愿	make a wish	烧香	burn incense sticks
标志性建筑	landmark	重要的历史遗址	historic site
……的故居	the historic residence of…	裂缝	cracks

（对历史建筑进行的）翻新　renovation　　状况完好的　in good condition

中间有庭院的住宅，例如"四合院儿"　courtyard house（庭院就叫作 courtyard）

优雅的　elegant　　　　　私密的　private

充足的阳光　plenty of sunlight　　更加接近自然界　get closer to nature

即使你不是曼联（Manchester United）的球迷，这个网站上关于 historic buildings in Manchester 的信息也一定会让你着迷：

www. visitmanchester. com/what-to-do/attractions/heritage/

Pat 的海外生活英语实录

如果要说一个历史建筑"保存完好的"，地道英文里最常用的形容词就是 well-preserved。

[剑桥例句] The building is well-preserved and in good condition

☆ 一个图书馆（双语感悟）Bilingual Reflections on Libraries

> Describe a library.
>
> You should say:
>
> where the library is
>
> what facilities it has
>
> how often you go there
>
> and explain whether you like the library or not.

Part 2 里有时会考到校园建筑，可以说的选择很多，比如 cafeteria / canteen（食堂），dorm / dormitory / hall of residence（学生宿舍楼），gym（体育馆或健身房），administration building（行政楼），student union building（学生会大楼）等等。至于教学楼，在英语里一般不叫 teaching building ✗，而是叫作某某 Hall 或者某某 faculty building。

library 是校园建筑里比较好说的一种，光是图书馆里的设施（facilities）和喜欢图书馆的原因（why you like it）就可以谈不少了，而且还可以结合我们在 Day 7 里谈过的与 library 有关的内容（p. 144）。

中国学校里的图书馆通常外观看起来很平淡，但内部明亮整洁（From the outside, it looks plain, but the inside is bright and clean.），但近年来英美的图书馆却有变得越来越"张扬"（bold and daring）的趋势，Pat 个人最喜欢的是 Seattle Public Library（右图），真正属于 the Information Age（信息时代）的建筑。

如果一个图书馆是校园里的标志性建筑，英文就要说 It's a landmark on our campus。如果图书馆的外面全都是玻璃，英文会说 It's wrapped in glass on all sides. 如果还有曲线的墙面，那么就是 curved walls。外观很漂亮可以说 It has a beautiful exterior. 室内井然有序要说 The interior is well-organised. 入口处的大厅是 entrance hall 或者 lobby，大厅里的大柱子叫 tall, thick columns。图书馆的借书柜台叫 the circulation desk 或者直接说 the front desk，还书则没那么麻烦，直接放进 drop box 就好了。阅览室你说 reading room 考官就能听懂，英美大学图书馆里还有一种 group study room，则是进行集体讨论（group discussions）用的，但一般需要提前预订（reserve）。有的图书馆还有 study carrels，就是用木板分开的小隔间，可以自己坐在那里安静地看书。

国外的图书馆按照书库类型分两种：一种是 open-stack library（读者可以自己入库取书），另一种 closed-stack library 只能图书管理员入库取书。图书馆的目录室叫作 catalogue room，复印室叫 photocopy room，计算机房是 computer lab，多媒体室可以叫 multi-media center。图书管理员当然是 librarians，借书请说 check out books，也有些人会说 sign out books，还书就是 return books。过期不还必须交 late fee。

如果你说图书馆的气氛很让人放松，就是 It offers a relaxing atmosphere. 说图书馆有多种多样的书籍和光盘就说 It has a wide variety of books, CDs and DVDs. 如果还提供免费无线上网 It provides free Wi-Fi. 是爱书者的乐园就叫 It's a mecca for book-lovers！

超短线

The Ultra-Short Track

我们可以把下面这个"不按常理出牌"（a wild card）的卡片也放在本节一起准备：

Describe a famous architect（建筑师）.

让中国孩子们用中文描述一个建筑师都是难题，更别说用英语了。

别急，其实你可以用几分钟就解决它。分两步走：

（a）牢记说艺术家的几个英文必备词：talented 有才华的，prolific 高产的，作品"源源不断的"，creative designs 很有创意的设计，be passionate about 对……满腔热忱的，和 masterpiece 杰作；

（b）适当了解一个建筑师的生平，比如有个网站是世界顶级建筑师大全 www.greatbuildings. com/architects. html。人名都是按英文姓氏的首字母排列的，点击其中一个然后下拉到 Biography 就行了，比如找找华人的骄傲 I. M. Pei（贝聿铭）吧。

更棒的是，准备好了这道题，我们就一起把看似很难的另外两道题 Describe an artist. 和 Describe a creative person. 也同时准备好了。

B 组织和个人

Pat 解题　Pat's Thought

这一节我们学习对于 organisation 和 individuals 的描述。

其实最好说的 organisation 就是一个 English learning club 了，说说它在哪里，什么人爱去，再谈谈自己熟悉的 English lectures，English corner 和 the importance of English 就够了。不过我想中国孩子们最感兴趣的 organisation 之一是 the NBA，所以今天我们会好好看看这个组织。其实描述什么 organisation 都是可以的，我们的本质任务是要练出用平实、自然的英文进行描述的能力。

至于 individual，当然就是"个人"。每天咱们都和个人打交道，但其实描述个人并不容易。比如一个"胖"英语就有很多词，除了 fat（很贬义），还有 overweight（语气稍客气一点），chubby（胖乎乎的），pudgy（又矮又胖的），stout（粗壮的），怎一个"胖"字了得。

又比如"外向的"，"内向的"，Pat 经常听到国内孩子们用 extroverted 和 introverted，但这两个词其实有点大，在国外生活中虽然有时听到但用得并不算很频繁。生活口语说"外向的"其实可以说 He's very sociable.（= outgoing），而"内向的"则可以说 He's quiet around people he doesn't know well.（= not so outgoing），反而更自然。

本节咱们就要研究各种不同的人。

OK. Here we go.

本类最有代表性的方向　Typical Topics

✳ Describe a family member.

✳ Describe an elderly person.

✳ Describe a teacher who helped you before.

✳ Describe a famous person who you admire.

✳ Describe an ideal job.

展开本类话题的思维导图　Mind Maps

（如果卡片上的 4 个提示问题仍然不能让你说出充实的答案，那么下面的思维导图可以帮助你继续扩展出扣题、充实的 ideas）

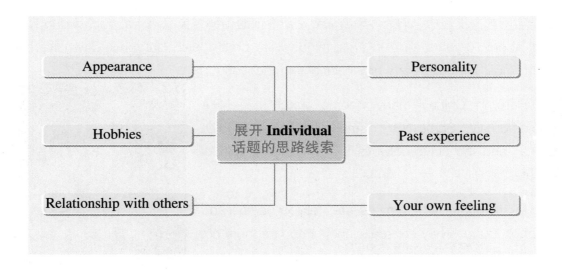

分级演示　Sample Answers

1. 组织（organisation）

> Describe an organisation.
>
> You should say:
>
> which organisation it is
>
> what kind of organisation it is
>
> whether it is popular
>
> and explain whether you like it or not.

☆ 一个组织之　**NBA**

难度指数：★ ★ ★ ☆ ☆

Pat 的答案

I'd like to talk about the NBA, which stands for the National Basketball Association.

As far as I know（国内孩子说卡片的一个问题就是口气总像该领域的权威似的，但其实听起来挺假的，因为并没有人会是所有问题上的专家），it was founded in New York about 70 years ago. At first, things were pretty hard, but these days, it's one of the most famous sports organisations in the world.

Here in China，many people watch live NBA games on TV. Some NBA games are even played in China，and the tickets always sell out in a couple of minutes.

My favourite NBA players are LeBron James and Stephen Curry. They are really cool. I admire them not just for their success, but also for their spirit, you know, their sportsmanship. They're real legends in my eyes.

The NBA is also a legend because it's so successful, and NBA games are always exciting to watch. I really hope more NBA players will come to China and show us their amazing basketball skills.

轮到你了

▶ Word Bank on This Topic

| 联合会 | association | 是……的缩写 | stand for... |

成立于……　was founded in... (这个 founded 不是 "被找到"，而是 "被成立")

现场直播的比赛　live / laiv / games

（门票）卖光　sell out (地道英文里这个短语一般不用被动)

运动员精神　sportsmanship　　　传奇　legend

扩展词汇

常规赛	regular season	季后赛	playoffs
受到热捧	enjoy a huge following	最有价值球员	MVP
有影响力的	influential	团队精神	team spirit

队员们都很团结　There's real team spirit.

激励年轻人	inspire young people	励志的	inspiring
热情	passion	管理得很完善的	well-managed
很有娱乐性的	entertaining	金州勇士队	Golden State Warriors
芝加哥公牛队	Chicago Bulls		

达拉斯小牛队　Dallas Mavericks (地道英文里也常简称为 the Mavs)

迈阿密热火队	Miami Heat	休斯敦火箭队	Houston Rockets
波士顿凯尔特人队	Boston Celtics	洛杉矶湖人队	L. A. Lakers
洛杉矶快船队	Los Angeles Clippers	克里夫兰骑士队	Cleveland Cavaliers
奥兰多魔术队	Orlando Magic	底特律活塞队	Detroit Pistons

组　织

圣安东尼奥马刺队　San Antonio Spurs（简称 the Spurs）

俄克拉荷马雷霆队　Oklahoma City Thunder

菲尼克斯太阳队　Phoenix Suns（这个州的夏天超热，这大概也锻炼了
　　　　　　　　球员们的顽强精神）

　　如果您是一位铁杆儿的足球迷（a passionate football fan），那么
这个网站可以解答您关于 FIFA 的各种问题：www. fifa. com/faq. html

请参考Pat的思路，并适当借鉴这个词汇表里的单词，思考如果是您将会怎么说

Pat 的海外生活英语实录

　　两支球队"棋逢对手"应该怎样表达呢？跟 chess 或者 opponents 都没关系，
而应该用 **evenly-matched** 这个简单却地道的词。

　　【剑桥例句】The two teams were really evenly-matched.

请仔细听音频文件里这些 NBA 球星的名字怎么发音（并且猜一猜他们是谁）：

LeBron James

Stephen Curry

Paul George

Kyrie Irving

Draymond Green

Blake Griffin

Derrick Rose

Russell Westbrook

Kevin Durant

Ricky Rubio

顺着这道题的思路，我们把下面这道题一起快速准备一下。

☞ **Describe a sports star you admire.**

同时身为 one of the fastest-rising NBA stars，a Harvard graduate 和粉丝们心目当中的"Lin-sanity"，大男孩林书豪让不少老美主动把地道英文的"双赢"（win-win situation）改成了 Lin-win situation。虽然因为膝盖受伤（knee injury）不得不中途退出去年的常规赛（missed his team's last 14 games of the regular season），但他无疑是真心英雄（a true hero）。

Fast Facts about Jeremy Lin:

He's a Chinese-American NBA player, born and raised in California, and is very proud of being Chinese.

His parents moved to the U. S. in the 1970s.

Both of his parents are just average height, but Jeremy Lin is well over 6 feet tall. (1 foot =30. 5cm)

Although he played basketball at a high school very close to Stanford University, he ended up in Harvard.

He got a degree in economics from Harvard and is now a professional player for the Charlotte Hornets.

Some sports reporters called him "the most surprising story in the NBA".

Jeremy Lin became a famous NBA player at the age of 23, and he definitely has an even more brilliant basketball career ahead of him.

I hope Jeremy Lin will become a point guard as great as Magic Johnson.

I really love this quote from Jeremy Lin，"When I'm on the basketball court, I try to play with all my emotion and heart."

☆ 一个组织之 健身俱乐部

难度指数：★★★★☆

┌─────────┐
Pat 的答案
└─────────┘

Let me talk about the fitness club I attend. It's very close to where I live. I go there almost every afternoon. Some friends of mine also go there to work out.

组 织

It offers a wide variety of memberships, and the membership fees are pretty reasonable. They even have three-day guest passes for people who visit their club for the first time. The club also provides group exercise classes and yoga classes.

I like this fitness club because it's well-managed. It has lots of exercise machines, including treadmills, exercise bikes and steppers. The equipment is very clean and in good condition. All the employees, from the front-desk people to the trainers, are friendly and helpful. And with my membership, I can also use the swimming pool in the club for free, so it's really good value for money.

My only complaint is sometimes it's a bit too crowded. But most of the time, there's plenty of space for everyone so it's not a big problem.

轮到你了

It's Your Turn.

▶ Word Bank on This Topic

健身俱乐部	fitness club / health club	健身	work out
会员资格	membership	瑜伽	yoga
合理的	reasonable	免费体验券	guest pass
跑步机	treadmill		
固定健身单车	exercise bike / stationary bike		
踏步机	steppers	设备	equipment
健身教练	trainer	它的性价比很高	It's good value for money.
抱怨	complaint	拥挤的	crowded

扩展词汇

保持体格强健	keep fit	增强肌肉	build muscles
减轻压力，"减压"	reduce stress	减肥	lose weight

请参考Pat的思路，并适当借鉴这个词汇表里的单词，思考如果是您将会怎么说

organisation

普拉提　Pilates　　　　　　尊巴舞　Zumba dance

推荐　　recommend

www. olympic. org/athletes 这个网站提供了很多体育明星的介绍，比如在右上角的 Quick search 里输入 Dan Lin，点击 Go，然后点击 Athlete Profile 和右下角的 More About Dan Lin，您就能看到对林丹的详细介绍了。

Pat 的海外生活英语实录

您出国之后立马就会发现：健身对于年轻白人来说实在是生活里太重要的一个部分了，Pat 的很多朋友都是命可以不要，但是不能不去 gym，如果有几天没去健身就开始 "hold 不住" 甚至 feel guilty（有负罪感）。大家参加健身俱乐部的目标多半是为了让自己 "变得更有形儿"，用地道英语介绍这种健身目的绝不能说 give myself more shape ✗，而要说 get toned。假如你的考官正好也是一年轻白人，考试时你能在扣题的前提下用出这两个表达，会立刻让他/她 "心有戚戚焉"，不信你就试试。

【剑桥例句】Leo is exercising regularly to get toned.

2. 个人

> Describe a famous singer.
>
> You should say:
>
> 　who the singer is
>
> 　when the singer became famous
>
> 　how the singer became famous
>
> and explain whether you like the singer or not.

☆ 娱乐人物之　歌手（a）

王菲对媒体出了名的不友好，作 "王的男人" 也是有目共睹的困难，前男友窦唯骑电摩穿行胡同儿的照片已经神似动漫里的大叔。但是，内什么，仍然还是有人喜欢王菲，正

人　物

是因为她性格中的不完美吧（She's not a perfect person，but she's always been true to herself.）。不论是否喜欢她，咱们都不能否认：她是传奇（She's a legend.）。

难度指数：★ ★ ★ ☆ ☆

Pat 的答案

I'm going to talk about a famous singer in China, called Faye Wong.

She was born and grew up in Beijing. Her father took her to Hong Kong when she was 18. At first, she took some modelling classes because she was tall and slim. But she soon lost interest in modelling.

She enjoyed humming to herself because she felt it was relaxing. A songwriter noticed that and was really impressed by her voice. So he encouraged her to sign a recording contract, and she did.

She released her first album at the age of 19. Then a very important album was produced. Several songs in that album were big hits and won lots of awards for her. She's been a famous singer in China for more than 20 years, and almost all of her albums have received good reviews from her fans and music critics.

I like Faye Wong not just because she's talented, but also because she's a rebel who is always true to herself. Unlike many other singers in China, she ignores the press. But interestingly, it seems people like her even more because of that.

轮到你了

It's Your Turn.

▶ **Word Bank on This Topic**

王　Wong（您出国之后会经常看到一些香港或者广东移民的 last name 是 Wong，而不是 Wang）

模特班　modelling class

很高很苗条的　tall and slim（地道英文里说人 thin 是贬义，而说人 slim 却是褒义）

person

自己小声哼唱　hum to herself　　　　　歌曲创作人　songwriter

签唱片合同，"签约"　sign a recording contract

发行专辑，"出专辑"　release an album　　很受欢迎的作品　big hit

奖项　award　　　　　　　　　　　受到好评　receive good reviews

乐评人　music critic　　　　　　　　　有才华的　talented

叛逆的人　rebel（作名词时它的读音是/ˈrebəl/）

拒绝迎合主流媒体　ignore the press

扩展词汇

有魅力的　attractive　　　　　　　　　吸引力　appeal

多才多艺的　multi-talented

> 请参考Pat的思路，并适当借鉴这个词汇表里的单词，思考如果是您将会怎么说

　　喜欢欧美音乐的朋友应该经常看看这个有趣又有用的网站：www. biography. com/people/groups/singer，例如，请您迅速找出 Taylor Swift, Ed Sheeran 和 the Weekend 这几位 2016 年格莱美奖热门人物的详细介绍

Pat 的海外生活英语实录

　　95% 以上的国内考生都知道 idol 是"偶像"的意思，但地道英语里其实还有一个比偶像地位更高的词：**icon**，是指文化、艺术、娱乐、体育等领域里最具代表性的人。它在英美文化里是个很地道的词，谈明星时将会给考官带来"心灵的撞击"。

　　【剑桥例句】Kobe Bryant is a basketball icon. He has inspired（激励）a lot of young athletes.

☆ *娱乐人物之　歌手*（**b**）

难度指数：★★★☆☆

Pat 的答案

I guess you've heard a lot about Jay Chou because he's so famous in China.

人物

He grew up in a single-parent family. When he was little, Jay didn't get good grades at school. His mother was really concerned about him. When he felt down or lonely, he looked for nice music to cheer him up.

He was kind of average-looking, so no one really expected him to make it as a singer. He started out as a songwriter and wrote songs for many popular singers, like Karen Mok（莫文蔚）and Vivian Hsu（徐若瑄）.

Then he released his first album, "Jay". His voice was so unique. That album became an instant hit. So far all of his albums have received great reviews.

I like Jay Chou because his music is very different from other musicians'. He likes to blend a wide variety of music styles, such as R&B, hip-hop, and folk music — very creative and memorable. I guess that's why the tickets to his concerts always sell out in a couple of hours.

轮到你了

It's Your Turn.

▶ Word Bank on This Topic

在校成绩	grades at school	担心，忧虑	be concerned about…
让某人振作起来	cheer sb. up	外表普通的	average-looking
获得成功	make it	音乐创作人	songwriter
出专辑	release an album	独特的	unique
一发行就立刻热卖的作品	an instant hit	获得很高的评价	receive great reviews
结合	blend	节奏布鲁斯	R & B (Rhythm & Blues)
嘻哈音乐	hip-hop music	民间音乐	folk music
有创意的	creative	很容易记住的	memorable

卖光了　sell out（地道英文里这个短语一般不用被动）

扩展词汇

创作型歌手　a singer-songwriter

单曲　single

歌词　lyrics

感人的　touching

励志的　inspiring

名望与财富　fame and wealth

勤奋敬业的　hardworking and dedicated

一夜成名　an overnight success

多才多艺的　multi-talented

乐队成员　band members

主唱　lead singer / lead vocalist

吉他手　guitarist

贝斯手　bassist

鼓手　drummer

键盘手　keyboard player

关系很好，很"合得来"　get on very well

男孩组合（比如英国的 One Direction 和中国的 TFBOYS）
　boy band（地道英文里不说 boys' band ✗）

请参考Pat的思路，并适当借鉴这个词汇表里的单词，思考如果是您将会怎么说

　　欧美乐迷都有自己喜欢的乐队，这个网站详细介绍了会让任何一个真正的欧美乐迷震撼的 bands：today. msnbc. msn. com/id/4595384/ns/today-entertainment/t/best-rock-bands-ever/#. UD06ZcHibBR

Pat 的海外生活英语实录

　　周董已经不是"范特西"（*Fantasy*）年代的"小鲜肉"（a fresh-faced young man），但他的音乐不知不觉地火了十多年，而且始终保持着很高的质量，影响了整整一代人，堪称是音乐界的传奇人物，他与昆凌（Hannah Quinlivan）在 Selby Abbey 的婚礼更是占据了娱乐媒体的头条（made entertainment headlines）。"音乐界"的英文叫作 the music scene，而"传奇人物"则是 a legend。

　　【剑桥例句】Jazz legend, Ella Fitzgerald, once sang in this bar.

人物

☆ *娱乐人物之 影星*（英美观众熟知的刘玉玲）

难度指数：★★★★☆

┌─────────┐
│ Pat 的答案 │
└─────────┘

Let me talk about my favourite actress, Lucy Liu. Having experienced some ups and downs in her career, now she's one of the most successful Chinese-American actresses in Hollywood.

Lucy Liu's straight black hair makes her very different from the blonde actresses in Hollywood. I think she really knows what she looks good in. For example, she often wears slim jeans because she has long legs. This makes her look even more confident and attractive.

Lucy Liu usually plays roles in action films. Her most famous role was in *Charlie's Angels* as an intelligent and confident "Angel". She looked really cool fighting all the bad guys and saving people's lives.

The 21st century is often called the Chinese Century. And now China is the second-largest market for Hollywood films. I'm sure there'll be more and more Chinese stars becoming successful in Hollywood.

轮到你了

It's Your Turn.

▶ Word Bank on This Topic

起起落落 ups and downs（这么 "有哲理" 的概念，地道英文的说法就是这么简单）

事业 career   金发的 blonde

牛仔裤 jeans   自信的 confident

有吸引力的 attractive   聪明的 intelligent

┌─────────┐
│ 🔍 扩展词汇 │
└─────────┘

名人 celebrity   家喻户晓的名字 a household name

person

208

名望与财富 fame and wealth	勤奋敬业的 hardworking and dedicated
优雅的 elegant	时尚的 fashionable / stylish
大片儿 blockbuster	高票房电影 box-office hit
海报 posters	狗仔队 paparazzi
侵犯他 / 她的隐私 invade his / her privacy	
访谈 interview	魅力四射的 glamorous

请参考Pat的思路，并适当借鉴这个词汇表里的单词，思考如果是您将会怎么说

这个网址可以说是英美影星介绍大全：www. biography. com/people/groups/actors-and-actresses-film-actor-and-film-actress 例如，请点击页面右上角的放大镜，迅速找出对 2016 年奥斯卡最佳男主角奖得主 Leonardo DiCaprio 和最佳女主角奖得主 Brie Larson 的详细介绍

Pat 的海外生活英语实录

在好莱坞，Lucy Liu 是能够获得高票房电影（box-office hits）里的角色的少数华裔演员之一，这种地位（status）真够让人羡慕的。其实不仅是明星，对任何让你"羡慕"的人，比如对拿到了牛津全奖的大牛、或者对复议后单科提高了 1 分的幸运儿，你都可以发自内心地说，"I really envy you!"

[剑桥例句] I really envy her ability to talk to people she's never met before.

☆ 艺术家之 梵高

难度指数：★ ★ ★ ☆ ☆

Pat 的答案

I'm going to talk about an artist I admire, Vincent Van Gogh （梵高）. He was a 19th-century Dutch painter.

Van Gogh was very talented and creative. Instead of just trying to copy what he saw, he used colours freely in order to better express his feelings. His painting style influenced and inspired many other painters. And now he's considered one of the greatest artists in history.

I admire Van Gogh not just because he was so talented, but also because he had great sympathy for the poor. He often painted farmers and workers in his paintings. He even gave away most of his own money to help poor people.

Van Gogh sold only one painting during his lifetime. But I think he's much more than a great painter. He's one of the greatest cultural heroes of modern times.

轮到你了

It's Your Turn.

▶ Word Bank on This Topic

荷兰的	Dutch	有才华的	talented
有创意的	creative	表达他的感受	express his feelings
激励	inspire	同情心	sympathy
泛指贫穷的人们	the poor	他在世的时候	during his lifetime

扩展词汇

很有同情心的	compassionate	名誉	fame
抽象的	abstract	（艺术家）多产的	prolific
受到很高的评价	receive great reviews	天才	genius
杰作	masterpiece		

这个网站不仅覆盖了欧美历史上最著名的艺术家们的生平，而且还提供了大量图片帮你亲眼"见证"这些艺术家们的独特风格：
totallyhistory. com/art-history/famous-artists/

请参考Pat的思路，并适当借鉴这个词汇表里的单词，思考如果是您将会怎么说

person

Pat 的海外生活英语实录

　　成功的艺术家通常都会有很独特的风格。基础一般的国内同学会用 He/She has a very special style. 来表达这个意思，基础好的同学们则多半会讲 He/She has a unique style. （请注意："very unique" ✗ 是中式英语，因为 unique 本身就不能再比较程度了）。但其实，在地道英文里还有 instantly recognisable （一眼就能辨认出来的）这样更形象的说法。

　　【剑桥例句】The Eiffel Tower in Paris is an instantly recognisable landmark.

Pat 指南

　　关于艺术家，这个网站最大的优点是内容相当专业，可英文却简单得跟玩儿似的：library. thinkquest. org/J001159/famart. htm

☆ 成功的领袖之 Steve Jobs

难度指数 ★ ★ ★ ☆ ☆

Pat 的答案

He founded Apple with two friends in the late 1970s, and they made lots of money selling Apple I and Apple II computers. Then he was forced to leave the company after a power struggle. But later Steve Jobs returned to the company, and helped Apple grow to be one of the biggest companies in the world.

I admire him because he was a very hardworking and dedicated leader. He worked long hours, and expected his employees to work hard, too.

He was also a talented and creative leader, almost like a great artist. He was always working on new ideas. Over the years, his company brought us many beautifully-designed products, such as iPod, iPhone and MacBook.

Steve Jobs was a great public speaker as well. I remember him saying in a

人　物

speech，"Don't waste time living the result of someone else's thinking. " That really inspired me a lot. He showed us the importance of following our own heart. He was not just a successful business leader，but also an excellent role model for young people.

轮到你了   It's Your Turn.

▶ Word Bank on This Topic

前任的　former   建立　found（过去时是 founded）

【剑桥例句】I'd like to talk about Steve Jobs，the former CEO of Apple.

权力斗争　a power struggle   勤奋敬业的　hardworking and dedicated

长时间地工作　work long hours（看起来很"弱"，但这个短语其实是英文里说努力工作最常用的地道 phrase 之一，您有机会跟 native speakers 一试便知 ☺）

有才华而且很有创意的　talented and creative

设计得非常美观的　beautifually-designed

公共演讲者　public speaker   激励　inspire

榜样　role model

🔍 扩展词汇

创业者　entrepreneur

完全凭借自身努力成功的人　a self-made man / a self-made woman

领导才能　leadership skills   谦虚低调的　humble and modest

员工　employees   感觉很有动力的　feel motivated

高科技产品　high-tech products   感人的、励志的　touching and inspiring

勇气　courage

崇拜　worship（这个动词的崇拜程度比 admire 还要强）

传记　biography   自传　autobiography

最畅销作品　bestseller

请参考Pat的思路，并适当借鉴这个词汇表里的单词，思考如果是您将会怎么说

person

"保持对新事物的渴望，并敢于承担风险。" "Stay hungry. Stay foolish."

这个网址提供了大量当代著名商业领袖的详尽介绍：www. biography. com/people/groups/business-leaders 例如，您可以用页面右上角的放大镜轻松地找到对苹果现任 CEO Tim Cook 和 "特斯拉"（Tesla） CEO Elon Musk 的完整介绍。

Part 2 里面有时还会考到你喜欢的一本书。你的选择当然很多，而且只要坚持用浅显易懂的英语那么也不会很难。但描述一个名人的传记（biography）仍然是其中最轻松的选择之一，因为你只要说明自己是在哪里看到的这本书，价格如何，你为什么决定要买，读了之后有什么感受就好了。其中的第3点和第4点可以和描述一个你崇拜的 leader 或者 artist 充分结合起来准备，是 "省时、省事" 的好方法（当然也别忘了 p. 125 关于 reading 的内容）

Pat 的海外生活英语实录

真正成功的领袖必然是有魅力的，但 "魅力" 一词如果用国内朋友们使用过度的 charm 来表达却实在是相当地没有 "魅力"。请改用 *charisma* /kəˈrizmə/ 来描述政治家、企业家或者明星们等公众人物的 "范儿" 吧，考官对这个词的反应绝不会让你后悔。

【剑桥例句】How did a man of so little personal charisma get to be a leader?

☆ 家庭成员之 *母亲*（可以同时准备描述老师的词汇和短语）

难度指数：★★★★☆

Pat 的答案

Let me talk about my mother. She's of average height and build. She has long hair and wears glasses.

My mother is a high school teacher. She's caring and understanding, and she's always ready to help others, including her students and

人 物

her colleagues.

She's very good at sharing her knowledge with her students because she can explain things in a simple and clear way. She also has a good sense of humour and always tries to make her classes fun and interesting. She's a teacher who really cares about her students, and she always has a smile on her face. I think that's why her students like her so much.

As a wife and a mother, she loves her family and takes good care of everyone. When I was a child, she often helped me with homework, and told me interesting stories at bedtime. Now she still likes to share her ideas and opinions with me. But she's never forced her opinions on me. She respects me and supports me in everything I do.

My mother also has amazing cooking skills. The food she cooks is simple, but tastes really good. So she's not just an excellent teacher, but also a great mother, and a person I can always turn to for good advice. And everyone says I take after her...

轮到你了　　　　　　　　　　　　　　　　　　It's Your Turn.

> ### ▶ **Word Bank on This Topic**

中等身材　is of average height and build（这个固定说法里的 build 是作名词）

关心别人而且善解人意的　caring and understanding

同事　colleague（请您注意听音频里 colleagues 的正确发音，很多中国同学会说错
　　　　这个词）

分享知识　share her knowledge　　　　很有幽默感　has a good sense of humour

关心　care about　　　　　　　　　　面带微笑　has a smile on her face

照顾　take good care of...

准备睡觉的时候　at bedtime（家长给孩子讲的"睡前故事"英文里就叫 bedtime
　　　　　　　　　　stories）

把她的意见强加给 …… force her opinions on...

厨艺 cooking skills

很好的建议 good advice / sound advice

孩子像父母 take after（my mother / my father）

扩展词汇

友善的、耐心的 kind and patient

勤奋的、敬业的 hardworking and dedicated

生活态度很积极 has a positive outlook on life

外向的，喜欢社交的 sociable

很好的榜样 a good role model

要求严格但是很公平的 strict but fair

鼓励学生独立地思考 encourage her students to think independently

鼓励学生有创意地思考 encourage her students to think creatively

帮助学生树立自信 help students build self-confidence

让学生们总是很有动力去学习 keep students motivated to learn

很好接近的，平易近人的 approachable

和家长们紧密合作 work closely with parents

不听讲的学生，"捣乱"的学生 disruptive students

给老师的苹果 an apple for the teacher（国外的学生常用一个苹果来表示对某个老师的喜爱）

请参考Pat的思路，并适当借鉴这个词汇表里的单词，思考如果是您将会怎么说

时间充裕的同学还可以看看这个网址：www. theguardian. com/teacher-network/teacher-blog/2014/oct/31/effective-teaching-10-tips 看看英国人对真正行之有效的教学（effetive teaching）的理解和国内老师们有什么相同和不同

人物

Pat 的海外生活英语实录

在英美文化里，人们公认的一个好老师的标准除了 patient（耐心的），confident（自信的），know his / her subject well（对自己的教学科目有深入的了解）之外，"口齿清晰、表达能力强" 也是必不可少的要求之一。所以当准备 a teacher 这个话题的时候，请务必记牢 articulate /ɑːˈtikjələt/ 这个单词，因为它就是在国外生活里形容一个人口齿清晰、表达能力强最常用的那个词。

[剑桥例句] This young lady was intelligent and articulate.

Time to Branch Out.
推而广之

Describe a person who helped you before.

Describe a person who speaks a foreign language.

Describe your ideal job.（理想的工作）

补充弹药

intelligent 聪明的

well-organised 做事很有条理的

friendly and helpful 友好的、乐于助人的

advice and encouragement 建议和鼓励

Extra Ammo

启发

Part 2 里还有这样一个卡片：Describe a job that can make the world a better place. "能够让世界变得更美好的工作"，这话题真能让考生当场 pass out。其实仔细想想，教师不就是这样的工作么？或者说一个跟环保有关的工作也是扣题的：www. renewableenergyjobs. com/content/what-is-a-green-job 点击这个网页上面的任何一个工作，您就能立刻找到对它的详细描述。

person   216

☆ 老人与孩子（双语感悟）Bilingual Reflections

描述老人时当然也可以借用我们在前面一道题里谈到的地道词汇和短语，例如 kind and patient，a good role model，friendly and helpful 等。但英文里还有些好词和好短语则是描述老年人的时候专用的。

老人身体很好，我们除了可以说 He's / She's healthy and active. 地道英文里还专门有 He's / She's hale and hearty. 这个说法，是特指老年人的身体好，"老当益壮"。但如果老人走路已经需要拐杖，地道英文则会说 He / She walks slowly with a walking stick.

白发就是 white hair，灰发是 grey hair，而"花白的头发"在地道英文里则叫 salt and pepper hair。如果已经秃顶，英文会用形容词 bald. 如果有白胡子，就说 He has a white beard. 脸上有皱纹英文要说 He / She has some wrinkles on his / her face.

说老年人很乐观，除了大词 optimistic 之外，还可以用更简单的英文说 He / She always looks on the bright side of things. 老人心态年轻要说 He's / She's young at heart. 很有幽默感当然就说 has a good sense of humour 最地道。老年人下棋是 play chess，打麻将是 play mahjong，经常锻炼就是 exercise regularly，打太极叫 practise taichi，遛狗是 walk his（or her）dog，悠闲地散步、"遛弯儿"是 take a stroll，"跳广场舞"则要叫 practise their Square Dance routine。

要说老人"睿智"，那么仅仅用 bright 可就不够了，应该说 wise 才对。老人的记忆力还是很好就说 He / She still has a great memory. 老人的思维依然清晰是 His / Her mind is still sharp. 老人还是非常好学要说 He's / She's still eager to learn. 老年人的人生经历丰富是 He / She has a lot of life experience. 如果要说"我总是可以从他 / 她那里获得很好的建议"，地道英文里常会说 I can always count on him（or her）for good advice.

对于儿童，地道英文里同样有很多形象的词汇和短语，而且也都不难。

小朋友胖乎乎的叫 chubby，比较瘦的叫 slim（如果说 thin 则听起来会略带贬义），描述小朋友很可爱除了 cute 之外也可以说 adorable。

小朋友的身心都很健康就说 is happy and

人 物

healthy，喜欢户外活动是 likes outdoor activities，小朋友很有活力在地道英文里会说 He's / She's full of energy 或者 lively and energetic，性格很外向叫 He's / She's very sociable. 跟谁都能玩儿得来是 He / She gets on well with everybody. 喜欢和别人合作就说 He / She is a team player. 如果小朋友跟自己不熟悉的人在一起时会比较安静，则说 He / She tends to be quiet around people he / she doesn't know well.

小朋友在学校成绩好要说 He / She gets good grades at school. 很守规矩的叫 well-behaved，有礼貌而且尊敬别人的叫 polite and respectful，是同班同学们的榜样英文是 He's / She's a role model for his / her classmates，聪明而且又有创造力的叫 intelligent and creative，在某方面有天赋要说 has a talent for（music，painting，maths 等），说一个小朋友学习努力，虽然也可以说 studies hard，但在真实的英美生活里还是 He / She works hard. 更常用。

小朋友的求知欲很强，凡事总爱问个为什么，英文里说 He / She has an inquiring mind. 孩子是父母的"掌上明珠"，地道英文叫 He's / She's the apple of his（or her）parents' eye. 这是个生活里的惯用说法，apple 和 eye 都用单数听起来才 native。

另类话题 Off-the-Wall Topics

Joe Wong（黄西）这位"70 后大哥"的英语并不 native，而且他在说英语时的发音还带有浓重的东北口音。可他却登上了美国最著名的 late night TV talk show — *The Late Show with David Letterman*，并且成了近期最受美国观众注意的 stand-up comedians 之一。Joe Wong 的成功故事再次告诉我们：英语说得简单易懂，反而能让你和 native speakers 进行更加充分的沟通。

I（Joe Wong）came to the United States when I was 24, to study at Rice University in Texas.

Like many other immigrants, we want our son to become the President of this country and we try to make him bilingual（双语的），you know, Chinese at home and English in public, which is really tough to do.

In America they say that all men are created equal, but after birth, it kind of depends on the parents' income, or early education and health care.

person

I'm honored to meet Vice President Joe Biden here tonight. I actually read your autobiography（自传）, and today I see you. I think the book is much better.

So to be honest, I'm really honored to be here tonight, and I prepared for months for tonight's show. And I showed the White House my jokes about President Obama, and that is when he decided not to come… And I started to think maybe I should run for president myself. We have a president who is half black half white, it just gives me a lot of hope, because I'm half not black and half not white. Two negatives make a positive.

So guys, do you still find IELTS scary? Just give it your best shot and you'll be fine. ☺

人 物

C　人与自然

Pat 解题　Pat's Thought

natural beauty 这个词在英文中其实有两个意思，一个是指自然的美景，另一个是指"素颜"的美。当然两个意思都挺好，但这一节咱们只说第一个。

英美的生活离自然还是挺近的。Pat 在 BC 开车时还见过一只灰熊（grizzly bear）妈妈带着两只熊宝（bear cubs）慢悠悠地违章横穿马路，如果真的不小心撞到（run over）它们，就要被动物权益主义者们（animal rights activists）告上法庭（be taken to court）了。

英国和北美的生活里最重要的娱乐也是 fishing，camping（野营），hiking（远足），skiing（滑雪）等接近大自然的活动，而且英国、美国和加拿大的国家公园都很多。Pat 个人最喜欢 Alberta 的 Banff，那里的自然美景真的把人的呼吸都带走了（The scenery is really breathtaking.）。

本类最有代表性的方向　Typical Topics

❧ Describe a park.

❧ Describe a good place to relax.

❧ Describe a short trip.

❧ Describe a river / lake / sea.

❧ Describe a place of natural beauty.

展开本类话题的思维导图　Mind Maps

（如果卡片上的 4 个提示问题仍然不能让你说出充实的答案，那么下面的思维导图可以帮助你继续扩展出扣题、充实的 ideas）

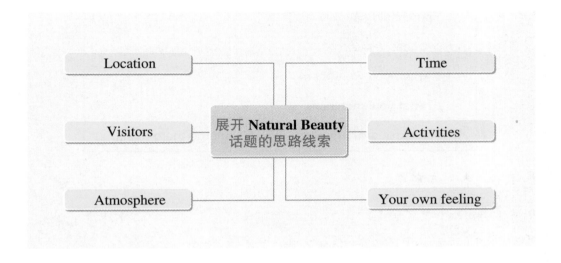

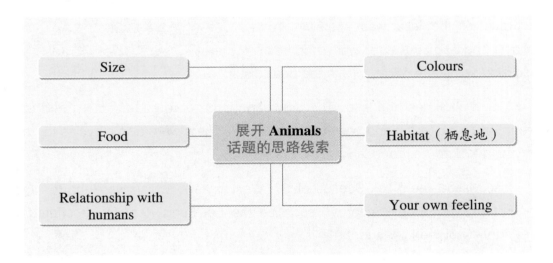

分级演示　Sample Answers

1. 一个有水的地方

☆ 西湖

> Describe a river, lake or sea you have visited.
>
> You should say:
>
> where it was
>
> when you went there
>
> what you saw there
>
> and explain whether you would like to go there again.

难度指数：★ ★ ★ ★ ☆

Pat 的答案

I visited the West Lake last September. It's close to downtown Hangzhou and very easy to get to by public transport.

I visited the lake on a clear, sunny day. The water of the lake was sparkling in the sunlight. The lake breeze felt warm and fresh. I could also see some rolling hills in the near distance.

I took a stroll near the lake. The grass and trees were well-trimmed, and there were many picnic tables and benches by the lake. There were also bicycles for rent. Everything looked neat and tidy.

I also visited the "Ten Scenes of the West Lake", which were the ten most famous tourist attractions nearby, such as the Lei Feng Pagoda. It offered an amazing view of the lake and the hills.

I really enjoyed the stroll. The lake and its surroundings felt so calm and peaceful. I took lots of photos there. I really hope I'll visit it again.

nature

轮到你了   It's Your Turn.

▶ **Word Bank on This Topic**

市中心	downtown	公共交通	public transport
闪亮	sparkling	微风	breeze
起伏的小山	rolling hill	在不远处	in the near distance
散步，很悠闲地走	take a stroll	修剪得很好的	well-trimmed
野餐桌	picnic table	室外的长椅	bench
干净整洁的	neat and tidy	旅游景点	tourist attractions
亚洲国家的古塔	pagoda	周围的环境	surroundings
宁静安详的	calm and peaceful		

📎 描述风景的扩展词汇

自然风景（注意：它是不可数的） scenery

清澈的	crystal-clear	壮观的	spectacular
非常美的	gorgeous / breathtaking	瀑布	waterfall
轰鸣	roar	岩石	rock

喜欢大自然的人们必去的地方 a must-see for nature lovers

峡谷	valley	山泉	mountain spring
温泉	hot spring	人造的喷泉	fountain
自然界的天然草地	meadow	人工维护的草地	lawn
亭子	gazebo	盛开的花	blooming flowers
芳香	fragrance	花坛	flowerbed

（鸟或昆虫）鸣叫 chirp

秋叶 autumn leaves / autumn foliage （注意 foliage 不可数）

野餐	have a picnic	去远足，徒步旅行	go hiking
去野营	go camping		

自然界

做日光浴　go sunbathing（注意听音频里它的正确读音）

宿营地　campsite　　　　　　　　烧烤　have a barbecue

在湖上划船　row a boat on the lake　　闪亮的水面　sparkling water

泛起波纹的水面　rippling water

光着脚在沙滩上走　walk barefoot on the beach

搭沙堡　build sandcastles　　　　捡贝壳　collect shells

海鸥　seagulls

摆脱繁忙的都市生活　get away from busy city life

更加接近大自然　get closer to nature

感觉心情平静并且很放松的　feel calm and relaxed

暂时忘掉工作　forget about work for a while

让疲劳的身心恢复良好的状态　recharge my batteries

小村庄　village　　　　　　　　当地人　locals

热情好客的　are welcoming and friendly

历史遗迹　historic sites　　　　维护得很好的　well-maintained

参观费　admission fee　　　　旅行纪念品　souvenirs

令人愉快的经历　an enjoyable experience

令人难忘的经历　a memorable experience

请参考Pat的思路，并适当借鉴这个词汇表里的单词，思考如果是您将会怎么说

　　Part 2 里面还有一道相关考题是Describe a place near water（一个靠近水的地方）. 其实只要描述一栋湖边的别墅或者一个海边的宾馆，我们就可以把学过的关于别墅和宾馆的地道词汇和短语自然而且扣题地使用起来。您还可以从 www. huffingtonpost. co. uk/2014/06/20/beach-hotels-britain-uk-good-hotel-guide_n_5515270. html 这个网址看到对英国最棒的一些水边宾馆的详细介绍。

nature

"风景如画的"，如果说 It looks like a picture. 并不严格对应，因为 picture 其实也可以很丑，但 picture 的形容词形式 picturesque /pɪktʃəˈresk/ 在地道口语中却是一个纯粹的褒义词。例如：

【剑桥例句】It's a picturesque village.

2. 公园/花园

> Describe a park / garden.
>
> You should say:
>
> > what it's called
> >
> > where it is
> >
> > what people do there
> >
> and explain whether you like the park / garden or not.

☆ 公园之 海洋公园

难度指数：★ ★ ★ ☆ ☆

Pat 的答案

I'd like to describe Ocean Park Hong Kong. It's about a 20-minute drive from downtown Hong Kong.

The park has many different sections. There's a lot to see and do as you walk around these sections.

For example, in the "Strait" section, you'll find thousands of sea creatures, including sharks, turtles and seahorses. In the outdoor "Wild Coast" section, you can see the exciting dolphin show. And in the play area, children

自然界

can even touch some of the sea creatures they like.

I like the Ocean Park because it has an amazing variety of sea creatures. It can really help visitors learn about sea life. The park is also very well-organised, and the employees are friendly and helpful. I think the park is good for all ages.

轮到你了

It's Your Turn.

▶ Word Bank on This Topic

部分	parts / sections	海峡	strait

海洋里的动物　sea creatures（地道英文也常用 creatures 来泛指动物）

鲨鱼	shark	龟	turtle
海马	seahorse	海豚	dolphin
井井有条的	well-organised		

扩展词汇

海狮	sea lion	海象	walrus
海豹	seal	虎鲸	orca / killer whale
水母	jellyfish	潜水员	diver
直接地体验	experience... first-hand	让人大开眼界的	eye-opening
野生动物园	safari park	野生生物保护区	wildlife reserve
自然保护区	nature reserve	栖息地	habitat

了解野生生物　learn about wildlife（wildlife 是泛指野生动植物）

请参考Pat的思路，并适当借鉴这个词汇表里的单词，思考如果是您将会怎么说

这个网址提供了英国各地区的自然保护区信息：www. wildlifetrusts. org/wildlife/reserves，沿着地图一路点击就可以看到你想了解的地区的 nature reserve 详情

Pat 的海外生活英语实录

泛指"海洋生物"，您不妨试试 sea life / marine life 这两种说法，它们会让考官紧皱着的眉头舒展开。

［剑桥例句］The children were amazed by the variety of sea life.

☆ 花园

难度指数：★ ★ ★ ☆ ☆

Pat 的答案

My favourite garden is the Classical Chinese Garden. It's just a short walk from where I live.

This garden is always a fun place to visit, and it's beautiful in every season.

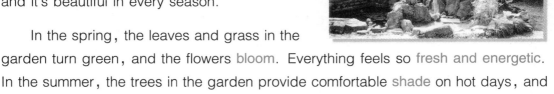

In the spring, the leaves and grass in the garden turn green, and the flowers bloom. Everything feels so fresh and energetic. In the summer, the trees in the garden provide comfortable shade on hot days, and visitors can watch the fish play in the lotus pond.

Most of the trees there change colours in the autumn, which looks amazing. The garden feels good even in the winter because the snow on the trees and on the ground makes it calm and peaceful.

I like this garden because it makes me feel relaxed and happy. And the air in the garden is always fresh and clean. It's like an oasis in the city. It's also a great place to learn about trees and plants.

轮到你了

It's Your Turn.

▶ **Word Bank on This Topic**

变成绿色	turn green	开花	bloom
充满生机和活力的	fresh and energetic	树荫	shade
莲花池	lotus pond	变颜色	change colours
安静祥和的	calm and peaceful		

城市里的一片"绿洲" an oasis in the city（地道英文里常用这个短语来形容可以躲开城市里的各种喧闹拥挤的地方）

自然界

扩展词汇

欣赏　appreciate

很悠闲地走，散步　take a stroll

挺拔的　tall and strong

岩石　rock

探索　explore

放松　unwind（请注意听音频里对它的读音）

botanical garden　植物园

优雅的　elegant

（植物）纤细的　slim

溪流　stream

发现　discover

这个网站提供了对伦敦的很多公园的介绍，而且网站上的图片用来考前放松也挺不错：www.allinlondon.co.uk/park.php

请参考Pat的思路，并适当借鉴这个词汇表里的单词，思考如果是您将会怎么说

Pat 的海外生活英语实录

有很多中国同学问 Pat "亭子"在英文里面叫什么。其实英美公园里的亭子并不是很多，而且即使有也远不如中国公园里面的亭子那么"惊艳"（breathtaking）。但只要您跟 native speakers 说 gazebo 这个词，他们就立刻能理解你是在说"亭子"了☺。

[剑桥例句] The area surrounding the gazebo is a popular place for children.

常见植物英文名称（如果想让答案更长，您当然还可以适当介绍一下自己在花园里最喜欢的植物，但不要太深入，因为毕竟这道题是考花园而不是考你最喜欢的植物，切记：扣题很重要）

tulip　郁金香

peony　牡丹

daffodil　水仙花

sunflower　向日葵

oak tree　橡树

willow　柳树

lily　百合

daisy　雏菊

orchid　兰花

carnation　康乃馨

palm tree　棕榈树

holly　冬青

nature

pine tree   松柏   petunia   喇叭花

申加拿大学校的读者们今后可一定别忘了 check out the maple syrup，超级好喝！

poinsettia   一品红，很红很漂亮的一种花，在英美 Christmas 的时候经常作装饰用

Time to Branch Out.
推而广之

Describe a walk that you took.

补充弹药

breeze   微风   take a stroll   散步，很休闲地走

chat   聊天   feel fresh and energetic   感觉焕然一新、精力充沛的

Extra Ammo

3. 动物

Describe an animal.

You should say:

what the animal is

where it can be found

what is special about it

and explain how people feel about it.

☆ 野生动物之   大象

难度指数：★ ★ ★ ☆ ☆

Pat 的答案

Elephants are fascinating creatures.

They are huge. African elephant can stand as tall as 4 meters. Actually, they

自然界

are the largest four-footed animals in the world. But they are very gentle and slow-moving. They don't "bully" other animals.

Elephants use their trunk to "grab" food and use their tusks to dig for water.

They are social animals, and the mothers lead the whole family group.

People say that elephants never forget. Trainers can even train them to use simple tools. For thousands of years, elephants have been trained to carry heavy stuff and carry people through the jungle. They are like hard-working employees for their owners. But they ask for bananas instead of cash...

轮到你了

It's Your Turn.

▶ Word Bank on This Topic

四足动物	four-footed animals	温和的	gentle
大象的鼻子	trunk	抓	grab
大象的牙齿	tusks	挖	dig
群居的动物	social animals	训练师	trainer
丛林	jungle	勤奋的员工	hard-working employees
主人	owner	现金	cash

扩展词汇

濒危物种	endangered species	偷猎	poaching
象牙交易	ivory trade	野生生物保护区	wildlife reserve
野生动物园	safari park		

WWF（世界自然基金会）的这个网址将会让您对濒危动物有更深入的了解：www. worldwildlife. org/species

请参考Pat的思路，并适当借鉴这个词汇表里的单词，思考如果是您将会怎么说

Pat 的海外生活英语实录

考到动物的话题，如果只是不停地说 animals 其实挺郁闷的。口试里绕开 animals 的好方法就是用 creatures 这个词，或者也可以说 living creatures。

[剑桥例句] Blue whales are the largest creatures ever to have lived.

☆ 野生动物之 狮子

难度指数：★ ★ ☆ ☆ ☆

Pat 的答案

Just like the tiger, the lion is also a member of the cat family and… in many ways lions are just big cats.

Humans have been so amazed by lions' size and strength that we call them the king of beasts. And a lion's roar can be heard up to 10 kilometers away.

Lions live in groups. Adult females look after their cubs together, hunt together and defend their hunting grounds together. But the males tend to be lazy, and some of them are actually troublemakers. Some cubs even get hurt by adult males when the adult females are away.

I like lions not really because they are strong, but because my girlfriend (for girls：boyfriend) is a Leo…

轮到你了

It's Your Turn.

► **Word Bank on This Topic**

猫科动物	the cat family	力量	strength
兽中之王	the king of beasts	吼叫	roar

照看	look after	小狮子／小老虎／小熊等	cub
捕猎	hunt	保护	defend
制造麻烦者	troublemaker	狮子座	Leo

🔍 **扩展词汇**

狮群　pride（地道英文里一群狮子经常被叫作 a pride of lions，可能跟雄狮看起来很"骄傲"有关 ☺)

星座　sign　　　　　　　　　　　凶猛的　fierce / ferocious

猎物　prey（注意：它是不可数的）

请参考Pat的思路，并适当借鉴这个词汇表里的单词，思考如果是您将会怎么说

这个网站提供了英格兰和苏格兰各主要动物园的详细介绍：
britishzoos.co.uk/

Pat 的海外生活英语实录

要表达"群居动物"，除了可以说 **They live together.** 之外，还有个很地道的说法：social animals。例如：

[剑桥例句] Lions are social animals that live in prides.

☆ **宠物之　鹦鹉**

难度指数：★ ★ ☆ ☆ ☆

Pat 的答案

Parrots have gorgeous feathers and a big tail.

They are good at copying human sounds. When you visit a pet shop, you'll probably find some parrots repeating "Hello! Hello!". And parrot owners often notice that their birds say

words like "goodnight" and "snack" at the right moment. Some parrots may even have the vocabulary of a two-year-old child.

Most of the time，parrots are very friendly. But be careful！Sometimes parrots do attack the people around them…

轮到你了

It's Your Turn.

▶ Word Bank on This Topic

非常漂亮的	gorgeous	羽毛	feathers
尾巴	tail	鹦鹉的主人	parrot owner
重复	repeat	攻击	attack

扩展词汇

可爱的	cute / adorable	烦人的	annoying
宠物的主人	owner	减少压力和孤独感	reduce stress and loneliness
耐心的	patient	责任感	a sense of responsibility
照看	look after		

这个网址为您提供了对英国最常见鸟类的详尽介绍：
birdsofbritain. co. uk/bird-guide/

请参考Pat的思路，并适当借鉴这个词汇表里的单词，思考如果是您将会怎么说

Pat 的海外生活英语实录

要说某种事物很"烦人"，除了 It's annoying. 之外，It really bothers me. 也是英美生活里的常用说法之一。

[剑桥例句] The noise in this area really bothers me.

Pat 指南

Describe an animal / pet you saw in your city.

在英美城市里见到最多的宠物永远都是 dogs，这个网站为"爱狗控"们提供了对各种狗狗最详尽的描述：www. terrificpets. com/dog_ breeds/

4. 重要的植物

> Describe an important plant in your country.
>
> You should say:
>
> what the plant is
>
> what it looks like
>
> whether you like it
>
> and explain why it is important in your country.

难度指数: ★ ★ ★ ☆ ☆

Pat 的答案

I'm going to talk about bamboo, which is one of the most important plants in China.

Bamboo is a kind of grass, but it can grow as tall as 30 meters — that's even taller than many trees. It grows very fast, like a couple of centimeters a day.

Another interesting thing about bamboo is although the bamboo stem is not thick, it's very strong.

It has been a symbol of vitality and honesty in the Chinese culture. It's also known as one of "The Three Friends of Winter" in China because it can survive cold winters.

Bamboo is also an important economic plant. Its use includes furniture making and building construction. It has contributed a lot to the Chinese economy.

And as you probably know, bamboo is the panda's main source of food. Bamboo shoots are also widely used in Chinese dishes. I love dishes that have bamboo shoots in them. They taste really good.

轮到你了 //// It's Your Turn.

▶ **Word Bank on This Topic**

厘米	centimeter	茎	stem
是生机的象征	a symbol of vitality	诚实	honesty
经济植物	economic plant	建造	construction
主要的食物来源	main source of food	竹笋	bamboo shoot

扩展词汇

常青的	evergreen	直立的	upright
松	pine	梅	plum
清淡的味道	a mild flavor		

备考时间充足的同学可以从这个网址看到对英国常见植物的详尽介绍：
www. plantlife. org. uk/wild_plants/plant_species

请参考Pat的思路，并适当借鉴这个词汇表里的单词，思考如果是您将会怎么说

Pat 的海外生活英语实录

　　Pat 注意到有很多中国的传统建筑外面会种竹子作为一种装饰。如果要用地道英文说"它可以成为很好的装饰"怎么说呢？native speakers 会说 It makes a good decoration. 这句话里的 make 不是制作，而是"可以成为"的意思。

　　[剑桥例句] The painting makes a good decoration in the living room.

☆ *野餐*（*双语感悟*）**Bilingual Reflections**

近期在亚太区经常有一只卡片熊出没：

Describe a picnic / an outdoor meal.

　　而且，这个答案如果说得比较有特色，就可以和另一道高频难题 Describe a special meal. 一起解决了，所以就更值得关注。

　　Pat 发现有很多中国同学不太了解野餐（picnic）的常用英文表达，其实 native speakers 在野餐时的用词并不"野"：

自然界

中文	地道英文表达
景色	scenery
家庭聚会	a family gathering
几家人一块儿聚餐（一般是每家都带些吃的，然后大家一起 share）	a potluck
公园里提供的野餐桌	picnic table
长椅	bench
小板凳儿	small stool
春天和秋天野餐时铺在地上的毯子（夏天则经常用 plaid sheet "格子布" 代替）	picnic blanket
铺开	spread out
背包	backpack
纸盘 / 纸杯	paper plate / paper cup
叉子	forks
刀	knife
勺子	spoons
装食品和餐具的篮子（在国外野餐时是必用的，考官听到会觉得很亲切）	picnic basket
烧烤（注意：barbecue 既可以做名词也可以做动词）	have a barbecue
烧烤用的原料	barbecue ingredients（常见的例如 chicken, lamb, shrimp 等）
烧烤的（后面加上肉类或者海鲜就行了）	grilled / barbecued（chicken, shrimp, salmon...）
调味酱	sauce
沙拉	salad
甜点（注意：它的发音和沙漠 desert 可不一样）	dessert（比如 cakes 和 biscuits）
水果	fruit（比如 strawberries 和 grapes）
瓶装水	bottled water
果汁	juice
垃圾袋	garbage bag
拍照片	take photos（过去时是 took photos）
玩游戏	play games
一次令人难忘的经历	a memorable experience
再加上你对于看到的景色和对自己感受的描述，早就够了……	

D 休闲娱乐

Pat 解题　Pat's Thought

很多同学在出国之前，都爱幻想（fantasise）国外是不是比中国好玩。

这个嘛……那得看你喜欢什么了。

如果您喜欢 sports 和 outdoor activities，那绝对应该出国，因为选择实在太多了。连 golfing 这样国内的"贵族运动"（high-class sports），在英美也不过只是大众运动（popular sports），因为价格并不贵（not very pricey）。

但如果您既不喜欢 sports，也不喜欢 outdoor activities，甚至都不喜欢 going to the cinema，那么你真有可能会觉得国外的生活挺单调的。西方人最喜欢的休闲活动除了 sports，基本上就是 hiking，fishing，camping，going to the cinema，clubbing，bar-hopping… 甚至连"看人"（people-watching）和"看鸟儿"（bird-

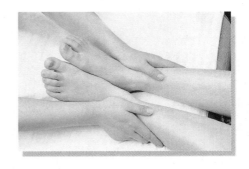

watching）都算是休闲活动。至于"洗脚城"（foot massage parlors）则少之又少，而卡拉 OK（karaoke）也并没有国内这么"火"（"in"）。

到底哪种娱乐更好玩儿？那只能说是"萝卜白菜，各有所爱"了（Different strokes for different folks.）☺。

本类最有代表性的方向　Typical Topics

✳ Describe a childhood game.

✳ Describe an outdoor activity.

✳ Describe your favourite sport.

✳ Describe a TV programme that you like / dislike.

✳ Describe a foreign country you wish to travel to.

展开本类话题的思维导图　Mind Map

（如果卡片上的 4 个提示问题仍然不能让你说出充实的答案，那么下面的思维导图可以帮助你继续扩展出扣题、充实的 ideas）

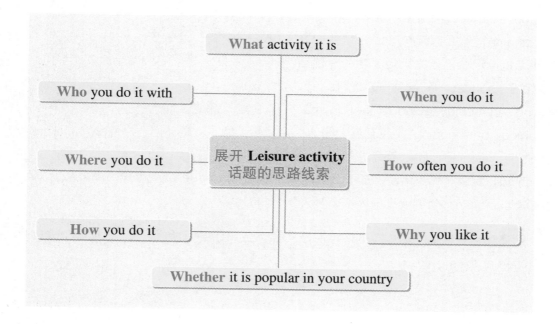

分级演示　Sample Answers

1. 童年时的游戏

> Describe a game you enjoyed as a child.
>
> You should say:
>
> where you played this game
>
> who you played it with
>
> how it was played
>
> and explain why you liked it.

☆ 游戏之　捉迷藏

难度指数：★ ★ ★ ☆ ☆

Pat 的答案

I often played hide-and-seek as a child. We usually played this game in a park or in a building with lots of rooms.

The game was like this: one of us, called the "seeker", searched around for the "hiders". The game started with the seeker covering his or her eyes and counting to 100, while everyone else ran away and found a place to hide.

After the counting was finished, the seeker opened his or her eyes and started searching for the hiders. And that was my favourite part of the game. The hiders tried their best to keep quiet. But then, there was always someone who got caught, and this person would be the next seeker.

I really enjoyed this game because it was simple but exciting, and it helped us stay active. These days, my friends and I have fun by sitting around and playing computer games, which can be unhealthy. Sometimes I really miss the simple fun of playing hide-and-seek.

轮到你了

It's Your Turn.

▶ Word Bank on This Topic

搜寻　search for…

躲起来　hide

数数字　count

保持安静　keep quiet

被抓到　get caught

保持活跃的，保持身体经常运动的　stay active

简单但是令人兴奋的　simple but exciting

简单的乐趣　the simple fun of…

扩展词汇

拔河　tug-of-war

追人　play tag

跑来跑去　run around

跳格子　hopscotch

提高孩子的平衡和协调能力　improve children's balance and coordination

在学校的操场上　on the school playground

在公园里　in a park

玩弹子球　play marbles

充满了悬念　is full of suspense

棋类游戏　board games

打败对方　defeat the other player

牌类游戏　card games

有趣而且令人愉快的　fun and enjoyable

玩得特别开心　have a great time / have a blast

团队精神　team spirit

和队友们紧密合作　work closely with their teammates

　　这个网站提供了对很多儿童游戏的描述，有时间的同学在集体追忆"少年时代"的同时，也可以对比一下中国小朋友和英语国家儿童们的游戏有哪些异同：www.activityvillage.co.uk/all-games-a-z

请参考Pat的思路，并适当借鉴这个词汇表里的单词，思考如果是您将会怎么说

Pat 的海外生活英语实录

小朋友玩户外游戏除了"好玩儿"（fun）之外，另一个重要的作用是可以锻炼孩子们的社会交往能力 social skills。

[剑桥例句] There're many online games that can help children improve their social skills.

2. 最喜欢的运动

☆ 最喜欢的运动之游泳

> Describe your favourite sport.
>
> You should say：
>
>   when you started this sport
>
>   how you learned to do it
>
>   whether you can do it well
>
> and explain why you like it.

难度指数：★ ★ ★ ☆ ☆

男生女生都可以说的常见运动的应该就是 swimming，而且描述游泳益处的词汇和短语也完全可以自然地用到很多其它运动上面。

:Pat 的答案:

My favourite sport is swimming.

I learned to swim when I was 8. My instructor was very patient and helpful. At first, I couldn't swim at all. I was even afraid of the water. My instructor told me to relax and concentrate. He showed me patiently how to move my arms and kick my legs. Little by little, I began to feel comfortable in the water. Then he taught me how to control my breathing. It took me a lot of practice to learn to breathe properly. But by the end of the swimming course, I'd become very confident in my swimming skills.

Now I'm a pretty good swimmer，and I go swimming every weekend. It helps me keep fit and improves my strength and balance. It's also a good way to relax and reduce stress. And I've made many friends at our local swimming center.

轮到你了

It's Your Turn.

▶ **Word Bank on This Topic**

游泳教练　swimming instructor

集中注意力　concentrate

适当地换气　breathe properly

保持身强体健　keep fit

减轻压力，"减压"　reduce stress

耐心的　patient

调节呼吸的节奏　control my breathing

自信的　confident

力量和平衡能力·strength and balance

扩展词汇

完全不会游泳　swim like a brick

很擅长游泳　swim like a fish

泳镜　goggles

仰泳　back-stroke

自由式　freestyle

增强肌肉　build muscles

提高我的耐力　boost my endurance

改善我的协调能力　improve my coordination

浮板　kickboard

树立自信　build self-confidence

蛙泳　breast-stroke

蝶泳　butterfly-stroke

潜水　dive

请参考Pat的思路，并适当借鉴这个词汇表里的单词，思考如果是您将会怎么说

　　如果有空，您还可以看看 BBC 怎样介绍常见的极限运动（extreme sports）：news. bbc. co. uk/cbbcnews/hi/find_out/guides/sport/extreme_sports，如果还觉得不够"刺激"，那么还可以再访问这个网站 www. buzzle. com/articles/list-of-extreme-sports. html，它对最常见的极限运动都给出了详尽的解释。

Pat 的海外生活英语实录

在 IELTS 口试里，谈到体育运动时往往会说到一项运动很"耗费体力的"，地道英文里有个常用词叫 strenuous，是个拿分效果明显的表达：

[剑桥例句] Hannah's doctor advised her not to take any strenuous exercise.

Time to Branch Out.
推而广之

Describe a skill.

Describe something that you are good at.

Describe a difficult thing that you can do well.

Describe something you hope to learn.

补充弹药

challenging　很有挑战的	build self-confidence　树立自信
overcome the difficulties　克服困难	get used to　适应

Extra Ammo

3. 有趣的新闻

☆ 一条有趣的新闻之　银行劫匪

Describe a piece of interesting news.

You should say:

　　when you heard the news

　　how you heard the news

　　who the news was about

and explain how you felt after you heard the news.

休闲娱乐

难度指数： ★ ★ ☆ ☆ ☆

如果你明白考官真正需要的其实只是一个扣题（to-the-point）、自然（natural-sounding）、清晰（direct and clear）的描述，就不应该让自己的答案里面充斥着大词和长难句，因为那样的答案不仅听起来会让 native speakers 费解，而且也和考官的期待背道而驰（run counter to what they expect）。

Pat 的答案

Let me share with you a piece of interesting news I heard on TV last weekend.

Last Friday afternoon, a man went into a bank in New York and tried to rob it. He was probably not a bad person. He wanted to rob the bank because he had lost his job, and then he lost his house and his car. The only thing he had was debt. So he decided to rob the bank and get some money.

"Fill the bag up?.. With what?!"

What made the news interesting was that he didn't have a gun. So this guy just took a banana and put it in his pocket. He thought that could fool the bank tellers.

He entered the bank, walked up to a teller, told her he had a gun and asked her to give him some cash. Of course the police came. This guy got so scared that he pulled out his "gun", I mean, his banana...

The news was interesting. But actually it was a sad story. These days, many people have lost their jobs because of the economy. I feel sorry for them.

轮到你了

It's Your Turn.

▶ **Word Bank on This Topic**

抢劫	rob	债务	debt
愚弄	fool (v.)	银行柜员	bank teller
现金	cash	害怕的	scared
面具	mask		

扩展词汇

新闻播音员	news presenter / anchor	值得信赖的	reliable
有误导性的	misleading	轰动的	sensational
丑闻	scandal	发人深思的	thought-provoking
侵犯他们的隐私	invade their privacy		

如果您对英语新闻有深入的兴趣，看 CNN 的官网当然是个好选择：www.cnn.com。如果您现在直接看 CNN 常规版还感觉吃力，那么也可以试试 CNN 的学生版：www.cnn.com/studentnews/，这个网站对于适应出国之后每天都要看、听英语新闻的生活是个不错的"试水"阶段。

请参考Pat的思路，并适当借鉴这个词汇表里的单词，思考如果是您将会怎么说

Pat 的海外生活英语实录

在地道英文里，fun 作形容词时是"有趣的"，而 funny 则是"搞笑的"。但如果您要说一件事情是"超级搞笑的"，请用 hilarious 这个形容词。考官听到这个词虽然出于职业准则不会放声大笑，但却会因为你的用词准确而会心地微笑。

Time to Branch Out.
推而广之

Describe something that made you laugh.

补充弹药

crack sb. up   让某人大笑

hilarious   超级搞笑的

punch line   一个笑话最后的那句话，"包袱"

休闲娱乐

4. 电视节目

> Describe a TV programme you like.
>
> You should say：
>
>   what kind of programme it is
>
>   what it is like
>
>   whether it is popular
>
> and explain why you like it.

☆ 电视节目之 家庭滑稽录像

难度指数：★ ★ ★ ☆ ☆

Pat 的答案

My favourite TV show is *America's Funniest Home Videos*. It's a very popular reality show.

The show is like ... people send in their funny homemade videos. Then the host plays the videos on a large screen and makes comments on the videos.

Many of the videos show funny moments at weddings or parties. Some people also send in videos showing the hilarious mistakes made by their young children. Sometimes the videos are organised around popular themes，such as pets，birthdays or vacations.

I like this show because the host has a great sense of humor. He keeps the viewers laughing throughout the show. I like the show also because it's all about family life and ordinary people. I guess that's why it attracts so many viewers.

轮到你了

▶ **Word Bank on This Topic**

真人秀	reality show	家庭录像	homemade video
主持人	host	评论	make comments
有趣的瞬间	funny moments	超级搞笑的	hilarious
围绕……组织起来	are organised around...	主题	theme
很强的幽默感	a great sense of humour	收看节目的人们	viewers
吸引	attract		

扩展词汇

竞赛节目	game show	有才华的	talented
参加竞赛节目的选手	contestants	说话很机敏的	witty
奖品	prize	综艺节目	variety show
问答节目	quiz show	选秀类节目	talent show
厨艺节目	cookery show	旅游节目	travel show
相亲节目	blind date show	缘来非诚勿扰	If You Are the One
嘉宾	guests	追求者	suitor
科学类真人秀	scientific reality show	最强大脑	The Brain
是街谈巷议的话题	is the talk of the town	很有争议性的节目	a controversial show

请参考Pat的思路，并适当借鉴这个词汇表里的单词，思考如果是您将会怎么说

时间充裕的同学可以在 www. dooyoo. co. uk/discussion/top-ten-quiz-shows/385040/和 www. dooyoo. co. uk/discussion/top-ten-quiz-shows/这两个网址看到英国观众到底怎样点评在英国收视率很高的 quiz show（问答节目）。

Pat 的海外生活英语实录

说电视节目或者广播节目"引人入胜的"，国内同学们一般会想到 interesting 或者 attractive，其实最准确的应该是 engaging 这个词。

[剑桥例句] A good radio show is always engaging.

休闲娱乐

Time to Branch Out.
推而广之

> Describe a radio programme.
>
> 描述一个广播节目

补充词汇和短语

talk show 聊天节目	a panel of guests 嘉宾团队
interviews 访谈	call-in show 观众打电话参与的节目
live phone calls 由观众现场打进的电话	
listener participation 听众的参与，注意这个地道短语里的 listener 可以不用复数或所有格	
lively conversations 气氛活跃的对话	broadcast 播放
attract lots of listeners 吸引大量的听众	well-received （节目）很受欢迎的
discussions about topical issues 关于热点话题展开的讨论	
weather information 天气信息	traffic information 交通信息
informative 信息大的	entertaining 娱乐性强的
educational 很有知识性的	

Extra Ammo

☆ 电视节目之 选秀节目

各种歌手选秀节目（singing talent shows）在中国引起了很多关注，这让 Pat 想到了正在美国大行其道的歌手选秀节目——The Voice。您不妨比较一下东西方同一类节目的形式（format）到底有哪些异同：

Pat 的答案

I'd like to talk about a popular singing talent show called "The Voice". It has three stages of competition：the blind auditions, the battles, and the live shows.

Only people with real singing talent are invited to the blind auditions，— the coaches can hear the singers perform, but they can't see the singers because they sit with their back to the singers. If a coach is impressed by a singer's voice, he or she pushes a button to select the singer for his or her team. Then the coach's chair turns around to face the singer.

Once the teams are formed, the battle is on. In this stage, the coaches focus on developing their singers' singing skills. They also have two of their team members compete against each other. Then the coaches decide which singers can get to the next stage. At the end of the battles, only the strongest members of each team go on to the live shows.

During the live shows, the top singers from each team compete against each other . The audience can vote to save their favourite singer. In the end, each team has only one member left to compete against the other teams. The winner of this final competition is then named "The Voice" and receives the prize of a recording contract.

I like this show because the singers are really talented, and they put in a lot of hard work to improve their singing skills. And their coaches also work very hard to help them improve. Watching this show is both relaxing and inspiring. That's why it attracts so many viewers.

轮到你了   It's Your Turn.

▶ Word Bank on This Topic

歌手选秀类节目	singing talent show	阶段	stage
盲选	the blind auditions	组内大战	the battles
现场对决	the live shows	导师	coach
表演	perform	按钮	button
挑选	select	竞争	compete（动词）/ competition（名词）

观众	audience	投票	vote
唱片合同	a recording contract	有才华的	talented
励志的	inspiring	吸引	attract

扩展词汇

激烈的竞争　fierce competition

出局，被淘汰　is eliminated

很有回报的经历　a rewarding experience

值得回忆的经历　a memorable experience

有趣而且令人愉快的　fun and enjoyable

> 请参考Pat的思路，并适当借鉴这个词汇表里的单词，思考如果是您将会怎么说

　　厨艺节目（cookery shows）是在中英两国都很流行的一类电视节目。这个网站是英国著名的"电视食神"（celebrity TV chef）Jamie Oliver 的官网：www. jamieoliver. com。他最擅长的就是用很简单的原料做出又好吃又健康的食品（cook tasty and healthy food with simple ingredients），即使你没学会那些 recipes（菜的做法），至少也能够对英国人喜欢的厨艺节目风格有更深入的了解 ☺

　　☆ *电视系列剧之　生活大爆炸*

难度指数：★ ★ ★ ☆ ☆

Pat 的答案

　　I'm going to talk about a sitcom I like, called *The Big Bang Theory*.

　　The two main characters of this sitcom are Leonard and Sheldon. Both of them are Caltech physicists and they share an apartment. Leonard has an IQ of 173 but has no problem communicating with the "average" people. Sheldon is even more intelligent, with an IQ of 187. But he really lacks social skills and often finds it hard to interact with the "ordinary" people.

　　Penny, their next-door neighbor, is a waitress who dreams of being an actress. Leonard has a crush on her, but they just seem to be completely different people.

So Penny starts to show the two geniuses what "real life" is all about.

I like this sitcom because it's hilarious. Every episode keeps me laughing non-stop. And many of the conversations in this sitcom are not only funny but also very witty. I have recommended it to many friends of mine.

轮到你了   It's Your Turn.

▶ **Word Bank on This Topic**

情景喜剧   sitcom   主要的   main

影视剧中的人物   character

加州理工   Caltech（The California Institute of Technology，美国的顶级牛校，去年该校物理专业的排名全美第一）

物理学家   physicist   聪明的   intelligent

缺乏   lack   社会交往的技能   social skills

与……沟通   communicate with   与……交流   interact with

梦想做某事   dream of doing sth.

暗恋某人   have a crush on someone（如果不明白这个短语的意思在 Facebook 上就是标准的"土人"）

天才   genius   超级搞笑的   hilarious

机智的   witty   （电视系列剧的）一集   an episode

不停地   non-stop   推荐   recommend

扩展词汇

书呆子   nerd   电视系列剧   TV series

娱乐性很强的   entertaining   （电视系列剧的）一季   a season

穿越剧   time-travel drama

绿箭侠   *Arrow*（这部 TV series 是在 Pat 最喜欢的城市之一 Vancouver 拍摄的）

绝命毒师   *Breaking Bad*   破产姐妹   *2 Broke Girls*

逍遥法外   *How to Get Away with Murder*

罪恶黑名单	*The Blacklist*	实习生格蕾	*Grey's Anatomy*
权利的游戏	*Game of Thrones*	特工卡特	*Agent Carter*
纸牌屋	*House of Cards*	绝望主妇	*Desperate Housewives*
英雄	*Heroes*	绯闻女孩	*Gossip Girl*
女子监狱	*Orange Is the New Black*	广告狂人	*Mad Men*
迷失	*Lost*	吸血鬼日记	*The Vampire Diaries*
尼基塔	*Nikita*	办公室	*The Office*
美少女的谎言	*Pretty Little Liars*	行尸走肉	*The Walking Dead*
皮囊	*Skins*	梅林传奇	*Merlin*

请参考Pat的思路，并适当借鉴这个词汇表里的单词，思考如果是您将会怎么说

　　时间充裕的同学还可以在这个网址看到英美观众最喜爱的经典电视剧

详情：www. imdb. com/chart/toptv/？ ref_ = nv_tp_tv250_2

Pat 的海外生活英语实录

　　《生活大爆炸》里的故事发生在加利福尼亚（California），它是以文化多样性（cultural diversity）而著称的一个州，所以我们在《生活大爆炸》第 9 季里也看到了华裔演员 Melissa Tang 的身影。

　　[剑桥例句] Manchester is well-known for its cultural diversity.

☆ 喜欢的电视节目之　海贼王

难度指数：★★★★☆

Pat 的答案

Let me talk about *One Piece*.

The main character of this anime series, Luffy, is the leader of the Straw Hat Pirates. He and his crew sail the seas in

search of the treasure called "One Piece", which can help him become the next King of the Pirates.

Luffy is unstoppable not only because he can gain superhuman abilities by eating the "devil fruit", but also because his crew members are very helpful. Together, they defeat strong enemies such as Crocodile and Rob Lucci.

The action in *One Piece* is fast-paced and exciting. But *One Piece* is not just about fighting. It's also about friendship, teamwork and ambition.

In other anime series, it's always like... the main character does everything. But in *One Piece*, the crew members, like Zoro, Sanji, Nami, Robin, Usopp and Chopper, are all COOL, which makes the team extremely powerful.

One Piece is a very long series, but it's not boring at all, because it really makes me think and inspires me a lot. That's why I'm a huge fan of OP.

轮到你了   It's Your Turn.

▶ Word Bank on This Topic

影视剧里的人物 character	日本动漫 anime
日本漫画 manga	系列剧 series
船员（或者机组成员）的统称 crew members	
海盗 pirate	
在海面上长时间地航行（固定短语）sail the seas	
超人类的能力 superhuman abilities	恶魔果实 devil fruit
打败 defeat	敌人 enemy
快节奏的 fast-paced	强大的 powerful
友情 friendship	团队合作 teamwork
志向，抱负 ambition	激励 inspire

休闲娱乐

扩展词汇

正面人物　hero（复数：heroes）	"反派"　villain（复数：villains）
尾田荣一郎　Eiichiro Oda	创作者　creator
妖精的尾巴　*Fairy Tail*	家庭教师　（*Hitman*）*Reborn!*
通灵王　*Shaman King*	
七龙珠　*Dragon Ball Z*（在英美有时被简称为 DBZ）	
火影忍者　*Naruto*	银魂　*Gin Tama*
周刊少年　*Jump Weekly Shōnen Jump*	死神　*Bleach*
犬夜叉　*InuYasha*	叛逆的鲁鲁修　*Code Geass*

请参考Pat的思路，并适当借鉴这个词汇表里的单词，思考如果是您将会怎么说

您还可以在这个网址看到对很多经典日本动漫的详细介绍，特别是每个介绍里的
Storyline 部分会对你很有帮助：www.imdb.com/list/ls054666938/

5. 电影

> Describe a film that you enjoyed watching.
>
> You should say:
>
>   what the film was called
>
>   what type of film it was
>
>   what it was about
>
> and explain why you enjoyed the film.

☆ 童年时看过的电影之　狮子王

难度指数：★★★☆☆

Pat 的答案

I first watched *The Lion King* as a young child, and then watched it again several times over the years.

This animated film is about a lion prince named Simba, whose uncle kills Simba's father and makes himself the ruler. But Simba is held responsible for the death of his father. So he runs away out of guilt.

Many years later, Simba is told that the kingdom is in serious trouble. So he faces up to the challenge and returns. With the help of his friends, he defeats his uncle and saves the kingdom.

I like this film because most of the characters are very cute, and the soundtrack to the film is amazing. I particularly like the song " Can You Feel the Love Tonight. " by Elton John.

The film also teaches valuable life lessons. For example, it teaches us that running away doesn't solve any problems. It also shows us the power of courage and friendship.

轮到你了　　　　　　　　　　　　　　　　　　　It's Your Turn.

▶ Word Bank on This Topic

动画片　animated film / animation	王子　prince
统治者　ruler	让某人负责任　hold sb. responsible
因为愧疚而躲开　run away out of guilt	王国　kingdom
勇敢地面对挑战　face up to the challenge	打败　defeat
电影原声专辑　soundtrack	尤其喜欢　particularly like
宝贵的　valuable	勇气　courage
友情　friendship	

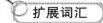
扩展词汇

剧情　plot / storyline　　　　　　　　　　小狮子（小老虎、小熊等）　cub

票房成功的电影，上座率很高的电影　a box office hit / a box office smash

小小兵，"小黄人儿"	_Minions_	功夫熊猫	_Kung Fu Panda_
很励志的	_inspiring_	续集	_sequel_
冰川时代	_Ice Age_	蓝精灵	_Smurfs_
格格巫	_Gargamel_	阿兹猫	_cat Azrael_
灰姑娘	_Cinderella_	童话	fairytale
怪物史瑞克	_Shrek_		

不能只看外表，不能以貌取人　Don't judge a book by its cover.

三维立体电影　a 3-D（它的读音就是 three-D） film

　　无论你是想了解怎样用英文描述剧情，还是想看英美观众对于一部电影的评论，这个"电影大全"都必不可少：www. imdb. com

请参考Pat的思路，并适当借鉴这个词汇表里的单词，思考如果是您将会怎么说

Pat 的海外生活英语实录

　　美版的卡通片（animation）与日版的卡通片（anime）不同，美版不论故事情节是什么，一定会有一两个可爱的卡通形象出现在电影里，但日系的则不一定。"可爱的"除了 cute 之外，adorable 也是 native speakers 形容小朋友、小动物或者卡通人物很可爱的一个常用词。

　　[**剑桥例句**] Theo is an absolutely adorable child.

☆ 搞笑电影之　失恋 33 天

难度指数：★★★★☆

Pat 的答案

I'm going to talk about _Love Is Not Blind_. It's a well-acted and well-directed romantic comedy.

It tells the story of Huang Xiao-xian, a wedding planner who finds out that her boyfriend has cheated on her. She's deeply hurt by that and she starts keeping a diary about the painful experience.

leisure

One of her colleagues, Wang Xiao-jian, has a crush on her but is often laughed at by her. Still, he helps her recover from the painful breakup, and finally wins her heart.

I enjoyed this film because the acting was good, and the story was very moving. At the same time, there were some really funny conversations between the characters. I enjoyed the film also because it reminded me of a famous saying, "Love is not blind — it just helps someone see things that others fail to see."

轮到你了　　　　　　　　　　　　　　　　It's Your Turn.

▶ **Word Bank on This Topic**

表演得很精彩的	well-acted	导演得很出色的	well-directed
情感喜剧	romantic comedy	出轨	cheat on someone
写日记	keep a diary	同事	colleague
暗恋某人	has a crush on someone	从……当中恢复过来	recover from
分手	breakup	感人的	moving
演技	acting	对话	conversation
让我想起……	remind me of...		

扩展词汇

取材自一个真实的故事　is based on a true story

改编自同名小说　is adapted from a novel of the same name

网络小说	web novel / online novel	是由……扮演的	played by...
由……执导	directed by...	拍摄得很美的	beautifully-shot
视觉上令人震撼的	is visually stunning	情节跌宕起伏的	full of twists and turns
剧情	plot / storyline	角色	part / role

前任男（女）友或者前任配偶　ex

剪刘海儿　trim someone's fringe（BrE）/ trim bangs（AmE）

小成本电影　small-budget film　　　巨大的票房成功　a huge box-office hit

（影视作品或者音乐作品）非常受欢迎的　well-received / well-liked

受到很高的评价　receive great reviews　　在（某一天）放映　was screened on…

单身人士　singles　　　　　　　　　引起……的共鸣　resonate with…

《老炮儿》　*Mr. Six*　　　　　　　　《美人鱼》　*The Mermaid*

《左耳》　*The Left Ear*　　　　　　　《匆匆那年》　*Fleet of Time*

《那些年，我们一起追的女孩》　*You Are the Apple of My Eye*

半自传体小说　semi-autobiography　　搞笑片　comedy / funny movie

超级搞笑的　hilarious　　　　　　　爱情喜剧　romantic comedy

浪漫和幽默之间的合理平衡　a right balance between romance and humour

动作片　action film　　　　　　　　充满紧张的动作场面　full of action scenes

特效　special effects　　　　　　　看起来很真实的　realistic

娱乐性很强的　entertaining　　　　　历史片　historical drama

战争片　war film　　　　　　　　　传记片　biopic

很有知识性的　educational　　　　　励志的　inspiring

令人难忘的　unforgettable　　　　　科幻片　sci-fi film

奇幻电影（像 *Harry Potter* 和 *The Lord of the Rings* 那种）　fantasy movie

恐怖片　horror film　　　　　　　　悬念片　suspense film

很有悬念的结尾　a cliffhanger ending　　贺岁片　New Year celebration film

很有喜庆气氛的　fun and festive（festival 的形容词形式）

电影的预告短片　trailer

强大的演员阵容　a strong cast（cast 就是"演员阵容"）

请参考 Pat 的思路，并适当借鉴这个词汇表里的单词，思考如果是您将会怎么说

　　Pat 的英美朋友们最喜欢的电影评论网站就是 www. rottentomatoes. com/top/，您可以在这里找到各种英美电影的 detailed reviews

在这个连影视作品也追求快节奏的年代里，虽然有一些电影的故事情节很出色（an outstanding storyline），但也有更多电影的故事情节是很"俗套的"（corny）。"剧情很俗套的"用地道英文的说法就是：The storyline is corny.

6. 歌曲之 加州明信片

> Describe a song or a piece of music you like.
>
> You should say:
>
>   what the song or piece of music is called
>
>   when you first heard it
>
>   where you first heard it
>
> and explain why you like it.

难度指数：★ ★ ★ ☆ ☆

Pat 的答案

I'm going to talk about a song I like, called *Picture Postcards from LA*. I first heard this song at a friend's home last month. Of course, LA stands for Los Angeles, the city where Hollywood is.

The lyrics of this song are about the singer himself and a waitress named Rachael. Rachael always dreams of becoming a superstar in Hollywood. And she often tells the singer about her dream. The singer is always like, " Sure, so send me picture postcards from LA. "

I like this song because it's about ordinary people and their simple lives. Both of them know this dream probably will never come true, but they're still happy and hopeful about the future. So it's a moving story.

I like this song also because the singer, Joshua Kadison, has a unique voice — a very deep and rich voice. The music of this song also makes me feel very calm and relaxed.

轮到你了　　　　　　　　　　　　　　　　　　　　It's Your Turn.

▶ Word Bank on This Topic

是……的缩写　stand for　　　　　　　　洛杉矶　Los Angeles

餐馆的女服务生　waitress　　　　　　　　歌词　lyrics

[剑桥例句]　The lyrics of this song are very moving.

……说　he's like, "…" / she's like, "…" （在英美日常生活里转述某人的话时
　　　　很常用）

普通人　ordinary people　　　　　　　　感人的　moving

独特的　unique　　　　　　　　　　　　低沉浑厚的嗓音　a deep and rich voice

⌖ 扩展词汇

给人印象深刻的，很容易记住的　very memorable

很励志的　inspiring　　　　　　　　舒缓的　slow and soothing

很有活力的　lively and energetic　　欢快的　happy and energetic

很有激情的　is full of passion　　　很有表现力的　very expressive

（歌词）寓意丰富的　very meaningful

（歌词）简单明了的　simple and straightforward

节拍　tempo　　　　　　　　　　　　旋律　rhythm

纯净自然的声音　a pure and natural voice

请参考Pat的思路，并适当借鉴这个词汇表里的单词，思考如果是您将会怎么说

　　喜欢英美音乐的朋友只要在这个网页的 search box 里输入你要找的歌名和 review 这个单词，就能够找到相关的乐评了：www.nme.com/search

　　Part 2 有时还会偷偷地把上面这个卡片题变形：Describe a song you liked as a child. 这个网站提供了世界各地的大量儿歌：www.mamalisa.com，您按照国家找到 China 就可以看到中国的儿歌了，从"小燕子"到"两只老虎"都有

Pat 的海外生活英语实录

Pat 有时会在线收听来自国内的音乐节目。现在很流行说一位歌手的表演（performance）很"给力"，那么用地道英文怎么表达呢？native speakers 会说：It's phenomenal.（phenomenal /fəˈnɔminl/ 这个词貌似很书面，其实在当代英美日常口语里的使用已经相当普及）。另外，国内影视圈最近流行说的"现象级电视节目"，其实就是 a phenomenal TV show 的对应表达。

7. 广告

> Describe an interesting advertisement you have seen.
>
> You should say：
>
>   when you first saw it
>
>   where you first saw it
>
>   what it was like
>
> and explain why it was interesting.

难度指数：★ ★ ★ ☆ ☆

Pat 的答案

I'm going to talk about an interesting commercial I saw on TV last weekend.

It was like… a man rushes to the airport，hops on a plane and flies to another city for a job interview.

After arriving at an office building，he gets into a lift and goes up to the 20th floor，looking very nervous. He looks down at his shoes，only to notice that they don't match each other. But he goes in for the interview anyway.

The man looks sad after the interview. But all of

a sudden, his mobile phone rings — he gets the job. He's so excited that he jumps into the air. Then the narrator says calmly, "Converse can always take you there."

This TV commercial was interesting because it was very creative, and the message was clear and powerful.

轮到你了

It's Your Turn.

► **Word Bank on This Topic**

在电视或者广播上面播出的广告　commercial

跳　hop

电梯　lift（英式英语）/ elevator（美式英语）

旁白　narrator　　　　　　匡威　Converse

广告要传达的信息　message　　清晰而且有说服力的　clear and powerful

扩展词汇

宣传海报　poster　　　　　　广告传单　flyer

很有效的　effective　　　　　拍摄得非常美的　beautifully-shot

可靠的　reliable　　　　　　推销新产品　promote new products

吸引人们的注意力　attract people's attention

很容易记住的广告词　a memorable slogan / a catchy slogan

有趣并且令人愉快的　fun and enjoyable

请参考Pat的思路，并适当借鉴这个词汇表里的单词，思考如果是您将会怎么说

　　如果您觉得看有创意的广告是一种享受，那就不妨看看著名的商业网站 Business Insider 评出的 2015 年度十大最佳广告：www.businessinsider.com/business-insiders-10-best-ads-of-2015-2015-12

Pat 的海外生活英语实录

　　如果要说某个广告是"针对"某类人的，地道英文里会用 is aimed at 这个短语。

　　[剑桥例句] This fast-food commercial is aimed at children.

8. 自己喜欢的网站

> Describe your favourite website.
>
> You should say:
>
> > which website it is
> >
> > how often you visited this website
> >
> > whether it's popular or not
>
> and explain why you like it.

每个人喜爱的网站并不一样，但好消息是：native speakers 在描述网站时常用的词汇和短语却相当集中，完全可以在短时间内快速掌握。

难度指数：★ ★ ★ ★ ☆

Pat 的答案

My favourite website is Yahoo.com. I'm sure you've heard a lot about it because it's one of the most popular websites in the world. I visit it every day, and I have its app on my mobile phone.

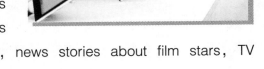

I like this website because it's very informative and entertaining. It provides a wide variety of information, like the latest world news, business updates and reports about important sports events. It also offers the latest entertainment stories, you know, news stories about film stars, TV celebrities and famous singers.

This website also has a Question-and-Answer（Q & A）section. It's like an online community where people ask questions and interact with each other. Lots of people go there to ask questions. They usually get answers very quickly. And it seems most of the answers are detailed and helpful.

休闲娱乐

Another reason I like this website is that its layout is clear and well-organised. It's user-friendly and always easy to navigate.

I like this website also because its founders, Jerry Yang and David Filo, started the website when they were just 24. Their success has inspired many young people to create new ideas and start their own businesses. So the website is not only informative but also inspiring.

轮到你了

It's Your Turn.

▶ Word Bank on This Topic

应用程序　app	信息量很大的　informative
娱乐性很强的　entertaining	最新发生的　latest
消息的更新　update	报导　report
名人　celebrities	问答部分　Q & A section
网络社区　online community	互动　interact
详细的，具体的　detailed	网站内容的布局　website layout
网页　webpage	井井有条的　well-organised
很方便使用的，"用户友好的"　user-friendly	
（网站的）导航很明确，内容很便于查找　is easy to navigate	
创建者　founder	激励（动词）　inspire
励志的（形容词）　inspiring	创造出新的想法　create new ideas

扩展词汇

点击率　hits	网络购物　online shopping
购物网站　shopping website	
社交网站　social networking website （例如：Facebook 和 Twitter）	
视频共享网站　video-sharing website （例如：YouTube 和 Youku）	
图片共享网站　photo-sharing website （例如：Instagram）	

请参考Pat的思路，并适当借鉴这个词汇表里的单词，思考如果是您将会怎么说

请求加好友　send a friend request	用户的注册信息　profile
个人信息　personal information	盗用用户名　ID theft
微博　micro-blog	名人之间的骂战　celebrity spat
关注某人　follow sb.	对某人取消关注，"取关"　unfollow sb.
"僵尸粉"　"zombie followers"	网络论坛　online forum
聊天室　chatroom	分享想法和观点　share ideas and opinions
结识新朋友　make new friends	楼主　OP

帖子　post

已经被转帖了很多次　has been reposted many times

获得很多个"赞"　get many "likes"

在网上疯传　go viral （它是最近几年在英美口语里非常流行的一个新 phrase）

上传　upload　　　　　下载　download

安装　install

收藏一个网站的网址　bookmark a site （英美口语里也常把 website 简称为 site）

热门词　buzzword　　　　虚拟的世界　the virtual world

沉迷于　be addicted to

　　著名的消费者报告（*Consumer Reports*）杂志的这个网址会让你对于网络购物有更深入的了解：www.consumerreports.org/cro/shopping-websites/buying-guide.htm

请参考Pat的思路，并适当借鉴这个词汇表里的单词，思考如果是您将会怎么说

Pat 的海外生活英语实录

　　谁都知道网站叫 website，可"网络公司"的英文是……？除了可以说 Internet company 之外，dotcom 也是地道英文里对网络公司的一种常用称呼。

[剑桥例句] A survey found that 20 of the top 150 European dotcoms could run out of cash within a year.

9. 故事

☆ 童年时听过的故事之三只小猪

> Describe a story you heard as a child.
>
> You should say：
>
> who first told you this story
>
> whether you heard it again later
>
> what the story was about
>
> and explain why you still remember this story.

难度指数：★ ★ ★ ☆ ☆

Pat 的答案

Let me talk about one of my favourite childhood stories, called *The Three Little Pigs*. I first heard the story from my grandpa, and I also heard it from some other relatives.

The story goes like this：Once upon a time there were three little pigs. They moved to a new village and built their own houses.

The first little pig built a straw house because that was easy. But the house was not strong at all. The second little pig built a stick house for himself. He didn't spend much time on it, and the house was not strong either. The third little pig was hardworking. He built a brick house. It took him a lot of time, and the house was very strong.

Then a wolf came along and blew down the first pig's straw house. The pig ran to the stick house. Then the wolf also blew down the stick house and chased the two pigs to the brick house.

The brick house was very strong. The wolf couldn't blow it down. He then tried to enter the house through the chimney and got killed in a pot of boiling water. And the three little pigs lived happily ever after.

I still remember this story because it's interesting and meaningful. It teaches us to hope for the best but prepare for the worst. It also teaches us that hard work always pays off.

轮到你了

▶ Word Bank on This Topic

在很久很久以前　Once upon a time…

从此之后快乐地生活着　lived happily ever after（经典英文童话的最常用开头和结尾，英美小朋友们全都会背）

亲戚	relatives	稻草屋	straw house
木棍搭成的屋子	stick house	用砖盖成的屋子	brick house
吹倒	blow down	追赶，追逐	chase
烟囱	chimney	沸水	boiling water

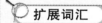 扩展词汇

寓言	fable	伊索寓言	*Aesop's Fables*
童话	fairytale		

白雪公主和七个小矮人　*Snow White and the Seven Dwarfs*

灰姑娘	*Cinderella*	皇帝的新装	*The Emperor's New Clothes*
美人鱼	*The Little Mermaid*	丑小鸭	*The Ugly Duckling*
安徒生	Hans Christian Andersen	孙悟空	The Monkey King
忠诚的	loyal	打妖精	fight against demons

童话故事的"寓意"英文怎么讲？请用 moral 这个词。注意：作"寓意"的意思时 moral 是名词。

[剑桥例句] The moral of the story is that honesty is always the best policy.

如果您还对其他儿童故事有兴趣，可以看看这个网站：etc. usf. edu/lit2go/68/fairy-tales-and-other-traditional-stories，而且还是既能读又能听

请参考Pat的思路，并适当借鉴这个词汇表里的单词，思考如果是您将会怎么说

休闲娱乐

10. 喜欢的外国文化

> Describe a foreign culture you're interested in.
>
> You should say：
>
>   which culture it is
>
>   how you learned about this culture
>
>   what you know about this culture
>
> and explain why you feel this culture is interesting.

    很多中国同学对这道题感到恐惧，因为 culture 是一个比较抽象的概念。但如果你理解考官的期待其实只是一个扣题、清晰、并适当含有细节的答案，就完全可以通过简洁的语言和适当举例来描述清楚一种外国文化。绝不要听起来活像是一位"异域文化权威"（如果你都已经深谙外国文化，那还何必非要拼尽全力考雅思出国呢?）。请牢记：IELTS 考官真正关注的是——你的英语能力。

难度指数：★ ★ ★ ☆ ☆

Pat 的答案

I'm going to talk about British culture.

I learn about British culture mostly from newspapers, magazines and television. And I have some online friends from the UK, who often share their ideas about their culture with me.

The first thing that comes to mind when I think about British culture is the historic buildings. There're many world-famous historic buildings in Britain, like Buckingham Palace and the British Museum. I really hope I can visit them someday.

I'm also very interested in British literature. So many good novels were written by British writers, such as *Pride and Prejudice*, *Robinson Crusoe*, and of course, *Harry Potter*.

Some of my favourite bands are also from the UK, like Coldplay and One

Direction. It seems there're many musically-talented people there. I also know that a lot of people in the UK like football, and I'm a big fan of Manchester United.

I'm interested in British culture because it's very different from Chinese culture. For example, Easter is an important festival in the UK, but not many people in China celebrate Easter. Another interesting difference is British people drive on the left side of the road, but we drive on the right side of the road.

I'm interested in British culture also because a good understanding of British culture can really help me improve my English skills. So I always want to learn more about it.

轮到你了   It's Your Turn.

▶ **Word Bank on This Topic**

了解······　learn about...（在英美生活口语里，learn 并不总是"学习"，也经常用来指"了解"）

网友　online friends

有重要历史意义的建筑　historic buildings

举世闻名的　world-famous / world-renowned

文学　literature

傲慢与偏见　*Pride and Prejudice*

鲁滨逊漂流记　*Robinson Crusoe*

哈利·波特　*Harry Potter*

很有音乐天赋的　musically-talented

曼联队　Manchester United

复活节　Easter

扩展词汇

旅游景点　tourist attractions

议会大楼　the Houses of Parliament（这个 house 习惯用复数，伦敦本地人也经常称它为 the Palace of Westminster）

泰晤士河　the Thames

"伦敦眼"　the London Eye（伦敦很有名的一个摩天轮 ferris wheel）

大本钟	Big Ben	去观光	go sightseeing
作者	author	简·奥斯汀	Jane Austen
丹尼尔·笛福	Daniel Defoe	罗琳	J. K. Rowling
大卫. 贝克汉姆	David Beckham	偶像	idol

非常喜欢　adore

切尔西队　Chelsea Football Club（生活里经常简称为 Chelsea）

利物浦队　Liverpool Football Club（常简称为 Liverpool）

阿森纳队　Arsenal Football Club（简称 Arsenal）

请参考Pat的思路，并适当借鉴这个词汇表里的单词，思考如果是您将会怎么说

伦敦人对伦敦地铁的昵称	"the Tube"	公共交通	public transport
高效率的	very efficient	友好而且有礼貌的	friendly and polite
性格内敛的	reserved	很有幽默感	have a good sense of humour
世界级的大学	world-class universities	炸鱼土豆条	fish and chips
传统与风俗	traditions and customs	文化遗产	cultural heritage
纪录片	documentary		

　　IELTS 口语的目标是尽可能准确地测试出你的英文口语能力，所以描述文化并不需要太深刻。但如果您考前时间充裕而且又对 culture 有深入的兴趣，就应该抽出时间来听一听 TED 嘉宾们关于文化的长篇探讨：www. ted. com/topics/world + cultures

Pat 的海外生活英语实录

　　说起英国人，中国同学们往往会想到"彬彬有礼"这个词。尽管这个词并不适合所有的英国人，但总体而言还是比较准确的。英文短语 polite and well-mannered 就等于中文"彬彬有礼的"。

　　[剑桥例句] He's polite and well mannered, and pleasant to hang out with.

Time to Branch Out.
推而广之

Describe a foreign country you wish to travel to.

补充弹药

by air　乘飞机

travel half way around the globe　到地球的另一侧

explore　探索

11. 一件艺术品之　雕塑

Describe a sculpture.

You should say：

　　where you saw the sculpture

　　what kind of sculpture it was

　　what it looked like

and explain whether you liked it or not.

难度指数：★ ★ ★ ★ ☆

Pat 的答案

I'm going to talk about a sculpture I saw at a sculpture exhibition last month. The theme of the exhibition was "The Environment".

It was an abstract sculpture dealing with the subject of environmental pollution. It looked a bit like a person sitting in a relaxed pose.

The sculpture looked calm and peaceful from a distance. But as I moved closer to it, I noticed it had cracks all over it. These cracks made the beautiful sculpture look ugly and made me feel uncomfortable.

Some working drawings for this sculpture were also on display, which I found helpful. They showed that the ugly cracks were actually designed by the artist to represent the terrible damage that pollution caused to the environment.

I liked this sculpture because it was very meaningful. And although it was an abstract sculpture, its message was strong and clear. I liked it also because it was made from recycled materials which were very eco-friendly.

轮到你了

It's Your Turn.

► Word Bank on This Topic

展览　exhibition　　　　　　　　　主题　theme

抽象雕塑　abstract sculpture

（艺术品）是关于某一主题的　deal with the subject of...

摆出很放松的姿态，摆出很放松的"pose"　in a relaxed pose

平静安详的　calm and peaceful　　　从远处　from a distance

裂缝　cracks　　　　　　　　　　布满……　all over...

雕塑家画的草图，设计雕塑用的草图　working drawings

展示　on display　　　　　　　　设计　design

象征着……　represent... / symbolise...　　寓意深刻的　meaningful

雕塑要表达的信息　message　　　循环使用的材料　recycled materials

有益于环保的　eco-friendly

扩展词汇

观赏雕塑　view the sculptures　　　雕塑家　sculptor

标题 title	具象的雕塑 realistic sculptures
看起来很逼真的 is true to life	空间 space
细节 detail	石膏 plaster
粘土 clay	石头 stone
光滑的 smooth	粗糙的 rough
直的 straight	弯曲的 curved
优雅的 elegant	很有创意的 creative
轰动效应 shock value	探索 explore
美术馆，画廊 art gallery	参观者 visitors
花园 garden	

请参考Pat的思路，并适当借鉴这个词汇表里的单词，思考如果是您将会怎么说

Part 2 有时也会考查关于 painting 的话题，这个网址可以帮助您了解很多世界名画的描述方法：totallyhistory.com/art-history/famous-paintings/

Pat 的海外生活英语实录

有很多雕塑是用金属制作的，例如 bronze sculptures（用青铜制作的雕塑），stainless steel sculptures（用不锈钢制作的雕塑）等。如果不想记那么多，也可以把所有用金属制作的雕塑统称为 metal sculptures。

[剑桥例句] We enjoyed viewing the metal sculptures in the park.

☆ 绘画（双语感悟）Bilingual Reflections

我们在 p. 135 讨论过的跟绘画有关的词汇和短语当然还可以继续用，同时可以进一步学习：

英美的 paintings 主要分成三种：风景画（landscape painting）、静物画（still life painting）和人像（portrait）。自画像叫 self-portrait，中国的水墨画我会把它叫作 Chinese ink painting。

画面的构图叫 composition，光线叫 lighting，笔触叫作 brush strokes，画布叫

休闲娱乐

canvas，画框叫 frame，画室是 a painter's studio，而画廊当然就是 gallery 了。

一幅"杰作"叫 a masterpiece。具象画叫 realistic painting，而抽象画是 abstract painting。美术欣赏课在英文里叫作 art appreciation classes。

如果画的颜色很浓，说 It has intense colours. 如果画面的颜色很鲜明，叫 It has bright，vivid colours.

全世界最有名的一幅画肯定是 *Mona Lisa*。它是一幅半身像（a half-length portrait），是大约 500 年前由达芬奇创作的（It was painted by Leonardo da Vinci about 500 years ago.）。Now it hangs in the Louvre（挂在卢浮宫里）and attracts art lovers from around the world（吸引着来自于世界各地的艺术爱好者们）.

这幅画最有名的特点就是 Mona Lisa 神秘的微笑（The most famous feature of this painting is Mona Lisa's mysterious smile.）。有的人觉得这幅画很真实（realistic），但是也有人认为她的微笑太梦幻了（a dreamy smile）。但是不管怎样，这幅画一定会在你的心里产生强烈的感受（It evokes strong feelings.）。

◣ E 物质诱惑

Pat 解题　Pat's Thought

本节我们会学到很多描述物品的地道词汇和短语。

谁都知道服装的拼写是 clothes，但却有很多同学不知道它的正确发音应该是 /kləʊðz/ √，而不是 /kləʊðiz/ ✗，因为 clothes 里面的 e 不发音。而人身上戴的配饰在地道英文里则叫 accessories，比如 earrings（耳环），bracelet（手镯），wristband（腕带）等。

在本节里我们还会学到很多 electronic devices。地道英文里还有一个很棒的名词专门指电子的小东西，叫作 gadget，考试的时候如果遇到电子产品话题不妨用 1~2 次。

当然我们还会学习更大型的 objects，比如 cars。Pat 的学生当中车迷（car buff）从来都不少，咱们可以看两种这辈子还能买得起的车型。

handicrafts（手工制作）一直是个难点，我们在本节也要突破。

一口气谈了这么多的 objects，希望我们不会变得 too materialistic（过于物质化）！

本类最有代表性的方向　Typical Topics

❋ Describe a vehicle.

❋ Describe a photo.

❋ Describe something that was made by yourself.

❋ Describe a childhood toy.

❋ Describe a gift you received.

展开本类话题的思维导图　Mind Map

（如果卡片上的 4 个提示问题仍然不能让你说出充实的答案，那么下面的思维导图可以帮助你继续扩展出扣题、充实的 ideas）

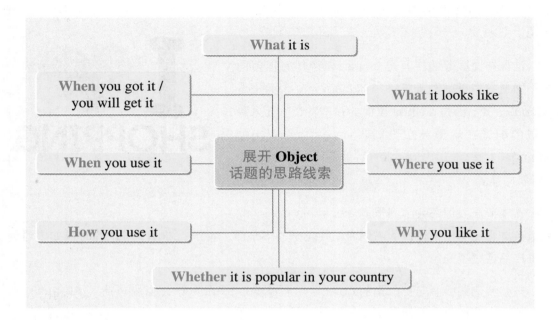

分级演示　Sample Answers

1. 交通工具

☆ 交通工具之　森林人

> Describe a vehicle you'd like to own.
>
> You should say：
>
> what the vehicle is
>
> what it is like
>
> whether it would be expensive to buy
>
> and explain why you'd like to own it.

Pat 发现国内的男同学们一提起真正适合"男僧"开的车就会立刻想到"悍马"（Hummer），可在油价飞涨、全球都"Go green."的年代里，像 Hummer 这样的"油老虎"（gas-guzzler）即使真能买得起也不是谁都能养得起的。去年在美国和加拿大进行的一项最新调查显示，Subaru Forester 拥有很多受过良好教育（well-educated）的男性车主（male car owners），它的左右对称全时四轮驱动（symmetrical all wheel drive）也正在悄悄地改变着英美传统观念中的"猛男"形象。

当然，你说什么车型考官都会欣然接受，因为考官真正关心的问题只是你有没有能力用地道的英语给出一个扣题、清晰、自然的描述。

Porsche 911

classic style

难度指数 ★★★☆☆

Pat 的答案

I'm going to describe a car I'd like to own, which is a Subaru Forester.

The outside of the car looks sporty and attractive, and the build quality feels good.

The inside is spacious and practical. The headroom and legroom are perfect for me, and there's a lot of cargo room in the back. The handling of the car is also very good.

I'd like to own a Forester because it looks nice and it's fun to drive. It also has comfortable seats and plenty of cargo space. But it costs much less than a luxury SUV like a BMW X3 or an Audi Q5. So it's good value for money.

I test-drove a Forester last week and was very impressed with it. I'm pretty sure I'll buy one later this year or sometime next year.

轮到你了

It's Your Turn.

► Word Bank on This Topic

有运动感的　sporty

有吸引力的　attractive

物品

车身的工艺　build quality（注意：在这个固定短语里不要用 building）

宽敞而且实用的　spacious and practical

头顶距离顶棚的空间　headroom

腿部的活动空间　legroom（这两个词里的 room 不是指房间而是指空间）

车身后部的储物空间　cargo room / cargo space

操控性能　handling　　　　　　　　　能够提供驾驶乐趣　is fun to drive

舒适的座椅　comfortable seats　　　　豪华级 SUV　luxury SUV

它的性价比很高　It's good value for money.

试驾　test-drive（过去时 test-drove）

扩展词汇

发动机　engine　　　　　　　　　　　动力很足　It has plenty of power.

可靠耐用的　reliable　　　　　　　　　省油的　fuel-efficient

时尚的　stylish　　　　　　　　　　　车或建筑的外观　exterior

内部空间　interior　　　　　　　　　　车的各项功能非常齐全　It's fully-loaded.

行车时的噪音很小　It's quiet on the road.　豪华的　luxurious

豪华车，高端车（固定短语）　luxury car　经济型车　affordable car

跑车　sports car　　　　　　　　　　　电动车　electric car

房车　RV / motor home

全驱系统　the all-wheel-drive system/ the AWD system（全驱系统在冰天雪地或者路
　　　　　面湿滑的地方很有用，而森林人特有的 symmetrical AWD system 更是连续
　　　　　数年被评为雪地表现最佳的全驱系统）

四驱　four wheel drive（对付雨雪天气这个也还行）

前驱　front wheel drive（它对付雨雪天气就会有点吃力了）

车的转向性能　steering　　　　　　反应很灵敏的　very responsive

请参考Pat的思路，并适当借鉴这个词汇表里的单词，思考如果是您将会怎么说

object　　　　　　　　　　　　278

二手车的售出价格　resale value（有些人把"老外"全想象成富翁，其实在英美"负翁"也不少，开二手车甚至五、六手车的励志哥们也不在少数）

您可以在这个网站看到所有英国常见车型的详细介绍（页面左上角 Choose a make 里面的 make 是名词，指车的品牌，model 则是指车的具体型号）：www. autocar. co. uk/car-reviews

Pat 的海外生活英语实录

如果要说车或者其他物品"定价合理的"，地道英文里常用合成词 reasonably-priced。

[剑桥例句] The car is fun to drive and reasonably-priced.

☆ 交通工具之 Mini-Cooper

Pat 发现国内的女同学们在说这道题时也总爱抛出一堆超级难词，彪悍程度已经不亚于一些猛男。"女汉子们"真应该试试用简单但是地道的英文更加清晰地描述这个话题。

难度指数：★★★☆☆

Pat 的答案

I'd really like to buy a Mini Cooper. A friend of mine bought a Mini Cooper last month. It cost her around 250, 000 *yuan*. But I would say it looks like a 500, 000 *yuan* car. （在真实的英文谈话里像 I would say…这类小短语特别多，其实并不是真就"非说不可"，但说了就更像是人与人之间的交谈，而不再是机器与机器之间的互殴）

The car looks very cute, like a chubby baby because it looks solid and compact. The inside is actually pretty spacious. The front seats feel very comfortable, and there's plenty of headroom. The back seats are a bit small, but I guess they would be large enough for children.

物　品

The car is well-equipped. I particularly like the backup camera because it makes parking easier and safer. The speakers also sound very impressive.

Unlike Beetles，Mini has a powerful engine. It's also fuel-efficient. That's really good news when the petrol price is still very high.

I'm sure I'll buy a Mini Cooper too because it's so fun and comfortable to drive，and it offers good value for money.

轮到你了

It's Your Turn.

▶ **Word Bank on This Topic**

胖乎乎的　chubby	结实紧凑的　solid and compact
宽敞的　spacious	前排座椅　front seats
后排座椅　back seats	头顶到顶棚的空间　headroom
设备先进的　well-equipped	倒车摄像头　backup camera / rearview camera
扬声器　speakers	停车　parking
与……不一样　unlike…	"甲壳虫"　Beetle
弧线型的车身　curved body	强劲的发动机　a powerful engine
省油的　fuel-efficient	
汽油价格　petrol price（英式英语）/ gas price（美式英语）	
它的性价比很高　It is（或者 It offers）good value for money.	

🔍 扩展词汇

车或建筑的外观　exterior	车或建筑的内部　interior
皮座椅　leather seats	停车位　parking spot / parking space
低油耗　good gas mileage / good fuel economy	
羡慕　envy	方向盘　steering wheel
手动档　stick shift / manual	自动挡　automatic（transmission）
敞篷车　convertible	跑车　sports car

object

流线型的　streamlined

底盘　chassis（真正爱车的人都明白：engine 和 chassis 其实才是最重要的，车的外观其实真心不值多少钱）

商务用车（车的正面是倾斜的那种长面包车）　minivan / MPV（可别说成 MVP ☺）

车的品牌　make（这时它作名词）车的型号　model

Pat 自己买车的时候通常会先到这个网站上比较 car reviews（车评）然后再"出手"：www.thecarconnection.com/new-cars。您在出国之前可以把它作为熟悉用英文介绍汽车的好工具，出国之后如果确实需要买车也不妨把它作为有用的参考。

国内同学们经常会发错音的汽车品牌（请注意听音频）

Mercedes Benz　（英文口语里经常只用前面的第一个词来指"奔驰"）

Volkswagen　大众	Hyundai　现代	Lexus　雷克萨斯
Lamborghini　兰博基尼	Cadillac　卡迪拉克	Volvo　沃尔沃
Porsche　保时捷	Farrari　法拉利	Audi　奥迪
Land Rover　陆虎	Rolls Royce　劳斯莱斯	Bentley　宾利
Renault　雷诺	Citroen　雪铁龙	Mazda　马自达
Nissan　日产	Toyota　丰田	

Chevrolet　（生活里也经常简称为 Chevy）雪佛兰

下面这两个品牌同学们一般不会说错，但也一起列出来吧：

BMW　宝马　　　　　　　　Honda　本田

请参考Pat的思路，并适当借鉴这个词汇表里的单词，思考如果是您将会怎么说

Pat 的海外生活英语实录

Pat 在新泽西的加油站加油时每次都会听到不堪汽油涨价之苦的哥们儿骂上几句。应该怎样用地道的英文来说一辆车"很费油"？地道英文里常用 It's a gas-guzzler（发音/gæsˈgʌzlə/）. 来表达对喝油无极限的"油老虎"的无奈。

[剑桥例句] Gas-guzzlers are expensive to drive because they use more fuel.

物　品

2. 电子产品

> Describe something electronic that you use often.
>
> You should say:
>
> what it is
>
> where you bought it
>
> what you use it for
>
> and explain why you like it.

☆ 电子产品之　**iPhone**

Pat 指南

"安卓粉" 也不必 complain，因为您不但可以借鉴这个答案的 ideas 和 words and phrases，而且还可以在"扩展词汇"里看到对描述安卓手机很有用的地道词汇和短语 ☺

难度指数：★ ★ ★ ☆ ☆

Pat 的答案

I'm going to describe my iPhone. I waited in line outside our local Apple store for hours to buy it. It's really worth the waiting!

I've used many smartphones. My iPhone is definitely the best. It's thin and light, and the Retina display is sharp and clear.

I use it to browse the Web, play music and games, and take pictures. The image quality of the 8-megapixel camera is amazing.

And of course, I use it for phone calls and text messages. The call quality is pretty good. Sometimes I also use the maps on my phone to get directions.

object

I like my iPhone because it's fun to use and looks great. It's also very easy to carry. It helps me keep in touch with family and friends.

轮到你了 It's Your Turn.

▶ Word Bank on This Topic

电子用品 electronic device / electronic gadget（后面这个数码迷们更爱用）

排队 wait in line

确实值得等这么久 It's really worth the waiting.

智能手机 smartphone

很薄而且很轻的 thin and light

"视网膜" 显示屏 Retina display

（显示效果）锐利清晰的 sharp and clear

上网 browse the Web / surf the Internet

（相机的）成像质量 image quality

百万像素 megapixel

短信 text messages

通话质量 call quality

确定行进路线 get directions

和亲友们保持联系 keep in touch with family and friends / stay connected with family and friends

扩展词汇

做工精美的 well-built

便于携带的 portable

非常漂亮的 gorgeous

很时尚的 stylish

触摸屏 touch screen

铃声 ring tone

令人愉快的 pleasant

屏幕 screen / display

高分辨率的 HD / high-definition

（色彩）鲜明的 vivid

（色彩）准确的 accurate

内置相机 built-in camera

存储容量 storage capacity

接听电话的效果 reception quality

电池充一次电之后的使用时间 battery life（不要只看字面误解为电池的终生寿命）

特色功能　features

触摸验证功能　Touch ID

语音激活的　voice-activated

世界上销量最大的智能手机　the world's top selling smartphone

使用安卓系统的手机　an Android phone / an Android-based phone

不像苹果手机那么贵　is less expensive than an iPhone

设计得很合理的　well-designed

方便使用的　user-friendly

把它轻松地放进口袋　slip it into my pocket

它的性价比很高　It's good value for money.

天气预报应用程序　weather app

视频播放应用程序　video-player app

健身应用程序　fitness app / work-out app

重要事务列表应用程序　to-do list app

穿戴设备　wearable device

健身手环　fitness band 或者 fitness tracker

指纹传感器　fingerprint sensor

私人助理　personal assistant

限量版　limited edition / special edition

可靠耐用的　reliable

SD 卡槽　SD card slot

应用程序　apps

音乐播放应用程序　music-player app

打视频电话　make video calls

地图应用程序　map app

简单实用的　simple and practical

智能手表　smartwatch

> 请参考Pat的思路，并适当借鉴这个词汇表里的单词，思考如果是您将会怎么说

　　喜欢数码产品的朋友应该经常登录这个网站，因为它不仅对备考 Part 2 有帮助，更是数码爱好者们的乐园：www. engadget. com/reviews/cellphones

Time to Branch Out.
推而广之

Describe a gift you received.

Describe something that you lost.

补充弹药

Extra Ammo

a thoughtful gift　很"贴心"的礼物　　precious　珍贵的

It's the thought that counts. 　（固定习语）最重要的是心意。

brings back fond memories　唤起美好的回忆

looked high and low for…　到处找……

upset　心烦的，"很郁闷的"　　　regret doing sth. 　后悔做某事

☆ 电子产品之　*iPad Air*

Pat 指南

在英美生活过的人都知道：Apple 在当地大学生当中确实拥有相当高的忠诚度（enjoys such a high level of loyalty among university students）。每次做集体 presentation 的时候，放眼望去尽是一个个闪亮的 Mac 大白苹果。很多英美年轻人虽然躺在沙发上用 iPad 的时候经常砸到鼻子或者门牙，可还是痴心不改（They're hooked on Apple's stuff.）。

Pat 并不关心您是一个"果粉"（an Apple fan）还是一个"果黑"（an Apple detractor）。我只想向您证明：只要思路清晰、扣题，即使是像电子产品这样的"技术性卡片"也同样可以用浅显易懂的英文来清楚地描述。

难度指数　★ ★ ★ ☆ ☆

Pat 的答案

I'm going to talk about my iPad Air. I bought it from the Apple online store.

It's very thin and light. I can easily carry it with just one hand. I guess that's why it's called iPad "Air".

The screen looks sharp and clear. Colours are bright and vivid. And I have to say the iSight camera is almost too good for a tablet. The image quality is amazing，and it can also record HD videos.

物　品

What else? The battery life... I can spend a whole afternoon on my iPad Air and still don't need to recharge the battery. So the battery life is pretty good.

I use my iPad to send and receive emails, watch films, read e-books and play games. I also often use it to take pictures and record videos. It's always easy to carry and fun to use.

轮到你了

It's Your Turn.

▶ Word Bank on This Topic

网店　online store	很薄而且很轻的　thin and light
（屏幕的显示效果）锐利清晰的　sharp and clear	
（色彩）鲜明的　vivid	（相机的）成像质量　image quality
拍摄高清晰的视频　record HD videos	给电池充电　recharge the battery
一次充电之后能够使用的时间　battery life　（注意：不要误解成"电池寿命"）	
看电子书　read e-books	拍视频　record videos

扩展词汇

使用安卓系统的平板电脑　Android tablet / Android-based tablet

可靠耐用的　reliable

便于携带的　portable　（反义词：bulky /ˈbʌlki / 笨重的，不方便携带的）

存储容量　storage capacity	笔记本电脑　laptop

操作系统　operating system　（例如 Windows 和 Mac）

处理器　processor

上网　browse the Web / surf the Internet

电子游戏机　game console　（在英美家庭玩得比较多的是 Wii /wiː/，PlayStation Vita, Xbox One 和 Nintendo 3DS）

数码相机　digital camera	可以轻松地放进口袋的　pocket-sized
触摸屏　touch screen	光学变焦　optical zoom
数码变焦　digital zoom	感光器　sensor

捕捉人生里的宝贵瞬间　capture precious moments in life

网络摄像头　webcam　　　　　打视频电话　make vide calls

优盘　USB disk（native speakers 有时也把它称为 USB drive）

USB 接口　USB port

把它和电脑连接起来　connect it to a computer

传输速度　transfer rate

　　这个网址堪称"英伦家电大全"，而且对各种产品都提供了详细的 product information：www. dixons. co. uk/gbuk/index. html

请参考Pat的思路，并适当借鉴这个词汇表里的单词，思考如果是您将会怎么说

Pat 的海外生活英语实录

　　Apple 的很多产品已经超出了生活必需品（necessities）的范围，而是为我们提供了更多休闲放松的选择。"休闲放松"除了 relax 之外，还有个 native speakers 相当常用的动词叫 unwind（发音/ʌnˈwaind/）。

　　[剑桥例句] Cooking a meal is a good way to unwind after a stressful day at work.

3. 照片

☆ 照片之　与人合影

> Describe a photo that you like.
>
> You should say:
>
> 　　what the photo is
>
> 　　when it was taken
>
> 　　where it was taken
>
> and explain why you like it.

物　品

Pat 指南 🔊

　　有很多同学喜欢 Ed Sheeran 的那首 Photograph，但却觉得这道题即使用中文说也绝难说到 1′30″以上，而且即使勉强说了一点也会很生硬（unnatural）。

　　确实，即使让考生用自己的母语描述一张 photo 都会很难，因为照片是平面的（two-dimensional），就算放大之后也就只有那么大，只能从照片的一个 corner 描述到另一个 corner。但题目里明确问了 when，where，why 等问题，所以适当谈谈拍照的经过和自己的感受不仅是扣题的，而且也是考官期待的。

　　比如描述过春节时全家人一起拍的一张照片，和父母一起度假时在一个旅游景点拍的一张照片，参加一个朋友的婚礼时与新娘（bride）和新郎（groom）一起拍的照片，参加某个考试拿到成绩之后的一张自拍（selfie）等等，都可以自然、扣题地谈出一些照片之外的内容。如果说拍到了一个名人（celebrity）的照片也不错，因为还可以合理合法地把这个名人描述 **2~3** 句（但不要太多 Less is more.）。

难度指数：★★★★☆

┌─────────────┐
│ Pat 的答案 │
└─────────────┘

I'm going to talk about a photo I like. It was taken last month while I was at the Hong Kong airport, waiting for my flight.

It was like… I was chatting with some friends. All of sudden, I noticed a man who looked exactly like… (*the celebrity's name*).

… is … （这里可以自然地加入 2~3 句介绍这个 celebrity 的内容，不要长，注意这部分可以用现在时）

So I became curious. I went up to him and asked if he was … He smiled politely and nodded. I was so excited because I'd never thought I could meet him in real life.

I told him I really liked his films (*or songs, music videos, TV shows*). I also took out my mobile phone and asked him if I could take a selfie with him.

He was like, " Sure！" Then he smiled and posed

object

for the picture. He even said "cheese"!

After I returned home, I printed out the picture and hung it on my living room wall, and I've shown it to many friends.

I like the picture because it reminds me of a very exciting experience. I'd never thought such a famous person could be so friendly and approachable.

轮到你了 — It's Your Turn.

▶ Word Bank on This Topic

机场 airport		航班 flight	
聊天 chat		突然间 all of a sudden	
好奇的 curious		很礼貌地微笑 smile politely	
点头 nod		拍自拍照 take a selfie	
摆姿势 pose			

说"茄子" say "cheese"（中文照相说"茄子"，英文照相说 cheese"奶酪"）

打印出来 print out　　把它挂在……上面 hang（过去时 hung）it on…

让我想起…… remind me of…　平易近人的 approachable

扩展词汇

把照片放在像框里 get the picture framed

很值得回忆的经历 a memorable experience

令人愉快的经历 an enjoyable experience

家庭照片 family photo　　集体的合影 group photo

（某个人或某个事物）让我一整天都很开心 … really made my day!

编辑照片 edit the photo　　图片编辑应用程序 photo-editing app

　　这个网址不仅含有很多与拍照有关的地道词汇和短语，而且也是"实用自拍指南"：www.wikihow.com/Take-Good-Selfies

请参考Pat的思路，并适当借鉴这个词汇表里的单词，思考如果是您将会怎么说

物品

Pat 的海外生活英语实录

说一个人 "很上镜"，不能说 very good on a camera，而要说 He's /She's very photogenic. (/ˌfəutəuˈdʒenik /)。而说一个人 "不喜欢照相"，在地道英文里则要说 He's / She's camera-shy. (面对镜头害羞)

[剑桥例句] Chloe is very photogenic. She has the type of face that looks attractive in a photo.

Time to Branch Out.
推而广之

Describe an important letter you received / you wrote.

补充弹药

a nice surprise   惊喜   an admission letter   录取通知

confirmed my place on the degree programme I applied for
确认我获得了我所申请的学位项目里的一个名额

a job offer letter   表示愿意提供一个工作职位的信

got the job I applied for   得到了我申请的工作职位

accept the job offer   接受该职位   an apology letter   道歉信

a thank-you letter   感谢信   moving   感人的

This letter really made my day.   这封信让我一整天都很高兴

Extra Ammo

4. 手工制作 (handicraft)

☆ 手工制作之 风筝

Describe something you made.

You should say:

what the thing was

> why you made it
>
> how you made it
>
> and explain whether you still have it today.

Pat 指南

北京给 Pat 印象最深的是什么？不是 the Forbidden City，也不是 the courtyard houses，更不是 Peking Roast Duck，而是晴天时北京天空上的风筝，那么自由，那么悠闲（carefree）。世界各地的城市我去了很多，但就是没有一个城市的人会像北京人这么爱放风筝，这是简单的快乐（the simple pleasures of life）。上课练习的时候，Pat 让很多孩子描述 making a kite，但怎么听都是像在背百科辞典（encyclopedia）。真想试试能不能用简单、清晰的英语来把这个过程说清楚。

难度指数：★ ★ ★ ☆ ☆

┌─ Pat 的答案 ─┐

Let me talk about a simple kite I made for my cousin last week. As I'd never made a kite before, I thought it would be hard. But it turned out that making a kite was actually easy and fun.

I decided on the shape of the kite first. It seemed to me that making a square kite would take less time. A square kite would also be easier for my cousin to carry.

So I went to an arts and crafts shop near my home and got a piece of coloured paper and two long plastic sticks.

I took them home and drew a large square on the paper with a pencil. And I asked my cousin to cut out the shape with scissors.

Then I tied the plastic sticks together with a piece of string to make a "T" shape. This would be the frame of the kite.

After that, I glued the paper square to the frame. I also attached the flying line

物 品

to the kite, and it was ready for its first flight.

We went to a park to fly it. The wind was pretty strong, so the kite went straight up and soared into the sky. Our hard work really paid off.

My cousin took the kite home. He really liked the kite, but I have no idea where it is now. Maybe he still keeps it at home, or maybe he's thrown it away. He's just an 8-year-old child, anyway...

轮到你了   It's Your Turn.

▶ **Word Bank on This Topic**

表弟/表妹/表姐/表哥	cousin	没想到却是……	It turned out that...
在……方面做出选择	decide on...	正方形	square
卖美术和手工用品的商店	arts and crafts shop	彩纸	coloured paper
塑料棍	plastic stick	画	draw（过去时：drew）
铅笔	pencil	剪出（某个图形）	cut out
剪刀	scissors	把……绑到一起	tie... together
线绳	string	支架	frame
粘起来	glue	固定到……上面	attach... to...
风筝的控制线	flying line	首次飞行	first flight / maiden flight
放风筝	fly the kite	冲上高空	soar into the sky
（努力）有回报	pay off（过去时：paid off）		

扩展词汇

圆形	circle	长方形	rectangle
三角形	triangle	椭圆形	oval
螺丝刀	screwdriver	镊子	tweezers
钳子	pliers	把……弄弯	bend
把……拧起来	twist	折纸	paper folding

请参考Pat的思路，并适当借鉴这个词汇表里的单词，思考如果是您将会怎么说

object   292

剪纸　paper cutting

缝制　knitting（其实有不少英美老奶奶也喜欢 "打毛衣"）

陶艺　pottery

　　这个网站提供了很多手工制作的详细过程，时间充分的同学不妨看一看：www. kidspot. com. au/things-to-do/collection/craft-activities？sort =title

Pat 的海外生活英语实录

　　自己动手制作物品可以提高人们，特别是儿童，解决实际问题的能力。在地道英文里怎样表达 "解决实际问题的能力" 呢？native speakers 就是用简单、自然的短语 problem-solving skills。

　　[剑桥例句] Educational toys can improve children's problem-solving skills.

Time to Branch Out.
推而广之

Describe a toy.

　　什么是 toys？*Longman* 和 *Oxford* 的定义是 objects for children to play with，所以 kite 本身也是 toy。您不妨再看看：www. toysrus. com ，在这里你将看到的玩具绝对比你这辈子见过的玩具都多，在页面左上角你既可以选择 Boys' Toys 或者 Girls' Toys，也可以根据不同的年龄（Age）来选择，更棒的是每个玩具的 Overview 下面还有 More details. 可以让你充分享受一次 "返老还童" 的感觉😊

补充弹药

Rubik's Cube　魔方（英语里 "拼魔方" 叫作 solve a Rubik's Cube）

puzzle　拼图游戏　　　　Lego blocks　乐高积木

educational toys　益智玩具

Extra Ammo

物　品

补充弹药

marbles　当它指玩具时并不是指大理石，而是指玻璃弹子

toy car　玩具汽车　　　　toy mobile phone　玩具手机

remote-controlled cars / radio-controlled cars　遥控汽车

Barbie doll　芭比娃娃

5．服装

☆ 服装之　旗袍／唐装

Describe an piece of clothing you like.

You should say：

　　what it is

　　what it looks like

　　when you wear it

and explain why you like it.

Pat 指南

Part 2 里还有一个题目是 Describe your favourite traditional clothing。所以如果准备旗袍（chi-pao）或者唐装，就把两个难题一起解决了。

Pat 在中国时看到唐装有很多翻译方法，但是多数的英文听起来都很别扭（They sound awkward.）。我会叫它 Tang suit，至少听起来还是自然地道的英文。

说唐装和旗袍会有一些相似的内容，但 Pat 个人感觉唐装比较宽松（loose-fitting），而且它的效果主要是让男士看起来更富贵（look wealthy and important），而旗袍是紧身的（close-fitting），而且效果主要是让女士看起来更优雅（elegant）。

难度指数：★ ★ ★ ★ ☆

object

Pat 的答案

I'm going to talk about my chi-pao. It was a birthday gift from my parents.

It's basically a one-piece, close-fitting dress. But it looks special because it's made from silk which is smooth and shiny. The bell-like sleeves, the colourful pattern and the slits on the sides also make it very different from other dresses.

I only wear my chi-pao on special occasions. For example, I wear it during Spring Festival family celebrations and at formal parties, such as business parties. I also wore it at my best friend's wedding last year.

I like it because it's easy to slip on and comfortable to wear. I like it also because it's beautiful and elegant, and makes me feel special and confident.

轮到你了   It's Your Turn.

▶ Word Bank on This Topic

连衣裙　dress	宽松的　loose-fitting
丝绸　silk	光亮的　smooth and shiny
像铃铛那样的袖子　bell-like sleeves	花纹　pattern
服装侧面的窄缝，"开气儿"　slit	特殊的场合　special occasion
家庭的庆祝活动　family celebration	穿上　slip on / put on
优雅的　elegant	

扩展词汇

独特的　unique	代表　represent
"国宝"，一个国家特有的事物　national treasure	

请参考Pat的思路，并适当借鉴这个词汇表里的单词，思考如果是您将会怎么说

物　品

清朝	the Qing dynasty	满族女性	Manchurian women
身份和地位的象征	status symbol	面料	fabric
缎子	brocade	棉	cotton
长袖子	long sleeves	短袖子	short sleeves
姿态优美的	graceful	家庭团聚	family reunion
制服	uniform	餐馆的男服务生	waiter
餐馆的女服务生	waitress	复杂的花纹	complicated pattern
鲜花图案	floral pattern	服装上的条纹装饰	stripes
服装上的圆点装饰	polka dots	衬衣（男式）	shirt
衬衣（女式）	blouse	牛仔裤	jeans
牛仔上衣	denim jacket	毛衣（正面不带扣子的毛衣）	sweater
毛衣（正面有一排扣子的毛衣）	cardigan	适合春秋穿的长袖运动衫	sweatshirt
"帽衫儿"	hoodie	休闲的	casual

　　Part 2 里还有这样一张卡片：Describe a piece of jewellery（首饰）you like. 它的出现频率很低，如果赶上这个卡片，真要好好反思一下考前自己是否虐待过小动物或者坐公车时没给老年人让座了。但讲讲是谁送给你的，为什么要送给你，你收到时的心情和你为什么喜欢它，也已经能说出不少扣题的内容了。首饰的具体描述有时间的话可以看看伦敦著名的 Harrods 官网：www. harrods. com，在搜索栏输入 jewellery，您就可以在每个商品的页面上看到 Overview 和 Details 了。咱们不必考虑价格，因为"只看一看也是享受"（The website is a feast for the eyes. ☺）

Pat 的海外生活英语实录

　　"传统服装"除了可以叫 traditional clothing，地道英文里还有一个短语 traditional costume 也是指有特色的传统服装。

　　[剑桥例句] The child was dressed in a traditional costume.

下面是最有名的一些时尚名牌，很多还没有标准的中文翻译，请仔细听音频中的发音（它们当中大多数都不是英语，所以发音还是很 tricky 的 ☺）

BURBERRY	FENDI	CHANEL
GUCCI	CHOLE	HERMES
BVLGARI	DOLCE&GABBANA	LOUIS VUITTON
VERSACE	SALVATORE FERRAGAMO	MARC JACOBS
ANNA SUI	SWAROVSKI	GIVENCHY

☆ 自行车 （双语感悟）Bilingual Reflections

Describe an invention（before the age of computers）.

计算机之前的发明，bicycle 也许是最值得我们继续使用而且也最环保（eco-friendly）的一种了。

首先，It was invented in the late 19th century by some Frenchmen. 然后，It became popular soon after it was invented，because it didn't cost much and it was easy to ride. 立刻流行起来了，原因就是既不贵又好骑。

Now millions of people ride their bikes every day. Some people cycle to work or school.（骑自行车上班或者上学）Others ride their bikes just for fun.（另一些人就是为了骑车的乐趣）Cycling is also a good form of exercise.（骑车当然也是很好的锻炼方式）

再了解一下 bicycle 的各个部分（parts）：

铃铛叫 bell，不过好像我在北京骑过的几辆车铃铛都不响（The bell didn't work.）。车把叫作 handlebars，车闸叫 brakes，横梁是 crossbar，车座叫 saddle，脚踏板是 pedals，链条叫 chain，轮子当然就是 tyres（BrE）/tires（AmE）了。

有些比较贵的自行车还有变速器，native speakers 把这个东东叫作 shifter。

如果自行车很新就说 It's brand-new. 已经比较旧了就说 It's a bit worn-out.，如果已经很久没骑过了，就说 It's gathering dust now（在"积累灰尘"）。

物 品

　　国内同学们爱用的 biking 在英美其实也经常可以说成 cycling，很多英美小朋友在早晨出门之前甚至还会特意问父母，"Can I cycle to school today?"

　　在北京如果 cycling 时还戴头盔肯定会被认为是小题大做（make a fuss about nothing）。但在英美，骑自行车时戴头盔（wear a helmet while riding a bike）实在太常见了，在美国有些州甚至明确规定 18 岁以下的孩子不戴头盔是违法的，连警察叔叔都要管。所以如果坚定地说一句 I always wear a helmet while riding my bike.，会让 native speaker 考官觉得你这人特有责任感（You're a responsible and reliable person.）。

　　在 Day 7 里面我们讲过 cycling 的各种好处当然也都可以拿过来说一说，而且还可以继续扩展，比如：Bicycles don't need any fuel（不需要燃料），so they can help us save money. 当然还有环境原因：Cycling is very eco-friendly because it's zero-emission（零排放）.

F 事件和经历

Pat 解题　Pat's Thought

在英文里说到 an event 或者 an experience 的时候经常会用到下面这些短语（不一定每一个都会用到，但是常会用到其中的几个）：At first, …; But then, …; So…; After that, …; Then…; …shortly afterwards（很短的时间之后）; Finally, …这些短语可以帮助我们把事件的顺序讲得很清楚。

今天我们还会谈到人生中一个重要的 event — wedding。如果说东西方婚礼的差异，Pat 观察到的是西方的婚礼仪式（wedding ceremony）更强调 spirituality（精神意义），而中国的婚礼仪式则更务实（practical），比如"闹洞房"（The couple's friends mess around in their bedroom.）就有很喜庆的效果，好玩儿。

本类最有代表性的方向　Typical Topics

❋ Describe a sports event.

❋ Describe a special meal.

❋ Describe a happy event.

❋ Describe a success you achieved.

❋ Describe an important change in your life.

展开本类话题的思维导图　Mind Map

（如果卡片上的 4 个提示问题仍然不能让你说出充实的答案，那么下面的思维导图可以帮助你继续扩展出扣题、充实的 ideas）

经　历

分级演示　Sample Answers

1. 开心的事件之　毕业典礼

> Describe a happy event.
>
> You should say:
>
> > what it was
> >
> > where it was held
> >
> > who went to the event
>
> and explain why it was a happy event.

Pat 指南

中国同学们熟悉的 happy event 选择很多，比如生日聚会（birthday party），迎接新年的聚会（New Year's Eve party），婚礼（wedding）等等。只要扣题、清晰、自然的答案就是好答案。正如考官们自己常说的，"It's not what you say. It's how you say it."

难度指数：★ ★ ★ ★ ☆

Pat 的答案

Let me talk about my graduation ceremony. It was held at the main assembly hall of my university.

My classmates and I arrived at the assembly hall very early. We were really happy and excited, and all of us were dressed in caps and gowns.

After all the graduates and guests were seated, the chancellor gave a welcome speech and congratulated us on our success. Then he read out our names, one by one, shook hands with us, and handed us our degree certificates. That was one of the happiest moments of my life.

After the ceremony, my friends and I took lots of pictures together outside the assembly hall.

experience

300

The graduation ceremony was a really happy event because we'd worked so hard to earn our degrees. The ceremony was a celebration of our academic achievements. We were happy and excited also because the ceremony marked the beginning of a new stage in our lives.

轮到你了 It's Your Turn.

▶ **Word Bank on This Topic**

礼堂　assembly hall（在英美大学里通常都是用人名来命名教学楼或者礼堂，直接叫 … Hall）

毕业典礼用的 "博士帽" 和 "袍子"　cap and gown（这是在英美校园里最常听到的说法，如果想正式一点还可以说 mortarboard and gown，但也有些人就很轻松地说 hat and robe）

就座　be seated

大学的校长　chancellor（英）/ president（美）

副校长　vice-chancellor（英国的大学校长通常只在仪式上能看到，真正的 "实权派" 其实是副校长 ☺）

做欢迎演讲　give a welcome speech　　　　出席　attend

祝贺　congratuate（动词）/ congratulation（名词）

读出　read/riːd/ out（过去时：read /red/ out）

握手　shake hands（过去时：shook hands）

递给　hand（过去时：handed）　　　学位证书　degree certificates

人生里最高兴的时刻之一　one of the happiest moments of my life

通过努力获得学位　earn our degrees

庆祝　celebration（名词）/ celebrate（动词）

学业成就　academic achievements　　　标志着　mark

我们人生里的一个新阶段　a new stage in our lives

🔍 **扩展词汇**

中学校长　headmaster（英式）/ principal（美式）

毕业证书　diploma　　　　　登台　walk onto the stage

从台上一边走到另一边　walk across the stage

特邀演讲者　guest speaker　　　感人的演讲　a moving speech

励志的演讲　an inspiring speech

流下喜悦激动的泪水　cried tears of joy and excitement

相互拥抱　hug each other　　　分享喜悦　share the happiness

请参考Pat的思路，并适当借鉴这个词汇表里的单词，思考如果是您将会怎么说

　　这个网址堪称伦敦的 events 大全，而且其中有不少是 happy events：
www. timeout. com/london/things-to-do/events-festivals

Pat 的海外生活英语实录

　　毕业典礼之所以让人快乐，是因为它让我们感到"自己所有的辛勤努力都有了回报"，native speakers 会说 All of our hard work paid off.

2. 体育事件

> Describe a sports event.
>
> You should say:
>
> 　　what it was
>
> 　　where it was held
>
> 　　who went to the event
>
> and explain why it was special.

Pat 指南

　　最容易准备、不需要特别的专业知识的，肯定是 the Olympic Games。权威的朗文词典对 the Olympic Games 的英文定义就是：an international sports event held every four years。奥运会完全符合题目的各项要求，但关键是怎样用简单的英文把它描述清楚。

在历届奥运会里，给 Pat 印象最深的是伦敦奥运会（London Olympic Games），而且英国文化也与考官们有着密切的关系，但描述它却并不需要很难的词汇。无论您是想描述北京奥运还是里约奥运（Rio Olympic games），也是一样的道理——清晰、扣题、自然的答案才是考官期待的。

难度指数：★ ★ ★ ☆ ☆

Pat 的答案

I'd like to talk about the London Olympic Games.

The opening ceremony showed us the amazing contributions Britain had made to the world. I particularly like Mr. Bean's hilarious performance and Paul McCartney's performance of *Hey Jude*.

During the London Olympics, more than 10,000 world-class athletes competed for their nations. Swimming was my favourite sport to watch at the Olympics. I was so excited when Sun Yang got the gold medal in the men's 400-meter freestyle race. He really reminded me of the Olympic motto — "Faster, Higher, Stronger".

The event was very special because only the best athletes in the world went there. Most of them competed fairly and honestly. It was a very inspiring event, and it really helped to promote peace and understanding among nations.

轮到你了　　　　　　　　　　　　It's Your Turn.

▶ **Word Bank on This Topic**

开幕式	opening ceremony	贡献	contributions
超级搞笑的	hilarious	表演	performance
世界级的	world-class	运动员	athlete
金牌	gold medal	自由泳比赛	free-style race
让我想起……	reminded me of...	奥运格言	the Olympic motto
公正、诚实地竞争	compete fairly and honestly	励志的	inspiring

促进和平与理解　promote peace and understanding

扩展词汇

四分之一决赛　quarter final	半决赛　semi-final
决赛　final	被淘汰　be eliminated
击败　defeat	对手　opponent

通过艰苦的努力才获得的胜利　a hard-earned victory

金牌　gold medal	银牌　silver medal
铜牌　bronze medal	获奖运动员　medalist

站在优胜者的领奖台上　stand on the podium

国歌　national anthem

流下喜悦激动的泪水　cried the tears of joy and excitement

速度　speed	力量　strength

平衡和协调能力　balance and coordination

柔韧性　flexibility	团队精神　team spirit
奥林匹克公园　Olympic Park	奥运村　Olympic Village
奥运场馆　Olympic venues	特别精彩的部分，"亮点"　highlight

主办城市　the host city

国际奥委会　The International Olympic Committee（IOC）

吉祥物　mascot	奥运会的五环图案　the Olympic rings

离开幕式 100 天的倒计时　100-day countdown

闭幕式　closing ceremony	火炬传递　torch relay

点燃奥运圣火　light the Olympic Flame

各国运动员走队　the Parade of Nations

激烈的比赛　a fierce competition / a tight competition

势均力敌的比赛　an evenly matched competition

100-meter sprint	摔跤　wrestling

请参考Pat的思路，并适当借鉴这个词汇表里的单词，思考如果是您将会怎么说

柔道 judo	排球 volleyball
艺术体操 artistic gymnastics	花样游泳 synchronised swimming
跳水 diving	水球 water polo
射箭 archery	射击 shooting
击剑 fencing	田径项目 track and field events
跨栏比赛 hurdle race	残奥会 Paralympics / The Paralympic Games
看体育比赛的现场观众 spectators	志愿者 volunteers
代表他们／她们的国家 represent their countries	
感受比赛的气氛 enjoy the atmosphere of the game	
见证 witness	体育迷 sports buff
（某个地方）挤满了人的 was packed	

请参考Pat的思路，并适当借鉴这个词汇表里的单词，思考如果是您将会怎么说

Pat 的海外生活英语实录

真正的体育迷（sports buff）一定不会错过这个网址超短却内容超多的网站：espn.go.com 无论你是足球迷，篮球迷，网球迷甚至棒球迷，都能在这里找到最新相关体育事件的报导

"激烈的竞赛"，很多同学都知道 fierce competition 这个短语。另外在英文口语里还有个说法：a cliffhanger。想象一下被悬在悬崖上的感觉多么让人紧张，就知道这样的比赛会是多么"扣人心弦"。

[剑桥例句] The match was a cliffhanger until the final seconds.

3. 成功完成的一件事

☆ *成功的经历之* 课堂演示（**presentation**）

Describe something you did that was a success

You should say：

what you did

经 历

> when you did it
>
> what difficulties you faced
>
> and explain how you felt when you were successful.

Pat 指南

生活里的 success 有很多种。大的 success 比如找到了一份自己很喜欢的工作，或者成功地申请了自己理想的大学。小的 success 比如为好朋友举办了一个成功的生日聚会，考试得到了一个好成绩，或者人生里第一次为父母做出了好吃的饭菜等等。

这里 Pat 以一个成功的课堂演示为例，因为同时还可以准备好 Describe a speech. 这个比较难的题。

难度指数：★ ★ ★ ☆ ☆

Pat 的答案

I'm going to talk about a successful presentation I gave last week.

Two weeks ago, our English teacher asked us to prepare a group presentation on some famous British writers and their works. He also divided us into teams of two or three for the presentation.

My teammate and I discussed the topic and made a list of the main points we wanted to make. After class, we went to the library and found some books on those writers and their works.

We went through the materials and selected the information we wanted to include. Then we made some PowerPoint slides and note cards to help us organise and remember the information. We also practised presenting in front of some friends.

We gave the presentation in class last Wednesday. My teammate gave the introduction and I presented the main part. At first, I was a bit nervous. I was just reading from the note cards. But as I went on, I felt more comfortable and confident. I spoke loudly and clearly. I also smiled and made eye contact with my audience. And I just glanced at the note cards from time to time rather than reading from them.

My teacher and my classmates were very impressed with our presentation. When we finished, our teacher said, "Good job!" And our classmates clapped. We felt really happy and excited, and very proud of ourselves for the success.

轮到你了　　　　　　　　　　　　　　　　　　It's Your Turn.

▶ Word Bank on This Topic

作品　works		分开　divide	
含有两个或者三个成员的团队　teams of two or three			
队友　teammate		挑选　select	
"PPT" 幻灯片　PowerPoint slides		提示卡　note cards	
组织　organise		开场白，引言　introduction	
有信心的　confident		进行目光交流　make eye contact	
听众　audience		很快地看一眼　glance at	
鼓掌　clap			
感到自豪　feel（过去时：felt）proud of ourselves			

🔍 扩展词汇

很强的成就感　a strong sense of achievement

获得成功　achieve success　　　　　令人难忘的经历　a memorable experience

高效率的　efficient　　　　　　　很有效的　effective

我的辛勤努力有了回报　My hard work has paid off.

　　成功地申请自己理想的大学是多数"烤鸭"现在最急需的 success，这个网址会让你对英国大学生的真实生活有更加深入的了解：www.telegraph.co.uk/education/universityeducation

请参考Pat的思
，并适当（
这个词汇身
的单词，
如果是您
怎么说

Pat 的海外生活英语实录

地道英文里评价一个好的 speech 有很多标准，比如 moving（感人的），inspiring（励志的），witty（机敏的），insightful（有洞察力的，有"真知灼见"的），well-rehearsed（预先"演练"得很充分的），well-structured（结构很合理的），informative（信息量大的）等等。但是说到底，a good speech 的共同点就是 well-received（很受听众欢迎的）。

[剑桥例句] His speech was well-received — the audience response was very positive.

Time to Branch Out.
推而广之

Describe a skill.

补充弹药

rewarding　很有回报的

motivated　很有动力的

build self-confidence　树立自信

practise this skill as often as I can　尽可能地多练习这种技能

Extra Ammo

4. 有趣的科学课

Describe an interesting lesson you attended.

You should say

　　when you attended this lesson

　　where you attended it

　　what it was about

　nd explain why you found it interesting

Pat 指南

Pat 发现国内的朋友们普遍觉得这道题很"悲催"，跟学生们深入交流之后发现：其实"悲催"的主要原因是国内的科学课教学往往过于理论化（focus too much on theory），比较单调，甚至在有些同学的记忆里根本就没有过 an interesting science lesson。

如果您在国外上过中学的 science class，就会深感这边的科学课确实可以用 interesting 来形容。因为国外中学的科学课强调 hands-on science（实际动手的科学），重视实验和展示（experiments and demonstrations），而且上课时常会播放科学短片（show students science videos）。为了吸引学生的兴趣，science teachers 还经常拿可乐（coke），柠檬水（lemonade）、葡萄干（raisin）或者爆米花（popcorn）这类东西到教室做实验，甚至有时连微波炉（microwave）、烤箱（oven）这类厨具也会登场。最近在英美中学的科学课里还时髦用一些不可逆的化学反应（irreversible chemical reactions）来展示 Harry Potter 的魔法到底是怎么变出来的，完全是真实的 *Harry Potter* 3D 版。所以 Pat 非常建议大家把 an interesting science lesson 这道题说得轻松一点，如果说得过于理论化、抽象化，不仅有被判跑题（off-topic）的可能，也会让考官感到文化休克（culture shock）。

难度指数：★ ★ ★ ☆ ☆

Pat 的答案

I'm going to talk about a science lesson I attended at secondary school when I was about 16 years old.

My science teacher was a middle-aged man who was nice and patient. Just like many scientists, he wore thick glasses and spoke slowly. But he had a good sense of humour and his lessons were always fun.

One of the most interesting science lessons he taught us was about density. He came into the classroom with a large beaker, a bag of raisins and a bottle of Pepsi, which really attracted our attention. He said he was going to share with us the "top secrets" of

经 历

density.

He poured some Pepsi into the beaker, and then put a couple of raisins in it. Of course, the raisins sank to the bottom of the beaker. But then, to our surprise, after they hit the bottom of the beaker, they went back up and they just kept going up and down in the Pepsi, which was really interesting.

Our teacher then explained to us the reason for this. At first, the raisins were heavier than the Pepsi. But after some gas in the Pepsi went into the raisins, their density became lower than that of Pepsi, so they went up. Once the raisins reached the surface of the Pepsi, the gas in them was pushed out and their density became high again, so they started to sink again.

I found this lesson interesting because our teacher really made the concept of density come alive. The experiment was simple but really fun, and it made the concept of density very easy to understand.

轮到你了

It's Your Turn.

► Word Bank on This Topic

中年的 middle-aged	耐心的 patient
镜片很厚的眼镜 thick glasses	有很强的幽默感 has a good sense of humour
密度 density	烧杯 beaker
葡萄干 raisins	百事可乐 Pepsi
吸引了我们的注意力 attract our attention	
让我们感到惊奇的是 to our surprise	
表面 surface	（本来很枯燥的事物）变得很生动 come alive
实验 experiment	

扩展词汇

碳酸饮料 carbonated drink	固体 solid

experience

液体	liquid	悬挂	hang
加热	heat up	冷却	cool off
重量	weight	质量	mass
体积	volume	化学元素	chemical elements
周期表	the periodic table	化学公式	chemical equation
化学反应	chemical reaction	仪器	instrument
仪表	meter	天平	balance
镊子	tweezers	勺子	spoon
显微镜	microscope	秤	scale
滴管	dropper	试管	test tube
漏斗	funnel	温度计	thermometer
搅拌	stir	混合	mix

请参考Pat的思路，并适当借鉴这个词汇表里的单词，思考如果是您将会怎么说

您有空时应该看看每年有超过 300 万人参观的伦敦科学博物馆（the Science Museum of London）的官网：www. sciencemuseum. org. uk/educators/classroom-resources。选择你想要了解的学生年龄段，再选择 subject，您就可以看到考官们真正熟悉的 science lesson 到底是怎样教的了。

Pat 的海外生活英语实录

在地道英文里如果要说一节课"引人入胜的"，最准确的表达是 engaging 这个形容词，而且它也可以用来描述 a speech, a TV show, a book 甚至 a childhood story。

【英美实例】Although I was tired, I found the book very engaging, making me want to stay up and keep reading it.

经　历

5. 一场表演

☆ 一场表演之 音乐会

> Describe a performance, such as a dancing or singing performance.
>
> You should say:
>
> > what kind of performance it was
> >
> > when and where you watched it
> >
> > what it was like
>
> and explain how you felt about it.

Pat 指南

Pat 自己是个乐迷（I'm a music buff），对古典音乐和流行音乐都很喜欢。这里给您讲讲去看一个 rock concert 的经历吧，比古典音乐会（classical concert）更接近多数"烤鸭"朋友们的真实生活。您可以体会一下怎么用英文描述那种热烈的气氛（exciting atmosphere）。

难度指数：★ ★ ★ ★ ☆

Pat 的答案

I went to … (*the band's name*)'s concert last Friday night. It was held at the largest stadium in my city. I'd been a big fan of the band. I'd even made a poster to hold up during the concert.

Last Friday night, I arrived at the stadium early. But it took me about 40 minutes to get to my seat. The concert attracted people of all ages, and the stadium was packed!

When the band took the stage, everyone stood up, clapped and cheered. Many people screamed the band members' names at the top of their lungs. Some people were so excited they even cried.

The band played songs from many of their albums and even played some acoustic songs. Then they performed their latest single. We waved our arms and sang along. I think for many people, that was the most memorable moment of the concert.

It was really exciting and inspiring to be so close to the band. And the live music was amazing. The band members did notice my poster. They even waved to me from the stage, which made me feel like I was on top of the world.

轮到你了   It's Your Turn.

▶ Word Bank on This Topic

体育场　stadium   海报　poster

吸引各个年龄段的人们　attract people of all ages

挤满了人的　packed   登台　take（过去时：took）the stage

鼓掌欢呼　clap and cheer   乐队成员　band members

高声呼喊　scream... at the top of their lungs

专辑　album   单曲　single

不用电子合成的歌曲，"不插电"歌曲　acoustic songs

挥舞胳膊　wave our arms   一起跟着唱　sing along

最值得回忆的时刻　the most memorable moment

激励人的　inspiring

现场表演的音乐　live music（注意：在这个短语里 live 的正确发音是/laiv/）

向……挥手　wave to...   极度喜悦的（短语）　on top of the world

扩展词汇

现场音乐会　live concert   表演者　performer

经　历

（粉丝）变得狂热了　go wild（过去时：went wild）

偶像　idol

气氛　atmosphere

充满活力的　full of energy

极度兴奋的　thrilled

昏过去了　pass out

最精彩的部分，"亮点"　highlight

乐队和观众之间的互动　interaction between the band and the audience

弯腰去和粉丝握手　bend down to shake hands with their fans

特邀嘉宾　special guest

太"劲爆"了　It was a blast！

非常精彩的表演，"现象级"的表演　a phenomenal performance

请参考Pat的思路，并适当借鉴这个词汇表里的单词，思考如果是您将会怎么说

　　这个网址列出了对全世界最棒的 50 个音乐节的介绍，虽然不能全都去一遍，但却可以很快地全都"看"一遍：www. timeout. com/music-arts-culture/50-best-music-festivals-in-the-world/

Pat 的海外生活英语实录

　　演唱会上歌迷们挥舞的"荧光棒"用地道英文怎么说？glow sticks 就是口语里的"荧光棒"，"挥舞"则可以用动词 wave 来表达。

6. 帮别人准备的一个聚会

Describe a party you organised for another person.

You should say：

who you organised the party for

what kind of party it was

where it was held

and explain how you felt about the party

对于多数"烤鸭"来说，生日聚会是最有话可说的 party，只用"小词"就可以说得扣题、清晰、自然。

难度指数：★ ★ ☆ ☆ ☆

Pat 的答案

I'm going to talk about a party I organised for a good friend of mine named Mia. Last month, I noticed her birthday was coming up. I wanted her to have a really special birthday, so I decided to organise a surprise birthday party for her.

I called my friends Jillian, Chris, Evan and Matt who were also Mia's friends, and asked them if they'd like to join me in throwing a surprise birthday party for Mia. They were very excited to hear my ideas and promised they wouldn't tell anyone about my plan. I also called Mia's parents in advance to make sure they would be okay with my plan.

On Mia's birthday, we went to her home with a big birthday cake, colourful balloons and our presents for her. We also helped her parents decorate the living room. Then we hid behind doors or curtains.

About ten minutes later, we heard footsteps and Mia came in. We jumped out and shouted, "Surprise!" Mia was so surprised she was like, "Oh, my goodness! What's going on here?" Everyone said "Happy Birthday" to her. Then we brought out the cake, lit the candles, and started singing the birthday song to her.

Mia was so excited she was moved to tears. She thanked everyone for the party, and she said it was the most special birthday she ever had.

I was very glad Mia liked the party I organised for her. I felt all my planning really paid off.

经 历

轮到你了

It's Your Turn.

► **Word Bank on This Topic**

本文里所用的人名都是目前国外年轻人的常见名字

作为惊喜的生日聚会　a surprise birthday party （表达这个意思时，native speakers 不说 a surprising birthday party ✗）

为某人开派对　throw a party for...　　提前给……打电话　call... in advance

气球　balloons　　　　　　　　　生日礼物　birthday present

装饰　decorate　　　　　　　　藏起来　hide （过去时：hide）

窗帘　curtains　　　　　　　　　脚步　footsteps

点蜡烛　light （过去时：lit） the candles

天哪！　Oh my goodness！（中国的同学们都知道 Oh my God！，但是在真实的英美生活里语气比较含蓄的 My goodness！更常听到，只有感到"震惊"的时候 native speakers 才会说 Oh my God！）

感动地流泪　was moved to tears　　有回报　pay off （过去时：paid off）

扩展词汇

过生日的男孩／女孩　the birthday boy / the birthday girl

密友　close friends　　　　　　生日贺卡　birthday card

异口同声地说"生日快乐"　say "Happy Birthday" in unison

唱"祝你生日快乐"　sing （过去时：sang）"Happy Birthday"

许愿　make （过去时：made） a wish

吹蜡烛　blow out （过去时：blew out） the candles

彼此拥抱　hug each other　　　　切蛋糕　cut the cake

开礼物　open the presents

唱卡拉 OK　sing karaoke （过去时：sang karaoke，请注意听音频里 karaoke 的正确发音，很多同学会说错这个词）

非常值得回忆的经历　a memorable experience

请参考Pat的思路，并适当借鉴这个词汇表里的单词，思考如果是您将会怎么说

experience

Pat 的海外生活英语实录

准备 IELTS 口语最好的心态就是把它看成学习地道英文和了解英语文化的起点。您进入任何一所英联邦大学之后都会立刻明白 party 在当地的校园文化里扮演着何等重要的角色。这个网站也能为你提供很多 party ideas：www. partycity. com/category/party +ideas. do

如果要说一个聚会是"精心策划"的，除了 It was carefully planned / carefully organised / carefully arranged. 这三个地道短语之外，还有一个国内孩子很少用但在国外却挺常用的表达：This was a well-thought-out party.

[剑桥例句] Nothing can be more fun than going to a well-thought-out birthday party.

7. 婚礼

Describe a wedding you have attended.

You should say:

when it was

where it was

who got married

and explain what happened at the wedding.

Pat 指南

William 与 Kate（在英美生活里一般是简称他们为 Will and Kate）当年的 royal wedding 在全世界获得了 **20** 亿观众的收视率，现在都已经生"二胎"了，可见 wedding 永远是一个令人向往的主题。

中国同学们回答这道题的常见误区是把婚礼的每一步都很机械、呆板地罗列出来，导致考生听起来更像是专业婚礼司仪（地道英文里叫作 wedding MC）在讲解自己的服务项目。其实考官真正想听你说的是一个扣题、自然、有整体感和连贯性的描述（description）。

难度指数：★ ★ ★ ☆ ☆

Pat 的答案

I'm going to talk about a good friend's wedding I attended last month.

The wedding ceremony was held in a church. It began at 9 in the morning. There were around 150 people at the ceremony, including the bride and groom's family, friends and colleagues. We all dressed up for the occasion.

After the guests were seated, the Wedding March started and the bridesmaids entered. My friend, you know, the bride, entered last, in a white wedding dress. Many guests were moved to tears as the bride and groom met at the front of the room, exchanged wedding vows and kissed each other.

There were even more people at the wedding party, which was held in a hotel. The room was well decorated, with lots of flowers and a huge wedding cake. My friend and her husband walked around and greeted their guests. Everyone had a great time at the party.

轮到你了

It's Your Turn.

▶ Word Bank on This Topic

结婚仪式　wedding ceremony / marriage ceremony

婚宴　wedding party / wedding banquet（地道英文口语里也常叫作 wedding reception）

新郎新娘　the bride and groom（地道英文里的习惯顺序是 "新娘新郎"）

同事　colleagues / co-workers	穿着比较正式的服装　dress up
就座　were seated	婚礼进行曲　the *Wedding March*
伴娘　bridesmaids	婚纱　wedding dress / wedding gown

热泪盈眶　were moved to tears　　交换结婚誓言　exchange wedding vows

装饰得很好的　well-decorated　　婚礼蛋糕　wedding cake

问候客人们　greeted their guests

🔍 **扩展词汇**

司仪　MC　　　　　　　　　　　开场白　opening remarks

伴郎　best man　　　　　　　　　男士晚礼服（适合非常正式的场合）　tuxedo / tux

花童　flower girl

新人　the newly-wed couple / the newly-weds

祝福与祝贺　best wishes and congratulations

切蛋糕　cut the cake　　　　　　蜜月　honeymoon

扔花束　toss the bouquet（据说拿到花束的女孩会是下一个结婚的女孩）

向新婚夫妇撒米（或者纸片）　shower the couple with rice（orconfetti）

　　看了这个网址，您就真可以考虑把婚礼司仪（wedding MC）当成职业了，因为关于英国婚礼的那些事儿介绍得实在太全了：www.theguardian. com/lifeandstyle/weddings

请参考Pat的思路，并适当借鉴这个词汇表里的单词，思考如果是您将会怎么说

Pat 的海外生活英语实录

　　无论是在中国还是在英美，婚宴上面都会有人向新婚夫妇祝酒，地道英文叫 drink a toast to the happy couple。

　　[剑桥例句] The guests drank（drink 的过去时）a toast to the happy couple.

　　Pat 最近在一本介绍中国文化的书里看到一段英文，谈到了中国文化里人生的四大喜事，您可以看看是不是能猜出来它们分别是什么：

　　Marriage is known as one of the four happiest things in one's life. The other three are achievement in examinations, meeting old friends away from home and rainfall after a drought. ☺

经　历

8. 节日

> Describe a festival that is popular in your country.
>
> You should say：
>
> what the festival is
>
> when it is celebrated
>
> what people do during this festival
>
> and explain whether you like this festival or not.

Pat 指南

国内同学们描述 festival 的常见问题同样是机械地罗列节日的起源和相关活动，一听就是在背诵（像这样简单粗暴的答题方式，甚至即使不是在背都会让考官误以为你在背）。

只要扣题，无论说哪个节日都是可以的，但必须始终牢记：虽然 Part 2 是 "独白"，examiner 也希望听到你自然、真实地说话。

难度指数：★ ★ ★ ★ ☆

Pat 的答案

Let me talk about the Duan Wu Festival. It falls on the fifth day of the fifth month of the lunar calendar. It has become even more popular since it became a public holiday in China.

The festival is celebrated in honour of a famous poet in Chinese history, named Qu Yuan. His country was defeated in a war and even lost its capital. The poet was so sad he drowned himself. These days, during the festival people eat rice dumplings (or in Chinese, *zong zi*), to pay tribute to him. We all respect people who love their country, right?

Another popular way to celebrate the festival is dragon boat racing. It's like a number of teams rowing and competing against one another. The boats are decorated to look like dragons, so they're called dragon boats. To be honest, I've only watched dragon boat races on TV. From what I've seen on TV, they are very fun and exciting events.

I like the Duan Wu Festival because it celebrates loyalty and the circle of life. And *zong zi*, the main food we eat during the festival, tastes really good...

轮到你了   It's Your Turn.

▶ Word Bank on This Topic

起源 origin

很爱国的 patriotic

糯米 sticky rice / glutinous rice

（粽子、元宵或饺子里的）"馅儿" stuffing / filling

豆沙 bean paste

用竹叶包起来的 wrapped in bamboo leaves

节日的庆祝活动（名词） festivities

很喜庆的（形容词） festive

中秋节 the Mid-Autumn Festival

圆月，满月 full moon

月饼 mooncakes

元宵节 the Lantern Festival

驱难避邪 ward off evil spirits

灯展 display of lanterns

"年三十儿" the Lunar New Year's Eve

压岁钱 lucky money

红包 red envelope

收到礼物 receive gifts

饺子 dumplings

放鞭炮 set off firecrackers

传统服装 traditional costumes

对联 couplet

狮子舞 lion dance

舞龙 dragon dance

节日里最精彩的部分 the highlight of the festival

标志着 mark

象征着 represent / symbolise

被和……联系到一起 is associated with...

经 历

生机，生命的活力（名词） vitality

很有活力的（形容词） lively / energetic / vibrant

午夜零点倒计时 count down to midnight

许愿 make a wish   烟火表演 fireworks display

Pat 自己长期生活在国外，每年都可以最真实地感受到春节对英语国家文化的影响力确实越来越大。您不妨看看伦敦在 2016 年是怎样庆祝中国新年的，一起感受一下在海外过春节的 "节日气氛"（the festive atmosphere）：www. telegraph. co. uk/travel/festivals-and-events/Chinese-New-Year-London-celebrations

请参考Pat的思路，并适当借鉴这个词汇表里的单词，思考如果是您将会怎么说

Pat 的海外生活英语实录

每个传统节日的背后都有着丰富的故事（There're many interesting tales behind every traditional festival. ）。那么怎样用地道英文表示一个节日是我们的 "文化遗产" 的重要部分呢？native speakers 会说 It's an important part of our cultural heritage.

[剑桥例句] Folk music is an important part of our cultural heritage.

☆ 双语感悟之 人生里一个积极的变化

Describe a positive change in your life.

You should say：

what this change was

when this change happened

why it was positive

and explain how this change has influenced your life.

想说好 Part 2，首先必须扣题。

什么样的 change 算是 a positive change?

a positive change 可以是生活小事。比如自己以前不关心家长，甚至经常和家长吵架（often argued with my parents），有一次父亲或者母亲生病了才明白应该照顾父母，自己也变得更加关心、体贴别人了（became a more caring and understanding person）。

又比如说自己以前在足球队或者篮球队里不愿意和队友合作（was not a good team player），总想成为注意力的焦点（always wanted to be the center of attention），经常拒绝传球给队友（often refused to pass the ball to my teammates），而且也不关心队友的感受（didn't care about my teammates' feelings）。球队遭到一次惨败之后（after our team suffered a heavy defeat），自己才明白团队合作的重要性（the importance of teamwork），学会了尊重自己的队友（learned to respect my teammates），于是向队友们道歉（apologised to my teammates），并且开始和队友们密切地合作（started to work closely with my teammates）。球队获得了很大进步（Our team improved a lot.），自己与队友们也成了好朋友（I became good friends with my teammates.），直到现在还保持联系（I still keep in touch with most of them.）等等。

a positive change 同样也可以是对你的生活方式有深刻影响的大事。比如自己以前过度依赖家长（relied too much on my parents），而且从来都不帮家长做饭或者打扫房间（never helped my parents with cooking or cleaning），但后来离开家去别的城市上大学，让你变得更加独立而且更有责任感了（more independent and responsible）。

又比如你以前的生活方式很不健康（I used to lead an unhealthy lifestyle.），例如每天花很多时间打网络游戏（spent many hours playing online games），爱吃垃圾食品（ate lots of junk food，ate 是 eat 的过去时），还熬夜看电视（stayed up late watching TV）等等。但一个电视节目、一本书或者一篇报纸上的文章（a newspaper article）帮助你真正明白了不健康生活方式的危害（helped me better understand the damage caused by an unhealthy lifestyle）。你决定改变自己的不健康生活方式（decided to change my unhealthy lifestyle），例如减少玩网络游戏的时间（reduced the time I spent playing online games），远离垃圾食品（stayed away from junk food），多吃蔬菜水果（ate lots of fruit and vegetables），按时作息（kept a regular sleep schedule），开始经常锻炼身体（started to exercise regularly）等等。现在自己每天都感觉精力充沛（feel energetic every day），而且注意力也更集中了（can concentrate better）……

Day

9

Part 3：深入讨论的 勇气

Don't let Part 3 become your Achilles' heel.

I talk of freedom
You talk of the flag
I'll look at you, you'll look at me
This will be what we said
Yes, this will be what we said

* *http://blog.ted.com/2010/06/17/audio_podcasts/* *

考官在 Part 3 里提出的问题一般都比较"宏大",而且还要求你说出一些细节（details）,而不再只是像 Part 1 那样轻松愉快的闲谈。为了从心态上做好准备,您可以登录这个 TED 网站,它的话题已经覆盖了 Part 3 的全部常见话题,而且 TED talks 的用词风格本身就很接近 Part 3 的用词风格,认真听吧

* *http://www.bbc.co.uk/worldservice/learningenglish/general/sixminute/* *

BBC 著名的"6 Minute English"也是准备 Part 3 的好工具,而且全部都是用标准英音讲的,尽情地模仿发音你也不必担心"走火入魔" ☺

▶ *We take the test seriously, but we want to make it fun and interesting as well.*

Part 3 的高分答案长什么样

口语 Part 3 常被中国同学们戏称为"趴睡",除了因为中文的"趴睡"和英文的 Part 3 发音接近之外,还因为很多同学感觉 Part 3 的挑战太大,所以干脆选择了"就地卧倒"。

口语 Part 3 是深入讨论(detailed discussion),考官会提出 6 ~8 个和你之前拿到的卡片话题有关的问题。但与 Part 1 的提问不同的是:考官在 Part 3 的提问很少涉及你个人的"私生活",而是更关注社区、城市、社会、国家甚至国际层面的问题,并且还要求你在讨论过程中能够说出一些细节(details)。所以 Part 3 确实比 Part 1 的难度大,但这也正是为什么能否回答好 Part 3 往往是区分普通的口试表现(6 ~6.5 分)和优秀的口试表现(7 分或以上)的重要分水岭。

事实上,Part 3 虽然是深入讨论,但它毕竟还是口语而不是写作。你只要能确实针对考官的问题提出自己的看法,并适当支持自己的看法就已经很好了,不需要"长篇大论"。而且,雅思考试主办方给出的 Part 3 官方高分答案范例仍然有清晰的逻辑规律可循,并非"无厘头"。只要我们有勇气、有决心,Part 3 完全可以顺利过关。

从结构来说,一个完整的 Part 3 答案通常是这样的:

01　明确回答考官提出的问题,让考官放心你不会跑题;

02　给出你这样说的理由(reason);

03　支持你给出的理由,也就是传说当中的"细节"(detail)。有理有据的谈话才能叫作讨论(discussion),否则就成了"漫谈"(chit-chat)。口语对话里最常见的支持方式就是举例。如果想不出任何恰当的例子,或者对某个理由确实"无感",那么就换一种更简单的方式再转述一下自己的理由也同样能够让理由听起来更有说服力;

__04__ 如果你发现自己说"high"了，想到的理由居然还不止一个，那么可以继续再说出其它理由以及相应的支持。注意：这一步并不是必须的，如果没有想到更多的理由，那就只说一个理由并且给出支持也很好，口试里的最大敌人其实是"刻意为之"；

__05__ 考官在 Part 3 会持续发问，一般会问 6 ~ 8 个问题。对于其中的 2 ~ 3 个比较"有感觉"的问题，您还可以选择用"On the other hand, ... "，"But I also think ... "，"But it's also true ... "，"Without ... , ... would ... "，"If we don't ... , ... will ... "等方式再对问题的另一面简要地谈一谈。这一步同样不是必须的，"可以有"但是不必勉强。

Pat指南

作为一种英语语言能力测试，IELTS 口试最可贵之处就是它的目的是考查真实的交流技能而不是考"背诵技能"。上面这个结构并不是僵化的、一成不变的。比如，如果并没有想到恰当的例子，那么就不需要勉强举例。如果没想到"另一面"的内容，也不用"硬着头皮"非去谈另一面。衡量 Part 3 的好答案只有一个标准：认真回答考官的问题，不跑题，而且也能适当地给出理由，确实有"讨论"（discussion）、而不是"逃论"（escape from the discussion）的感觉，那么就是一个很好的 Part 3 答案（a well-structured Part 3 answer）。

怎样才能说得流畅而不机械？

Fluency & Coherence

Part 3 答案里的句子之间既可以用 because, For example, such as, like（比如……），so, if, and, also 等逻辑关系词来形成逻辑连接（如果不确定用法请复习 Day 4 和 Day 5），也可以用 they, I, we, it, that 等代词来形成自然的过渡（如果不确定用法请复习 Day 5）。还有些时候就用很"直白"的语言把前面一句话的意思再简要地转述一下，也同样可以实现句子之间自然、流畅的衔接效果。

★　　★　　★

我们一起来看 British Council 官方提供的 Part 3 高分实例：

What qualities make a person admirable?

I think kindness and honesty are important qualities that most people admire（回答考官的问题）<u>because</u> sometimes it's hard to put other people first, and sometimes it's not easy to tell the truth（给出自己这样认为的理由）. People who are prepared to do these things are very special people（这名高分考生在回答这个问题时并没有想到"另一面"的内容，那就不必强求，语言地道、风格自然的答案才是考官真正期待的）.

这是 British Council 给出的另一个 Part 3 高分实例：

Do you think men and women tend to respect different qualities?

Yes, <u>I</u> think men admire competence <u>and</u> women prefer personal qualities, <u>such as</u> kindness（回答考官的问题）. I suppose <u>it's</u> because of <u>their</u> traditional roles（给出自己这样认为的理由）. Women traditionally looked after the children（地道短语：照看孩子）<u>and</u> men worked to earn money（地道短语：挣钱）, <u>so</u> <u>they</u> grew to admire different qualities（解释自己的理由，虽然并不是很"细"，但还是让答案听起来有了一些细节的感觉）. <u>But I also think</u> this is changing <u>and</u> men and women are becoming more similar in <u>their</u> work and attitudes（还说了一句"另一面"的内容，让自己的观点听起来更客观，但这一步不是必须有的）.

更多来自 British Council 官方的 Part 3 高分实例：

Do you think having a guide improves the experience of visiting an unfamiliar place?

Yes, I think it's useful（回答考官的问题）<u>because</u> guides generally have more knowledge of the area and the special places in that region（给出

自己这样认为的理由）. But I've heard some guides take visitors to specific shops or hotels that they can earn money from. You need to find a reliable person to be your guide（适当补充了“另一面”，但请注意：这名高分考生在回答这道题时没想到合适的例子，就并没有强迫自己“举栗子”，其实语言地道、风格自然才是官方高分答案真正的共同点）.

Do you agree that working from home will be more common in the future?

Yes, I agree because working from home can give employees more freedom and help employers reduce office costs. In the future, the Internet will be faster and there'll be more apps to help people work from home. So it seems working from home will be even more popular in the future（既没有举例，也没有谈“另一面”，但确实是在很认真地回答考官的问题，并适当给出了细节，就仍然是 Part 3 里的好答案）

我们再来看《剑 11》Test 1 里的“趴睡”高分答案：

What do you think are the advantages of living in a house rather than an apartment?

Living in a house is more comfortable than living in an apartment（回答考官的问题）. You have more space and enjoy more privacy if you live in a house, and you're less likely to be bothered by noise（给出自己这样认为的理由）. I live in an apartment and the family upstairs often play loud music, which is very annoying. I hope I can move to a house someday（通过生活里的例子来支持前面给出的理由）.

Do you think everyone would like to live in a larger home？ Why?

I think most people would like to live in a larger home，but not everyone （回答考官提出的问题）. Living in a larger home gives people more space and privacy （给出自己这样认为的理由）. But cleaning a larger home takes more time and energy. Not everyone would enjoy cleaning a larger home （对"另一面"也进行了适当论述，但并不机械刻板）.

正因为是深入讨论（detailed discussion），所以考生经常会感到考官在 Part 3 里对一个话题"穷追不舍"。沿着上面的讨论，《剑 11》里又继续提出了下面的问题：

Do you think it's better to rent or to buy a place to live in?

I think it's better to buy a place to live in （回答考官提出的问题）. You don't need to pay rent to a landlord if you own the place. It also gives you more freedom （给出这样认为的理由）. For example，you can decorate your living room as you wish （举例子支持自己的理由）. It's true that many young people these days can't afford to buy their own place and have to rent （自然地提及了"另一面"）. But I think it's always better to be a homeowner than a tenant.

再请看《剑 10》Test 3 里面的高分答案：

How important do you think spending time together is for the relationships between parents and children?

I think it's very important （回答考官的问题）. Spending time together helps parents and children build strong family relationships （给出自己这样认为的理由）. For example，doing housework together gives them the chance to help each other. And when parents and children eat meals together，they can talk and share ideas and opinions. Things like playing sports together and going on holiday together can also help them build strong relationships (举例子支持自己的理由，注意这名高分考生因为没有想到"另一面"的内容就从容地选择了不说另一面，机械僵硬的结构反而会让考官厌烦).

我们再来看《剑10》Test 1 的 Part 3 高分答案：

**Which kinds of jobs have the highest salaries in your country?
Why is this?**

The CEOs and managers of large companies get the highest salaries in my country (回答考官的问题). They work hard and help their companies achieve success (给出自己这样认为的理由). They earn very high salaries for their hard work and business success, and that's fair (并不是每一个高分答案都必须"举例子"或者"谈另一面"，把前面的理由用简单的语言解释一下也同样能让答案更充实，口语如果"过于机械"就等于"自动缴械").

《剑10》Test 1 的 Part 3 还对上面的问题进行了"无耻"的追问，但只要思路清楚、风格自然，考生就能对严刑拷打泰然处之：

**Are there any other jobs that you think
should have high salaries?**

Yes, I think primary school and secondary school teachers should also be well paid (回答考官的问题). They help children and teenagers develop important skills, such as language skills, maths skills and communication skills (说明自己这样认为的理由). They contribute a lot to society but they don't have high salaries (支持自己的理由). I believe they should earn much more than they do now.

《剑 10》Test 2 里面的这个 Part 3 问题不谈国家和社会，却与社区有关：

> **Do you think local businesses are important**
> **for a neighbourhood?**
>
> Yes, I think they're very important. Local businesses make life more convenient for people who live in the neighbourhood. They also create jobs for local people and give local people a strong sense of community. For example, many people like to meet their friends and chat at local cafés.

再请看《剑 9》Test 3 的 Part 3 高分答案：

> **Can travel make a positive difference to the economy of a country?**
>
> Yes, it can because travellers spend money on hotels, food and transport. They contribute to the service and transport industries in many countries. Without tourism, the economy of these countries would suffer（用 Without … , … would … 来谈"另一面"）.

下面这道《剑 9》Test 4 的 Part 3 考题则考到了社区和人民政府：

> **Who do you think should pay for the services that**
> **are available to the people in a community?**
> **Should it be the government or individual people?**
>
> I think that depends on what kind of services they are. If the services can benefit most people in a community, such as a community library or a local school, then they should be paid for by the government. On the other hand（用 On the other hand, … 来引出"另一面"）, some community services, like children's summer camps and art classes, should be paid for by individual people because many community members don't use these services.

Do you think children should wear school uniforms?

Yes, I think they should. Uniforms can give children a sense of belonging and promote teamwork. Uniforms can also help children concentrate on their studies because they don't need to worry about what to wear. Parents can also save money on their children's clothing if their children wear school uniforms five days a week. （虽然还可以继续谈校服 look boring 看起来很枯燥，are uncomfortable 不舒适，take away students' freedom of expression 剥夺学生表达自己个性的自由等"另一面"的内容，但这名考生选择了只谈支持穿校服的理由，听起来自然的答案就是好答案，不必苛求"面面俱到"））

只有自然的结构听起来才会真实。但如果你确实想谈谈"另一面"，那么当然也不用跟考官客气：

Do you think parents should help their children make decisions?

Yes, I think they should（回答考官的问题）. Parents have more life experience than their children and they know their children very well, so they can give their children sound advice. On the other hand, it's important that parents just provide help and support but don't make decisions for their children.

Which do you think are more important,
art lessons or academic lessons?

I think academic lessons are more important than art lessons（回答考官的问题）. Academic lessons, such as maths, language and science lessons（举例子）, teach students the skills they'll need to find jobs（给出自己这样认为的理由）. It's true that art activities are fun and art lessons can help students develop art skills, <u>like</u> painting and drawing skills（也适当提及了"另一面"），<u>but</u> it seems these skills won't really help students when they enter the job market.

Do you think it's impolite to use mobile phones in public places?

<u>I</u> think it's impolite to use mobile phones in public places <u>like</u> cinemas, libraries and classrooms where people are supposed to be quiet. <u>But</u> I think it's okay to use mobile phones in other public places <u>such as</u> shopping centers and fitness centers where it's always noisy anyway, if we don't mind others hearing our phone conversation（对另一方面也适当论述，但前提是必须自然，而不能是"牵强附会" forced and far-fetched）.

Part 3 的绝大多数考题都是常规题，但偶尔也确实有可能出现少量比较"雷"的问题。比如，下面这道《剑9》Test 2 Part 3 的考题居然要你进行"心理分析"。如果真遇到这种"不可理喻"的问题，除了心里万马奔腾而且一出考场就买彩票之外，我们需要特别注意的是别被"带到沟里去"。请坚信：<u>IELTS 口试的本质是一个语言考试</u>，绝不要浪费时间去想弗洛伊德或者村上春树到底是怎么说的，<u>考官真正的关注焦点其实仍然是你的语言</u>（正如 British Council 官方明确指出：Remember, this is a test of speaking！）。只要你的英语表述得清楚、自然，即使 ideas 非常简单，在考官眼里你仍然是一个可敬的 candidate。

Why do you think some people like doing new things?

<u>I</u> think that's <u>because</u> doing new things is more fun and exciting than doing the same old things all the time. When people do new things，<u>they</u> feel excited. <u>It</u>'s almost like an adventure. <u>And</u> doing new things is <u>also</u> a good way to gain new knowledge，<u>such as</u> knowledge about a new place or a new tool.

再来看更多的 Part 3 高分答案实例：

> ### Why do many people like going to concerts?
>
> I suppose there're different reasons for different people. Some people want to experience good music. Others want to get close to the musicians they like. There're also people who go to concerts just to make new friends. For example, I made some new friends at a rock concert last week and that was exciting.

有效提高 Part 3 实力的 6 步
（A Six-step Approach to Success in Part 3）

A　回答 Why 原因类问题你应该熟悉的句型

Why 原因类问题在 Part 3 考试里每场必有。请熟记下面的句型，但只要记 1 ~ 2 种即可。“大牛”看看就行，自己说最好。

◇ That's because…

◇ The main reason is that…

◇ The most important reason is that …

◇ There're a couple of reasons. （如果这样回答，那就至少要给出两条原因并适当支持）

Pat 指南

☆ to the best of my knowledge 和 as far as I know 这两个短语都表示“据我所知”，可以帮助你缓解讨论你并不太了解的原因时的无助感：

e. g. Hmm, to the best of my knowledge, those languages are dying out because of the spread of English.

B 回答"今昔对比"类和"展望未来"类问题你应该熟悉的短语

Part 3 里的另一类常考问题是问你生活的某个方面在过去与现在，或者现在与将来有什么不同。回答这类问题时一定要特别注意：说过去、现在和将来的时态是不同的，而且下面的短语你也应该熟悉，仍然是每类知道 1~2 个就够了。

回顾过去的情况：

◇ In the past, …

◇ Traditionally, …

◇ People used to…

介绍现在的情况：

◇ These days, …

◇ Today, …

◇ But now, people …

展望将来的情况：

◇ In the future, …

◇ Maybe in the future, …

◇ In the future, people will probably …

C 回答 How should… ? 解决方案类考题的常用句型

解决方案类考题不一定每场都会出现，但也是 Part 3 的高频提问形式之一：

◇ To solve this problem, … should…

◇ The best way to address this problem would be…

◇ A long-term solution would be … (一个长期有效的解决方案是……)

Pat 指南

　　回答 "解决方法" 类考题一个很好用的句型是：Ideally, ... But in reality, ...（理想状态应该是……可实际上……）。听到你这么真诚（sincere），考官也会是一声叹息（sigh with sympathy）。

　　例：Ideally, all cars should be removed from this world because they are causing so many problems for us. But in reality, the number of cars just keeps increasing.

　　类似的地道英文句型还有两个，一旦有机会在回答 "解决方法" 类考题时用到必定拿分。当然，你最多只要知道一个就够了：

　　(1) Ideally, ...　　But in practice, ...

　　(2) In theory, ...　　But in practice, ...

D　回答 advantages 好处类考题常用的句型

　　在 Part 3 里，一旦被要求解释 advantages，就可以把 advantages 和 benefits 适当交替使用，以避免一再重复地使用 advantages 或者 benefits。

　　下面的句型常用来回答和 "好处" 有关的问题：

　　◇ The main benefit is…

　　◇ The most important benefit is…

　　◇ There are a couple of benefits.（如果这样回答，那就至少要给出两个好处并适当支持）

E　回答 disadvantages 弊端类考题的常用句型

　　如果感觉你的答案里有可能 disadvantages 会出现得过于频繁，不妨用 drawbacks 来替换。

　　◇ I suppose the main problem is…

　　◇ The main concern is…

　　◇ An important drawback is …

Pat 指南 🔊

中国同学们在 IELTS 口试里的最大敌人并不是说得太简单，而是说得过于呆板。其实只要努力针对考官的提问给出尽量明确的回答就好了，你真的不必纠结自己是不是每句话都用出了"好句型"和"好词汇"。每位考官都希望坐在他/她面前的是一个可以真实交流的人，而不是一个传声筒或者复读机。

F Part 3 必备的高分词汇和短语

请继续熟悉 Day 3 里面的实用短语，它们是保证您被问到任何话题都能有话可说的 building blocks。而且，您还可以在随本书附赠的《IELTS 口语高频词汇 & 短语速查手册》附录 C 里面看到 Pat 总结的 100 个 Part 3 高分词汇和短语。

超短线
The Ultra-Short Track

对于时间紧却面对 L. R. W. S 四座大山的考生来说，如果实在找不出时间去充分准备 the Speaking Test 的 Part 3 了，那么至少要好好听听剑 4 ~ 剑 11 官方真题里每套 Listening 的 Section 4，您会发现它的语言风格酷似口语 Part 3 的答案。例如剑桥官方真题里这个关于 recycling 的段子和口语 Part 3 里关于 recycling 的考题何其相似：

The high quality comes at a cost in terms of the waste produced during the process. Plastic causes problems because there're so many different types of plastic in use, and each one has to be dealt with differently. One of the solutions is recycling plastic bottles to make containers which are used all over the country.

如果您连通过听力 Section 4 来提高口语 Part 3 的时间都没了，那么最后的一道防线就是直接利用您的 Writing 基础来准备口语 Part 3 的问题。虽然这两个考试还真有不少话题是相似的，例如 Environment, Animals, Culture, Government 等，但全凭写作功底回答出来的 Part 3 会显得有点过于正式了，所以只可以作为 last resort（不得已之选）。

Day

口语高分考生的共同点
What It Takes to
Get a Good Score.

The play is done; the curtain drops
The actor stops
And looks around to say farewell

最后一天了。江淹的《别赋》说："黯然消魂者，唯别而已矣。"英文却说"Every ending can be a new beginning."中西方文化的差异，确实不是一两句话能够说清的。

Pat 写这本书的动力之一就是希望把自己多年来在英语国家的学习、生活里每天都听到、看到的真实英文传递给中国同学们，帮助同学们摆脱用"中式英语"说英文话题的苦恼。您可以放心地把从本书学到的英文用在 IELTS 口试以及出国之后的留学生活里，享受和 native speakers "无障碍交流"的乐趣（the pleasure of easy and effective communication）。

Pat 完成本书的另一个心愿是帮助中国同学们拨开种种迷雾，看清 IELTS 口语高分的本质要求：用英语去和你的考官进行一次真正的交流。正如很多口语考官们明确指出的，"It's not what you say. It's how you say it." ❶ 扣题，❷ 清晰，❸ 自然的答案才是坐在你对面的 examiner 真心期待的。

如果您仍然半信半疑，希望 Cambridge University Press 出版的 *The Official Cambridge Guide to IELTS* 提供的这个高分实例能最终说服您：

Describe a person who has been an important influence in your life.

You should say：

how long you have known this person

why you chose this person

how this person has influenced your life

and explain how you feel about this person.

由剑桥官方提供的高分答案实例：

> I've decided to talk about my grandmother. I've known her for all my life. She's an amazing person.
>
> I chose her because when I was young, she looked after me when my parents were busy at work. So I have a lot of good memories of her when I was growing up.
>
> She has influenced my life by being such a calm person. She also taught me how to read and write. And I think it's because of her that I work so hard now. She also taught me a lot about my culture. For example, she taught me how to cook some traditional dishes.
>
> When I think of my grandmother, I feel very happy. I love her very much and I feel a lot of respect for her. But sometimes I also feel worried about her because she is quite old now and still lives alone.

这样的答案扣题、清晰，而且语言也自然流畅，考官可以充分理解考生要表达的信息，形成了真正有效的交流，得高分实至名归（It does deserve a high score.）。

甚至即使遇到非常"虐心"（excruciatingly hard）的题，考官也希望你能说清晰、自然的英文，而不是给他／她同样"虐心"的答案：

> Describe a concert hall.
>
> You should say：
>
> where it is
>
> what it is like
>
> why you went there
>
> and explain whether you like it or not.

I'm going to tell you about a concert hall in my city. It's called the Centennial Center.

It's not quite in the city center, but is only a short walk away.

The building is old, but still in good condition. The main hall is very big. There're probably more than 800 seats in it. The seats are comfortable, and it's easy to see the stage from most of the seats.

The hall has a high ceiling and a wood floor. The sound is great from almost everywhere in the hall. I've seen many concerts at this hall, from classical to jazz. I've also seen some drama performances there.

I like this concert hall because it's a great place for music lovers. The concerts are always impressive. The employees there are friendly and helpful. And ticket prices are fairly reasonable.

追求扣题、清晰、自然，并且适当用地道的词汇和短语来点缀（但绝不是"充斥"）自己的答案，这就是 IELTS 口试高分考生的真正共同点。这样的答案向考官证明的是考生的英语沟通技能（English communication skills），而不是向考官炫耀自己的"机械记忆技能"（rote memorisation skills，俗称"狂背技能"）。

"用词难到让考官惊叹"的答案在 IELTS 口语备考路上只是缘木求鱼（a misguided effort）。而当你真正明白坐在你对面的那位职业是雅思考官的 native speaker 到底期待什么，你已经成功了一半（You're halfway there.）。

本书和它的姐妹篇《IELTS 写作完整真题库与范文全解》帮助很多中国考生朋友们实现了自己的梦想。这是"十天系列"的读者陈佳沛同学（口语8.5分）和朱梦平同学（口语7分）的成绩单。虽然两位同学的基础和分数不同，但有两个共同点：❶ 口语成绩分别超过了这两位同学自己的"传统强项"——阅读成绩和听力成绩；❷ 他们都非常重视和考官的交流（communication）。

其实不止是这两位同学，重视与考官的交流是 Pat 认识的每一位中国口语高分考生的共同点——simply because the IELTS speaking test is a test designed to assess English communication skills.

如果您在 IELTS 口语备考路上遇到任何问题，或者您也愿意和朋友们分享自己在"屠鸭"路上的点点滴滴，欢迎致信：ieltsguru@ sina. com。Pat 每天都收到来自世界各地很多朋友的邮件，但只要有时间一定会尽量回复您的—— simply because I'd like to know what my Chinese readers think. ☺

陈佳沛同学的心得

我目前就读于悉尼大学，Pat 的书籍让我的口语和写作获得了很大的进步。以下是我的一些备考心得：

首先，从心态上说，一定要勤奋，不能一边给自己"我已经够努力了"的幻觉，同时却浪费很多时间在玩手机或者其它对考试无用的事情上面，给自己拖延的借口。

关于写作和口语的语言点、易错点，Pat 的书里已经总结得很详细了，我就不再重复了。例如，我和考官说到天气时用出了一个很地道的词 drizzle，就是 Pat 的口语书里面讲的（Big thanks，Pat！）。这里想跟没有考过雅思的朋友们强调一下的就是：你的考官也是真实的人，不是机器（Your speaking examiner is a real

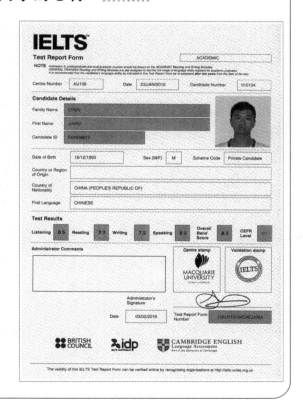

person，not a machine.），所以你和考官两个人之间的交流很关键。Treat your speaking examiner as a friend. 口试要得到高分就一定不能怕和考官分享你的真实想法和感受。

还有一点我想说的是语法的重要性。我自己来澳洲读本科之前都是在国内普通高中上学的，也见过有不少同学认为不应该花时间在毫无用处的语法上面，但我却不这么认为。比如在口语方面，语法并不需要说得很难，但是时态、单复数等容易错的语法点都会直接决定考官对你的说话内容的理解难易程度。有小错误也许是难免的（我自己至少在 Part 3 里也出现了少量的语法错误），但如果错误太多，就会让考官觉得理解你说的内容很困难了。

对于口试，我自己的切身感受就是勤奋很重要，但勤奋在点子上也很重要。Work hard and work smart！

∷∷∷∷∷∷ **朱梦平同学的心得** ∷∷∷∷∷∷

首战听力没考好，但总分和小分都够了就不打算再考了。关于口语我个人最重要的体会就是不要把它当成一个决定终生命运的考试，而是把它看成和一个外国朋友交谈的机会，认认真真地说出你的看法，这样反而能够发挥出最佳状态。当然充分的准备是必不可少的，我的做法就是认真看 Pat 书里的语言，同时让自己的表达变得更地道更自然。很多同学关心的语速，我的体会是让语速变得流利是逐步实现、水到渠成的，如果从一开始就追求语速流利，反而会很紧张，而且说出来其实还是磕磕绊绊的。口试时一定要保持自信和冷静！当然我自己未来学习的路还很长，我会继续加油的！谢谢 Pat！

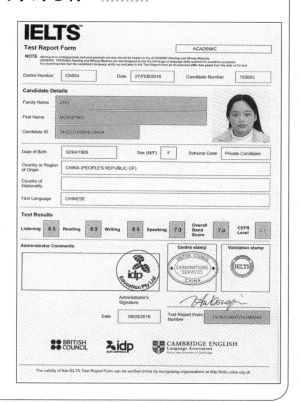